At War with the 16th Irish Division, 1914–1918

At War with the 16th Irish Division, 1914–1918

The Staniforth Letters

Edited by Richard S. Grayson

IMPERIAL WAR MUSEUMS

In association with Imperial War Museums

Pen & Sword
MILITARY

First published in Great Britain in 2012 by
Pen & Sword Military
an imprint of
Pen & Sword Books Ltd
47 Church Street
Barnsley
South Yorkshire
S70 2AS

ISBN 978 1 84884 634 0

A CIP catalogue record for this book is
available from the British Library

Typeset in Ehrhardt

Printed and bound in England by the MPG Books Group Ltd.

Pen & Sword Books Ltd incorporates the Imprints of Pen & Sword Aviation,
Pen & Sword Family History, Pen & Sword Maritime, Pen & Sword Military,
Pen & Sword Discovery, Wharncliffe Local History, Wharncliffe True Crime,
Wharncliffe Transport, Pen & Sword Select, Pen & Sword Military Classics,
Leo Cooper, The Praetorian Press, Remember When, Seaforth Publishing and
Frontline Publishing

For a complete list of Pen & Sword titles please contact
PEN & SWORD BOOKS LIMITED
47 Church Street, Barnsley, South Yorkshire, S70 2AS, England
E-mail: enquiries@pen-and-sword.co.uk
Website: www.pen-and-sword.co.uk

Contents

Editor's Introduction

Richard S. Grayson

During a house removal in the early 1970s, John 'Max'[1] Staniforth found a long-forgotten collection of letters. They were his own letters, written to his parents throughout the First World War. Some were damaged beyond legibility by damp and mice, but the vast majority were intact. Staniforth saw in his letters a story which he was keen to tell to the wider world, a story of both the horrors of war and of the war's day-to-day routines. So he typed up the letters into a volume, which he gave a working title of *Kitchener's Soldier, 1914-18: The Letters of John H.M. Staniforth*, and tried to have them published. Unfortunately, his efforts fell on deaf ears.[2] Temporarily, much of the world had lost interest in the First World War. Staniforth died in 1985, his letters unpublished, with the originals having been donated to the Imperial War Museum in 1981. He would never know that they would one day reach the audience he sought.

John Hamilton Maxwell Staniforth (known in the family as 'Max') was born on 23 June 1893 into a middle-class family at Hinderwell, on Yorkshire's north-east coast. His father, John William 'Jack' Staniforth, was a local general practitioner. Staniforth was educated at Charterhouse before becoming an undergraduate at Christ Church, Oxford, where he was when war broke out in August 1914.

Public school and Oxford-educated, Staniforth had all the credentials to enlist as an officer wherever he was needed. However, his mother, Mary 'May' Jane Dobbin Maxwell, was Irish by birth, born in County Cavan, and that connection was important to the twenty-one-year-old volunteer. He also felt that he should be trained as an ordinary soldier before he could consider leading men. So instead of following the path of so many Oxford undergraduates – seeking a commission – he took the unusual step of enlisting as a private in the Connaught Rangers. As the successor to the 88th Foot, the Connaughts were the heirs to the regiment in which his maternal great-grandfather had served. Even then, Staniforth's social background made him an unusual enlisted man, so much so that the officer who recruited Staniforth felt the need to explain to the Commanding Officer of the 6th Battalion, The Connaught Rangers, 'he wishes to make himself an efficient soldier before applying for a Commission.'[3]

Staniforth was rapidly attached to the 6/Connaughts, part of 47 Brigade in the 16th (Irish) Division. From his first days in the army, Staniforth wrote to his parents at least once a week, very often more. Promoted to corporal within weeks of enlisting, Staniforth was transferred to the 7th Battalion, The Prince of Wales's Leinster Regiment (Royal Canadians), who were also members of 47 Brigade. With this battalion he went through the basic training of an ordinary enlisted man before being commissioned in late November 1914.

Staniforth was far from the only 'English' officer in the 16th Division, even at the start of the war, and it should not be assumed that his Englishness would have been an issue for either fellow officers or men in the ranks. His background of public school and university was shared by the Irish officers, and some of them might have had scarcely any trace of an Irish accent. To the men, officers' social class rather than their accents might have been the defining officer characteristic, and there does not ever appear to have been any suggestion that Staniforth had any difficulty fitting in. Moreover, it should be remembered that British and Irish identities were considerably more multi-layered and inter-woven prior to the Easter Rising of 1916 and the subsequent fight for independence.[4] Thus Unionists, who were resolutely against Home Rule, could be comfortable with displays of Irish symbolism, and their own identities incorporated elements of Irishness. Meanwhile, Irish Nationalists joining the British Army in 1914 and 1915 comfortably sang 'God Save the King' and included the Union Flag in their own patriotic displays.[5] Joseph Devlin, the Nationalist MP for West Belfast, happily declared that, by taking part in the war effort, his supporters 'intend . . . to claim a full and an increasing share in the work and glory of the Empire, which the blood and brains of Irishmen have done so much to create.'[6]

Such features of Irish politics and military history are part of the context of the Staniforth letters, which are an extremely readable account of the training, battles and daily life of soldiers of the 16th (Irish) Division throughout the war. They include evocative accounts of trench life, show how the 16th Division was influenced by the contemporary politics of Ireland, and contain a detailed personal account of the effects and treatment of gas poisoning. In many of his letters, Staniforth gave voice to the experiences of the ordinary soldiers, especially through writing the story of their training in a way that was rare. Few private soldiers brought such a high level of education to the ranks, and Staniforth was able to use his skills to tell their story.

The collection published here contains key letters which Staniforth did not include in his typescript. In that, he said that between 21 May 1917 and 31 March 1918 only one letter (23 October 1917) had survived. However, there are in fact thirty-one additional letters from that period in the Staniforth papers held in the Imperial War Museum.[7] These extra letters are mostly legible, and amount to nearly 30,000 words, to add to the approximately 80,000 in Staniforth's typescript. Why were they omitted by Staniforth? They are certainly extremely interesting accounts. Indeed, they contain some of his best writing and cover the horrors of Passchendaele. It is possible that he found the memory of that battle too traumatic to recall and did not want to type them up. However, many letters from that time deal simply with day-to-day matters and it seems more likely that they had been misplaced when he typed up the rest of the collection.

This volume does not contain all of the original letters. Matters relating to family and friends, which would be of little interest to the general reader, have been left out, along with references where the meaning is unclear, such as to letters Staniforth received from his parents. Sections of letters which were so badly damaged as to require sizeable editorial insertions to make them readable (much of which would have been guess-work) have been excluded. Staniforth's fellow officer Billy Cullen[8] got to know his parents and wrote to them, but those letters are omitted, even though Staniforth put some in his typescript. While much about day-to-day life has been included, much else has been removed where it constitutes repetition or does little to illustrate the generalities of life in the army.

However, Staniforth's own style has been retained throughout, including its inconsistencies, so that the letters are as he wrote them. He used both Bosch and Bosche, while both whiskey and whisky are referred to in the same letter (with no obvious distinction being meant between Irish and Scotch). He used, for example, both wagon and waggon, and orderly-room and Orderly Room. Such differences have been kept. Mistakes in punctuation have also been retained to try to offer the letters in a form that is as close to their original as possible.

Any editorial addition has been placed in square brackets, including indications of where text (other than greetings and farewells) has been removed. Such omissions appear thus: [. . .]. The format of dates has been standardized (Staniforth used many different forms), and the location from which Staniforth wrote has been added if he was not able (due to censorship) to include it. References are the editor's except where stated.[9] Underlining in the original has been italicised. Removed from each letter is the opening address which was usually 'My dear ones' and the closing 'As ever' and other signings-off. But it should be noted that these were always very affectionate and, along with the general tone of the letters, suggest that Staniforth had a very close and loving relationship with his parents. That goes some way to explaining why the letters in this volume stand as such a vivid personal testimony of the war, offering the innermost thoughts of a man who witnessed horror at first hand.

Author's Foreword

J.H.M. Staniforth

The letters which follow were discovered, more than fifty years after they had been written, in the course of a house removal. Some were found to be irretrievably damaged by damp and mice, and there are consequently gaps here and there in the sequence; but with these exceptions they form a continuous record of the writer's experiences in the Great War, from his enlistment as a private in 1914 to his return as a major to civil[ian] life in 1918. For the historian, they constitute what is probably a uniquely detailed picture of military life in the New Armies of that era.

John Hamilton Maxwell Staniforth, the son of a country doctor, was born in 1893 and named after his maternal great-grandfather, the Irish writer William Hamilton Maxwell.[1] There is mention in the letters of the family home, The Anchorage, at Hinderwell on the north-east coast of Yorkshire, and of his two younger sisters Maisie[2] and Maureen ('Mornie'),[3] and familiar references to the near-by villages of Staithes, Runswick and Ellerby, which composed his father's practice. From Charterhouse, which he entered with a scholarship in 1906 and left as head of the school in 1912, he went with a classical scholarship to Christ Church, Oxford. He was thus one of that 'golden generation' of young Oxford and Cambridge men who hurried so eagerly to war at their country's call, and of whom so many never returned. Among the members of the lively but short-lived Shaftesbury Club (with its motto from Dryden, 'Sagacious, bold, and turbulent of wit') who made him their secretary were Philip Guedalla[4] and G.D.H. Cole[5] of Balliol, J.B.S. Haldane,[6] A.P. Herbert[7] and Douglas Jerrold[8] of New College, E.E. Bridges[9] of Magdalen (later to be Sir Edward Bridges, Secretary of the Treasury and Head of the Civil Service, and eventually 1st Baron Bridges) and H.G. Strauss[10] (afterwards Lord Conesford) of the House.[11]

In the Long Vacation of 1914 he accepted a holiday post as tutor to a pupil at Grassington, near Skipton. The declaration of war on August 4th found him committed to this engagement, so that it was not until October that he was free to follow the majority of his contemporaries into the fighting forces. At that time volunteers were still allowed to choose the unit they wished to join, and his decision was unhesitatingly for the Connaught Rangers, the old 88th Foot, in which his great-grandfather had been a captain. Accordingly, after being sworn in and given the King's shilling and a travelling warrant at the recruiting office in Whitby, he set off on the 15th of October for the regimental depot at Galway and his initiation into Army life. From that point his own letters take up the story.

Abbreviations

A.C.C.	Army Corps Commander
A.D.C.	Aide-de-camp, an adjutant to a higher ranking officer
Adj or Adjt	Adjutant
A.P.O.	Army Post Office
A.S.C.	Army Service Corps
Bde.	Brigade
B.E.F.	British Expeditionary Force
Bn.	Battalion
B.R.C.H.	British Red Cross Hospital
Brig.-Gen.	Brigadier General
C.B.	Confined to barracks
C.C.S.	Casualty Clearing Station
C-M	Court Martial
Cmdg.	Commanding
C.O.	Commanding Officer
Coy.	Company
D.D.B.	Divisional Depot Battalion
D.R.	Despatch Rider
D.S.C.	Distinguished Service Cross
G.O.C	General Officer Commanding
G.S.	General Service (fit for)
H.E.	High explosive
Hdqrs.	Headquarters
H.Q.	Headquarters
I.O.	Intelligence Officer
I.N.V.s	Irish National Volunteers
I.V.s	Irish Volunteers
Lieut.	Lieutenant
Lt.	Lieutenant
Lt. Col.	Lieutenant Colonel
Lt. Gen.	Lieutenant General
M.G.	Machine gun
M.O.	Medical Officer
N.C.O.	Non-Commissioned Officer

O.C.	Officer Commanding
O. i./c	Officer in command
O.T.C.	Officers' Training Corps
Q.M.	Quarter Master
R.A.M.C.	Royal Army Medical Corps
R.E.	Royal Engineers
R.F.A.	Royal Field Artillery
R.G.A.	Royal Garrison Artillery
R.O.D.	Railway Operating Division
R.T.O.	Regimental Transport Officer
S.A.A.	Small Arms Ammunition
Sig. Coy.	Signal Company
T.C.D.	Trinity College Dublin
T.C.O.	Train Conducting Officer
U.V.F.	Ulster Volunteer Force
V.A.D.	Voluntary Aid Detachment
W.A.A.C.	Women's Auxiliary Army Corps
W.O.	War Office

List of Illustrations

Staniforth aged five in 1898.

Staniforth is aged seventeen in 1910.

Staniforth's Connaught Rangers cap badge.

One of the Leinster Regiment badges Staniforth acquired on transfer.

Postcard of Staniforth on parade.

2nd Lieutenant J.H.M. Staniforth.

Kilworth Camp in early 1915.

Lieutenant J.H.M. Staniforth.

The road to Guillemont viewed from Waterlot Farm, 11 September 1916.

German dead scattered in the wreck of a machine-gun post near Guillemont, September 1916.

The Battle of Ginchy, 9 September 1916.

The 16th (Irish) Division memorial at Guillemont.

Captain J.H.M. Staniforth.

16th (Irish) Division Christmas card, 1917.

Ulster – No Surrender.

Biddie in her Women's Royal Naval Service uniform.

Biddie.

Biddie and Max on their wedding day, 1 July 1922.

Max Staniforth *c*. 1941–2.

Staniforth in his study in 1982–3.

Staniforth's 1914–15 Star, Victory and British War Medals.

Chapter 1

'A fearful mutiny': Training in the Ranks, October to November 1914

The 6/Connaughts were unlike most battalions in Kitchener's New Army in that they had an overtly political dimension. At the outbreak of the war, Ireland had been on the brink of civil war, with two rival private armies ready to fight each other over 'Home Rule', the plan by the Liberal government in Westminster to give Ireland a measure of devolution, while remaining part of the United Kingdom. The plan was bitterly opposed by Protestant Unionists, concentrated in what is now Northern Ireland. They were used to calling the shots in many aspects of Irish political life and feared that a Home Rule Parliament in Dublin would be Catholic-dominated and ride roughshod over the views of Protestants. Many argued that 'Home Rule' would mean 'Rome Rule'.

To offer resistance to Home Rule, the Ulster Unionist Council had formed the Ulster Volunteer Force in early 1913 and it soon had around 100,000 men armed and in uniform.[1] Despite their professed 'loyalty' to the British Crown, they were ready to fight against the rule of the British Parliament if it forced Ulster into a Home Rule Ireland. In response, Irish Nationalists, who backed Home Rule, formed the Irish Volunteers (IVs), which numbered at least the same as the UVF. Their initial purpose was to implement the will of Parliament if it passed Home Rule, so it is ironic that they are now seen as the forerunners of the Irish Republican Army.

By the summer of 1914, Parliament was about to pass Home Rule, for the whole of Ireland, and it looked as if civil war would ensue. This would not just have engulfed Ireland, but also threatened to draw in mainstream opinion in Britain. Andrew Bonar Law,[2] the leader of the Unionist Party[3] in Parliament, had already declared, 'the people of Ulster will resist, and I think they will be right', adding that 'If you shot down a hundred of them in Belfast to-morrow a thousand would be ready the next day to share the same fate.'[4] However, with British entry into the continental war on 4 August, eyes were forced to turn elsewhere. Despite their willingness to fight each other, both the UVF and the IVs were soon to find themselves in the British Army. By early September,

1

the Irish Unionist leader, Edward Carson,[5] had persuaded the War Office to create a separate division (around 16,000 soldiers) in which members of the UVF could enlist. This 36th (Ulster) Division soon became an active symbol of Ulster's loyalty to Britain and Unionist leaders hoped that such enthusiastic volunteering could help to persuade the British government not to force Ulster into a Home Rule Parliament.

When war was declared, Nationalist politics was thrown into turmoil, threatening the unity in its ranks. A traditional Nationalist view, associated first with Daniel O'Connell,[6] was that 'England's difficulty is Ireland's opportunity' in that it provided Irishmen with an opportunity to grasp power at home. However, in August 1914, John Redmond[7] interpreted that view very differently, arguing that Nationalists coming to Britain's aid in the war against Germany would advance the cause of Home Rule. So, the Irish Volunteers were initially offered for the defence of Irish shores. Redmond said in Parliament that the government:

> . . . may to-morrow withdraw every one of their troops from Ireland. I say that the coast of Ireland will be defended from foreign invasion by her armed sons, and for this purpose armed Nationalist Catholics in the South will be only too glad to join arms with the armed Protestant Ulstermen in the North.[8]

Of course, many Irish Nationalists joined the ranks individually. Some were called up because they were reservists, liable to join their regiments at the outbreak of war. From mid-August, others joined the newly formed non-political 10th (Irish) Division. However, the IVs were not joining as a group in the way that members of the UVF were and Nationalists began to feel they were losing the public relations war over recruitment. So in mid-September Redmond called for the creation of an 'Irish Brigade', drawing on language redolent of previous Irish service in so-called foreign armies.[9] With Home Rule passed as law (though its implementation was put on hold) Redmond took further steps in support of the government. On 20 September, in a speech at Woodenbridge, County Wicklow, Redmond told the Irish Volunteers assembled there that they had a 'two-fold duty' to defend Ireland's shores and also to fight 'wherever the firing line extends in defence of the right of freedom and religion in this war'.[10]

Redmond's support for enlistment in the British Army caused a split in the ranks of the IVs. Eoin MacNeill[11] and his supporters removed Redmond's nominees from the Volunteers' Provisional Committee. They said Redmond had violated the founding principles of the IV by advising them 'to take foreign *service under a Government which is not Irish'.[12] But across Ireland, approx-imately ninety-three per cent of the Volunteers backed Redmond.[13] By mid-October, Redmond had reaffirmed his control of the Irish Volunteers, renamed as the Irish National Volunteers (INVs).*

In the autumn of 1914 Redmond worked tirelessly to recruit IVs into the British Army. He had got his wish for a new division when, in mid-September, Lord Kitchener agreed to form the 16th (Irish) Division from troops recruited in Ireland. That was then enhanced by his instruction to its commanding officer to clear space in a Brigade (47 Brigade was eventually agreed) for men from the INV to be drafted into battalions together.[14] The Brigade consisted of four battalions: 6th Battalion, The Royal Irish Regiment; 8th Battalion, The Royal Munster Fusiliers; the 6/Connaughts and the 7/Leinsters. From October, their ranks were filled by volunteers from across Ireland. Among them, an atypical volunteer was J.H.M. Staniforth. He enlisted for the Connaughts in Whitby, having been initially told by the recruiting officer there that it was not clear if he could enlist in an Irish regiment in Yorkshire. Staniforth made it clear that if he could not, then he would go to Ireland to enlist, and so the officer sought special approval from the War Office, which was given.[15] Staniforth's letters from Ireland immediately offer a detailed picture of life during basic training.

Mallow [Co. Cork], 18 October 1914

The last two days have been more full of adventures than I have had for a long time, and they're not over yet.

On Friday morning I arrived at Galway, and went to the railway hotel for a last good breakfast before taking the plunge. When the irrevocable moment came, my spirits were very low. However, I braced myself up; if others had done it, why couldn't I? Anyway, I couldn't turn back now, so I paid my bill, shouldered my pack, and set off.

The barracks at Galway are a long way out of the town; a little cinder-path runs beside the railway, and it was fearfully hot, and the pack got heavier and heavier. But at last I got to the gate, took a long breath, and marched boldly in. I walked into the first room I saw, and handed in my two papers. I was taken to the C.O.,[16] who read my note and told me a draft of recruits was leaving the depot next day, and I was just in time to go with them. He also said he would write to the C.O. of the 6th Battalion and do what he could for me.

I loafed round the barrack square till one o'clock, and then a mess-sergeant sent me in to eat with the workmen who were doing some repairs. (There were only half-a-dozen staff-soldiers in the place, and [a] couple more who had been invalided back from the front.) We had a lump of stewed beef and potatoes in their jackets, and mustard etc. in tin lids. No table cloths, of course. We had a pint of porter for 2d from the canteen with it.

After the dinner I was sent to the tailor's and given a kit. We Kitchener's men have a plain blue serge coat, knickerbockers, puttees, and a saucy little forage-cap, rather like a slice of melon in shape, with the regimental badge. The general effect is Coast-Guardish or Naval-Brigadey to look at.

We were given a couple of incidental jobs or wood-carrying and sack-lifting to do for the Stores department, but otherwise left in peace.

I made friends with one of the invalids, who was recovered and going away next day, and we strolled out into the town, which is about as big as Whitby. The first thing we found was a Sinn-Fein-and-Redmondite[17] riot in full blast, with sticks and stones flying. However, we escaped from that with a little purely defensive fighting (!) and went into a shebeen for peace.[18] Over our drinks he told me a lot about the Germans and Mons.[19]

We came back at about 8, and I went to my barrack-room. It was open just for that night for a few of us recruits, so there was no fire and a general air of desolation about the place. I chose a bed and locked away my kit in the store-room, after adding to it [. . .] several of the things I had brought from home. (It's a pity about the blanket, but I couldn't possibly take it with me; I'll write for it when we go to the front. Also I believe I've left the pills etc. in a tin in the bag; if I have, please send them on.)

Then I turned in early, on an iron bed-cot, under two ragged brown verminous horse-blankets. I got my best sleep between then and midnight; and then the rest of my fellow-recruits began to come in, blind drunk. The place resembled a casual ward; about a dozen seedy, ragged, lousy, unshaven tramps, who lurched in and lay on their cots smoking, spitting, quarrelling, making water all over the room (excuse details), hiccupping and vomiting. It was after three before the last of them settled into a repulsive noisy slumber among his rags. It was the quaintest night I ever spent.

Next morning a proper corporal came in from the next barrack-room where the handful of soldiers were (lucky beggars!), and roused us up and told us to get our breakfast and be ready to leave at 9 o'clock. He fled back from our reeking shambles as soon as he could to his own civilised quarters.

So we crawled up, with blasphemy and expectoration; a few of us had a wash at the tap outside; and we put on our new kit – except two still drunken fellows who forgot it. Of course there was no breakfast for us, so at the last minute we rushed in and shared the mess of the soldiers, eating in our fingers from tin plates. Then we paraded. The regulars were going off to Kinsale, and we recruits to Fermoy.[20] We were in charge of an old colour-sergeant who had rejoined for the war.

Then the fun began. We all got to Limerick all right, and had three hours to wait there. We recruits were sent to the barracks there, occupied by the South Irish Horse (yeomanry), and told to wait there. Well, our sergeant was a mild, helpless old thing with a 'strong weakness' himself, so he let us get out of hand altogether and we scattered over the town, drinking hard. Consequently, when we got to the station at 4.30, we found that the train had gone with two of our party, leaving the rest of us behind. Also the kit-bags had been stacked on the platform and quite likely stolen since the departure of the two who had been posted to guard them.

However, another train went in half-an-hour, so we got into that; but it was slow, and we arrived in Limerick Junction just in time to see the last Fermoy train steam out of the station. We had another three hours to wait (7 till 10) before a train could take us on to Mallow, where it was decided we should spend the night. Of course there was a rush to the bar at once. There had been a couple of attempts to steal kit-bags already (by those who had forgotten or lost theirs), so I was appointed to guard them. I made a pile of nineteen and sat on them, and lit my pipe to wait.

Well, you can imagine the situation. The station is like Whitby Town, a big windy barn of a place. Night had fallen; a few lamps were lit, and the platform was filled with these filthy, sodden, smelling, staggering, slobbering lepers who sang and cursed and quarrelled and snored by turns. The colour-sergeant had given up the case and retired to the first-class refreshment-room to pass the time, poor old thing. It was like an unreal nightmare.

Well, they kept making idiotic attempts and pretexts to examine the kit-bags, so I [. . .] drew a line round my stack of bags and announced that the man who crossed it would get hurt. Bless me, though, in five minutes there was another of the scum padding round. Then I got suddenly mad with the whole absurd crowd that shuffled and whispered and slobbered and spat, and I smashed my fist into his face. He went down sideways, like a tree, and hit the platform a fearful smack, and lay there and howled. I sent another to keep him company (it was like hitting spongy rolls), and then I got the other two sober fellows and we formed a police picket and carried them off to the waiting-room, commandeered the keys from the station-master, and locked them up to rave and shout by themselves. Then we sat down and waited in peace for the train. When it came, we could only get as far as Mallow; so we arrived there at midnight and went to the deserted barracks there for shelter. There was a caretaker in charge, and he routed out a score of old blankets and opened a kind of loft for us. The other fellows made up shake-downs on the boards, lying almost in each other's arms; but I didn't fancy that, so I went exploring till I found a little room open, like the small harness-room at the Anchorage. It was dusty and cobwebby, just like the harness-room used to be, but at least it was private. I put my boot through the window, which was hermetically sealed (the damage will go down to 'act of God,' I suppose), and lay down in a corner. I had some experience of our fellows by that time, so I put my kit under my head and slept with my £5 in my fist and my boots (the heavy ones) at my hand. Sure enough, about three in the morning I heard the door open – fortunately it was too cold under one blanket to sleep deeply. I picked up my boot and slung it as hard as I could about where I judged a man's face would be. He wasn't long in the one place after that.

Next morning I had a wash and a shave from a tap in a sink below, and went up with the colour-sergeant to see if we could get any breakfast in the town. Remember we had had nothing since breakfast the previous morning, and only a bowl of tea and a lump of dry bread at that. We had to wait an hour at the station before the refreshment-room opened, and then we arranged for twenty sandwiches and twenty cups of tea. Also we found that there was no train to Fermoy till five in the afternoon. So we spent Sunday sitting in the old barrack-yard at Mallow counting the daisies. I began this letter in the afternoon, but we were marched off before I finished it.

So at last we came to Fermoy, and found more bread and tea waiting for us. I've had more bread and tea in the last few days than I care for. We were herded into a little room not the size of your sitting-room, ten of us, and given hay palliasses. There is just room for them all on the floor at once, head to toe. The barracks are very big, but quite full, so we are turned into what used to be the married quarters. Unfortunately I have got the two biggest villains of the lot in with me. We have to leave a man in the room all day, but lots of things have been stolen already. (These two jewels sold their kits as soon as they got them, got drunk on the proceeds, and reported the kits as 'missing, probably stolen, sir'!) We overheard them looking at one chap who was turning out his kit, and saying, 'That's a —— fine kit; we'll fix it.' We tipped the fellow the wink, and he slept with one eye open that night.

The thieving is simply incredible. Pat Cavanagh left his shirt on his bed to run into the next room for a light. He was back in thirty seconds, but the shirt was 'whipped on him,' as someone said. Fortunately nothing of mine has gone. I made my bed up on the trestle table, put my boots on it, and gave out fair warning to everyone before I went to sleep. However, nothing happened.

Since then we have had more regular times. Seven hours drill a day, and the evening to ourselves. The town is full of soldiers – it is a big depot – and the work is very interesting and the food excellent so far. The officers are mostly English, and very nice. But the regiment is supposed to have the worst character in the Army!

My address is 'Pte. J. Staniforth, C Company, 6th Battalion The Connaught Rangers, New Barracks, Fermoy, Co. Cork.' Will you send me back my pocket-book and the pills and Formamint, if they are in the pack? If it doesn't turn up in reasonable time, have enquiries made; I don't know how far Irish goods trains are to be depended on. It was despatched from Galway on Friday night, carriage forward, goods train, addressed to you.

Well, I'm very well, happy, and contented. The quartermaster-sergeant asked me this morning if I would like to be a corporal soon, as he wanted some who weren't 'in dread of the blackguards.' So perhaps I may get a step in a few weeks. Meantime I'm seeing life and enjoying it.

P.S. Much of this sounds like romance, but it's all cold fact. There are only three decent men in C Company. The rest are quite indescribable villains. However, it's all in the seven – or rather three.[21]

P.P.S. The next station to Fermoy, about 2½ miles away, is the renowned Ballyhooly.[22]

We are to move again before Christmas, I believe; possibly to Dublin.

New Barracks, Fermoy, 24 October 1914
[. . .] To take up my tale where (I believe) I left off, I slept in my barrack room, which is really not a barrack-room at all but a small living-room in the old married quarters, for three nights. They were bad nights for sleep, because of the damp and draughty floors, the two thin blankets, and the potential thieving – which however never materialised. One had to sleep in one's vest, pants, and shirt to keep warm, although I generally used the shirt to roll up with the woollen cardigan jacket as a pillow, to mitigate the austerity of a kit-bag packed with boots and brushes. The advantage was that one was not likely to oversleep the 6 a.m. call. We use no bugles yet, but in the middle of the night – or so it seems – an orderly

corporal bursts in and arouses us. Then we stretch and rub our eyes and sit up one by one, and somebody pulls up the blind. The feeble light of dawn struggles in and reveals, a dense cold fog outside, and shapes in blankets with dirty faces and rumpled hair lying or sitting up all round the room. Some have straws from the mattresses sticking in their hair, and all have grey-back Army shirts open at the throat. There is a certain amount of grey fog about the room, which has crept in through the 12 inches of open window we insist on. A dirty deal table and a couple of forms and an ordinary kitchen dresser and plate-rack complete the setting. Can't you imagine the scene? – 'Dawn in a Barrack-Room.'

We get up and pull on our breeches, slip up the braces, lace up our boots and struggle into a tunic, set a cap upon the tumbled hair, and the toilet of all but the most fastidious is complete. We cleanse the mouth by the simple and admirable process of hawking loudly and spitting on the floor. A few, however, patronise a tap at a sink in the scullery at the rear of the cottage and indulge in a wash, if they can face the water, which is very cold. We wash by holding our head under the tap and turning it on. Soap is looked upon rather askance.

By this time the orderly man for the day has gone to the cookhouse and brought back a pail of hot, sweet tea, which is very welcome; and when we have absorbed this, made our beds and stacked away the blankets, and wound up our legs in puttees (which, if you take a pride in doing it neatly, takes as long as a woman doing her hair), it is time for the first parade – 7 o'clock.

We turn out into the mist, and form up in two ranks in a paddock behind our cottages. In a minute the two company officers (2nd lieutenants about my age) appear from the fog, looking very fresh and clean in comparison with their men. The company-sergeant-major brings the squad to attention, salutes, and reports all present, except the orderly men for the day and one or two who have gone sick. The officer then gives him the order-book, and he reads out to us the battalion orders for the day, which may or may not contain anything to affect us – usually not.

Then, 'Squad . . . number! Form fours! Right turn! By the left . . . quick march!' and away we go in a straggling mass, half asleep and very cold and hungry; and the business of another day has begun.

We are led at once to a big 20-acre field, and double round it for ten minutes by the officer's watch. This sounds easy, but ten minutes is a long time to keep it up, and the old fat men are hideously distressed at the end of it. (On the morning after pay-night – Saturday morning, that is – the doubling is kept up for *twenty* minutes, with a short pause at half-time.

The object of this is to sweat the drink out of the men. It is admirably calculated to serve its purpose.)

Then we are given five minutes' 'easy,' and there is much gasping and blowing and spitting and wiping of red faces and sotto voce blasphemy. Gradually, however, we subside into a normal condition again, and are ready to go on once more. The fours are cast back into two lines again, the front rank 'makes a back' for the rear rank to leap over, and away we go across the field at leap-frog, each line stopping after its jump and making a back in its turn. This again upsets the old brigade some, but we go at it for a quarter of an hour before we get an 'easy.'

Finally, there is an obstacle course of about 200 yards, with odd and difficult jumps, vaults, hurdles, and a wooden wall to be escaladed. We go over this twice, up and then down. (You see, the idea of this first parade is not so much drill-instruction as to freshen us up for the work of the day, and ease the stiffness out of the muscles.)

Then we are formed up in fours again and marched back to our own lines, very much awake indeed and very different from the sleepy scarecrows of an hour before. The mists are clearing away, the world is up and about, it is eight o'clock, a civilised hour – which 6.30, we feel, emphatically is not – the orderly men have got breakfast waiting for us, and altogether life is very tolerable. There is more chaff in the ranks, and less profanity; and we are happier men.

'C Company . . . dis-miss!' says the officer, as glad to be finished as we are; we make a turn to the right, salute as one man (theoretically), break off, and the parade is over.

In the barrack-room, which has been aired, swept, and garnished by the orderly man and looks different now from the dank, stuffy sty of the night-time, there are clean white bowls of steaming tea, piles of fresh bread, a chunk of golden butter (margarine, but none the worse for that) and a couple of tins of sardines, or a plate of cheese, or tinned salmon, or a lump of brawn – or, on a few black days, none of these extras. Whatever it is, it doesn't last long. Our table manners may perhaps leave something to be desired, but they serve their purpose very adequately. The method is to fill your mouth as full as possible with a hunk of soft bread, buttered with the flat of an unwashed thumb in preference to a knife, imbibe as much tea as the bread will absorb, and then make conversation across the table. You probably choke cataclysmically, but that doesn't matter. Plates, of course, are dispensed with, and knives are used (if at all) as another world which I have long since forgotten used to employ spoons. I have seen a man drink spilt tea with his knife – though not very successfully.

Breakfast lasts about five minutes – crowded minutes in which much execution is done – and we are free till the next parade at 9. We turn out in a body and leave the orderly man to clean up our messings. An orderly's lot is not altogether a happy one. We smoke – on the amiable co-operative system. A Woodbine, half-smoked the night before, which has reposed behind its owner's ear and shared his slumbers, will be remembered, withdrawn, lighted with a borrowed match (always try half-a-dozen neighbours before you use one of your own matches; they are the scarcest commodity in barracks, although four boxes may be purchased for a penny at the grocery-canteen), and passed from mouth to mouth. This 'loving-smoke' is one of the few barrack institutions I have been unable to subscribe to. When a fellow requests a draw at my cigarette, I give it him for keeps. This is snobbery.

Now is the time for the nuts of the company to shave themselves. Somebody has a twopenny mirror, which is in great demand; but lids of biscuit-boxes do as well, and the scullery is crowded with jostling men, armed fortunately only with the harmless Army razor. (There is a legend of a man who once shaved himself with even such an one, but it is generally regarded as an ingenious fiction; we are content if, as Spud Murphy puts it – yes, we have a Spud Murphy – we 'take the clover and leave the grass.')

Shavers are divided into three classes: (i) the sensible being who shaves from the scullery tap, (ii) the needlessly particular crank who pours all the warm tea-dregs of the mess into one bowl and uses that, and (iii) the demented lunatic who takes a bowl and goes to the cook-house for a drop of really hot clean water. Even such an one there is in C Company.

So, between smoking, shaving, cleaning boots and 'keeping fourths'[23] [. . .] the time passes till 9 o'clock, and we fall in for the second parade. This is the really heavy work of the day, for it lasts till 12.30. For three-and-a-half hours we are gathered up, flung out, shuffled, and re-dealt over the parade-ground, forming, wheeling, extending, closing, and all the machine-made details of squad drill until we are sick to death of the tramp of our own feet. Every hour we have ten minutes 'easy,' and we fall out panting and sit about on logs and bricks and smoke Woodbines till the whistle goes and we start all over again.

However, we are dismissed at last, and rush off to our rooms to wait for dinner. At one o'clock the cook-house bugle blows (I said we didn't use bugles, but we do: just this one call, three times a day; and the most unmusical recruit knows 'Come to the cook-house door, boys!' when he hears it now) and the orderly man snatches up his tin pan and hares off for our dinner. When it comes, there is a universal shout of execration; stewed beef and baked spuds, and a pail of soup so thin that you wouldn't see it on a dark night. For all that, however, it disappears fairly fast. The orderly expels the men from the room, sets out the proper number of bowls and plates, tilts a splash of soup into each bowl and hacks off a cubical lump of beef for each plate, adds a couple of potatoes, and invites the mess to 'dive in.' Which they do, almost literally. Certainly the amount displaced on the floor and table could not be more if they did.

After dinner we lounge till 2, cleaning rifles, pipeclaying belts,[24] reading scraps of newspaper, removing beef-fat or gravy from the hair and clothing, etc., until the S.M. walks along the lines shouting 'Fall in!' That's a word we get to dislike. And so we obediently fall in for the third parade, which lasts till half-past four ('Half four,' in the vernacular) and consists of squad drill, physical drill, and lectures upon musketry and signalling. Most of the time is spent in wondering what the time is and how soon the parade will be over. But 4.30 comes at last and we dismiss, 'making a turn to the right, saluting as one man, and after a short pause dispersing quietly' for the last time; and the day is before us.

Tea is the first episode, and is correctly named, for tea it is, and nothing else. The provident mess will have secreted bread from its breakfast, and perhaps even a squashy pat of butter, but it is unlikely that there will be anything but the half of a bowlful of tea for us. Still, it is very eagerly accepted and drunk; and afterwards we brush our clothes, stick on a forage-cap with a saucy swagger, collect a silver-mounted cane from somewhere, and go forth to see the world. A few, of course, stay in, but not many. A stroll down the hill, over the bridge, and into the town, a look round the main square -which has about a dozen quite decent shops – a smart swagger down the main street and back, and then the haven of a pub is the usual programme. If possible one avoids the picket, who are too apt to arrest a man because he is merely merry.

I generally go to the Soldiers Home, where I submit to Moody & Sankey[25] and antimacassars[26] with a good grace for ten minutes, and then go for a chair by the fire in the reading-room with a magazine, or a supper at the coffee-bar below stairs, for the remainder of the evening.

By half-past nine we have to be back in barracks, and at ten the gas is turned off for the night. And so ends the day.

Of course there are incidentals every other day or so, such as the various fatigues, pickets, garrison duties, and night-guards; but I'll leave them for another letter.

I must just tell you of an incident of last night. Charlie and I (Charlie is a lad from the Irish Times; a compositor, and a good fellow; and by the way one of the volunteers who got their rifles at Howth[27] that day) were coming in at about twenty-five past nine. When we came in under the gate there were a couple of hundred men or so seething round the guard-room door, and enormous excitement. We found there were a dozen drink-maddened prisoners who had mutinied, got possession of the guardroom (the guard, young and untrained, had fled outside and locked them in), and were smashing their way out, armed with bayonets. Every pane of glass was shattered, and volleys of missiles came out into the darkness every minute, scattering the crowd like sheep, and the door was slowly coming to pieces under an improvised battering-ram inside. A picket was hastily falling in with rifles and bayonets to meet the rush. The sergeant of the guard was being carried away on a stretcher, laid out with two kicks below the belt, and one of the guard was having a great bayonet-gash in his wrist bound up. We got the order to form up and stand by in case of need; so we stood in a double rank under the stars and watched the door splintering. At last there was only one plank . . . then that went, and out they came in a great rush like wild animals. They were met by the picket, standing fast by its arms, and there was a priceless scrap. The Irish fight screaming, which adds to the effect. Of course they were secured at last and lodged in the cells, and there is to be a court-martial to-morrow. This is one of the little incidents you outsiders do not hear about. Oh, the Connaughts are a great regiment.

I'll stop now and send this off. On Thursday the officer told me I could get a lance-stripe sewn on my jacket, so my address is Lance-Corporal Staniforth now, and may perhaps be Corporal soon.

Fermoy, 30 October 1914
Cheero – great times – lance-corporal's stripe yesterday, and to-day shifted my quarters into sergeant-major's room. Luxury!

Fermoy, 1 November 1914
Many thanks for your parcel. It was extraordinarily well planned. The bootlaces and stamped envelopes were what I was wanting most of all.

If you are sending another, will you put in something sweet instead of the aperient[28] pills – we get no sugar in any form (except tea) all day long: no pudding for dinner or anything of that sort, so everybody devours chocolate whenever they can get hold of it.

Last Thursday, the 29th, I got my second (full corporal's) stripe, and with it the immediate consequence of orderly-corporal duty. And this is how I spent Friday – no, Saturday it was.

Up at 6 instead of 6.30 (and a damnable day it was too; wet and dark and abominably cold) and round all the lines to find out who was going sick for the day (you must make up your mind early if you intend to be an invalid in the Army) and making a note of every man's Christian name, age, and religion – G.O.K. [God Only Knows] what for, but you can't go sick without a religion; I suppose if anyone professed atheism he wouldn't be admitted to hospital.

Anyway, when I had a long roll of 'Egan, John, 25, R.C.' and 'Quinn, Michael, 32, R.C.' and many others – note cause and effect; the previous night had been pay-night, and most of the patients' diseases were easy to diagnose – and an intimate acquaintance with my company in its robes de nuit[29] (which are precisely the same as its robes de jour, only less so) and its moment of waking, I went off with it to the orderly sergeant. There is an orderly officer for the day for every company, an orderly sergeant for the week, an orderly corporal for the week (except when he is learning, like me), and an orderly man for every room every day. They are all slaves but the officer, who is an overseer.

Having got rid of my sick-roll, I hared off (haring off is an orderly corporal's long suit) and fished up an orderly man from each room in my company, and armed them with tin pans, pails, and one blanket.

Then away we went to the cook-house to draw rations, just as the others were falling-in in a drizzling mist on a puddly ground for the 7 o'clock parade. An orderly is excused all parades, because he would certainly die if he wasn't. Ostensibly he remains in his room on the alert, to protect it from thieves. Actually he puts the key in his pocket and goes off to the canteen, if he has any money; if he hasn't, he removes his boots (or not, to taste) and goes to bed. However, I digress. To resume, I formed up my little brigade and we marched away to the cook-house, and found other precisely similar little brigades waiting. We hung about and stamped ('clapping our webby feet and saying damn' is the Kipling expression, isn't it?) until H.M. the Orderly Officer sauntered along. The canteen sergeant called us up company by company, and we received due allowances of tea, sugar, cheese, sardines, and butter, while I stood by to see the correct weight. Then two men spread the blanket (still warm and hoppy from its owner) and massive cooks hurled 75 pounds of bread into it very rapidly, in princely great loaves whose frontage could be measured by the acre. The two men stooped and staggered and sweated and managed to sling it up between them somehow, I saluted respectfully to the officer-pup and reported all correct, and away we went home again, shedding the tea and sugar at the steamers round the cook-house corner to be made up into breakfast tea.

Back in our own quarters, the slaves hurled down several tons of fodder round my feet in silence and gaped expectantly. Apparently it was up to me to apportion the spoil with some semblance of fairness. I divided the cheese rudely with a coal-shovel, dealt out sardine-tins with a free hand, and scattered pounds of butter as you throw meal to hens. The bread we dismembered with fine strong black hands. Then the envoys departed, each to his own place.

In about ten minutes it was eight o'clock, and the company returned through the rain from parade and clamoured for food. The cookhouse bugle went, and each mess swiftly vomited up its orderly man, who ran like a rabbit and anon returned with the now 'assembled' tea in a pail, and we 'dived in.'

I had just begun, and was standing like the Mad Hatter with a basin in one hand and a bitten slice in the other, when there was a shout of 'Or'ly corp'ril! Letters!' Normally this would have been a bugle-call, but as I say, we use no bugles. So I dropped the breakfast and fled away to the regimental mail-sergeant's room, where he was sitting on his bed with a post-bag, dealing out letters to the orderlies of A, B and C companies. I collected a batch for our fellows, and made my third tour of the barrack-rooms delivering them.

This brought it up to 8.30, and there was a rush of business coming; I was getting behind time. I finished up the breakfast more quickly than I ever did at school (fortunately there wasn't much of it!) and hared off again to the orderly sergeant for the sick report, now duly made out on proper forms from my earlier pencil-scribble. I got this, and hunted out the men, marshalled them in fours, marched them off to the main barrack-square and paraded them there with the sick of the other companies, leaving them to the care of the 'sick sergeant', who took them away later to the hospital. Then back again to the orderly sergeant for the 'C Company parade-state' (a detailed form accounting for every man for the day: sick, guard, fatigue, absent on furlough,[30] available for ordinary duty, cooks, police, and what not). This has to be taken over to the regimental orderly-room before 9 o'clock for the Colonel's inspection. And *by* 9 o'clock I had to have my brigade of slaves with their tins at the cook-house to draw the dinner meat. I was moving quite some, about that time! However, we got there as the clock was striking, and had to wait another five minutes for the officer-pup. When he came we got to work, and in due time received copious dollops of extraordinarily repulsive-looking flesh, which we left as before to be cooked at the steamer.

Then I got a breathing-space, and made my bed, cleaned the grate, laid the fire, swept the room, brushed my teeth, shaved, and brushed my boots with a lump of stewed-beef fat. (God put fat on cows (? or horses) that soldiers' fires might be kindled, soldiers' boots greased, and soldiers' bayonets protected from rain – but not that soldiers' bellies might be filled. We do everything with it but eat it.) I had just time to wash the fat off my fingers and rush off to collect the slaves again to draw potatoes. This interesting ceremony takes place at 10 every morning, when soldiers of the King descend in pairs down through a trap-door, along a subterranean tunnel, and into a dark cellar, where a navvy, naked to the waist, shovels potatoes from a limitless pile by the light of a half-inch of candle stuck into one of the aforesaid potatoes themselves. When they are brought up to the light of day the slaves take them away and wash them in some purlieu of their own – I didn't go with them. In any country but this they would have to peel them as well, but we escape that.

And then I sat down – absolutely for the first moment that day!

My next duty wasn't till 1 o'clock, and that was only to take the slaves over to the cook-house for the dinner, and divide it up amongst the messes – rather a dirty job, for you seize a lump of meat as big as a coal-box in your hands and hack it into half-a-dozen gobbets. It is always the same: stewed beef. Some days it is less stewed than others; that is the only change. It is eaten with the fingers, by preference; rarely with a knife, never with a fork.

There is another post after dinner to be delivered, and then I am free until 4 o'clock – except of course that any officer who wants a message taken anywhere sends for the orderly corporal of his company. However, I got off with one journey to the Brigade Office in the town, so it might have been worse. After tea, which we draw at 4 and consume at 5.30, I had to get the Battalion Orders for the next day from the Orderly Room (that is, a big book in which the programme for the next day's work is drawn out, and any little bits of information or communications from the Colonel) and take it round to the quarters of our two Company officers before Mess, for them to read.

Then I had to remain 'within hearing' of our lines for the rest of the evening until 'Lights Out,' to quell any disturbance that might arise.

And in my 'spare time' it is the duty of every N.C.O. to 'inculcate amongst the men a soldierly spirit and a sense of discipline and honour!'

Now for some more important news. Hughes[31] (that's the Company officer) called me up after parade one day about a week ago, and urged me very strongly to apply for a commission. He explained that he was a barrister in Dublin when the war broke out (he's about 28) and at once enlisted in the Dublin Fusiliers as a private, like me, to see what the life was like. He was trained for a month at the Curragh in the ranks; and then, when he knew his work, sent in his application for a commission (temporary). He got one almost at once, and was posted to the Connaughts.

I asked him about money, and he said (i) that the allowance given is sufficient to cover the expense of a kit, but that it is not granted till the officer joins his regiment; in other words, you must strain your credit to purchase the outfit, and recoup yourself afterwards; (ii) that he is living on his pay quite comfortably under existing circumstances – and from what I have seen of the officers' mess and their quarters here, I believe him.

He was extraordinarily nice and helpful, and got me a form for the application. He said he was persuaded it was the best thing for me, that I need have no fears on the score of expense, and that the facts of my knowledge of drill, my practical experience, and my corporal's stripes would tell greatly in my favour.

So I thanked him and took away the form, and filled up a score of questions as to age, experience, qualifications, etc. Then I had to send it away to the Dean of Christ Church for his testimony to my character and educational standard, and also to Latter at Charterhouse for a similar one. They both sent back nice letters with their testimonials. Finally, I had to get the Colonel's signature. I went to him in the morning, and he said, 'Come again this evening.' I wondered why. That same afternoon the company was out on the big race-course practicing skirmishing and extended order, and the Colonel came out to look on.

In a minute or two he called me out and told me to take charge and carry on. I was knocked all of a heap, but I rallied all the swagger I could and tried to look as if I had drilled companies for the last twenty years. For a quarter of an hour I handled the company under the Colonel's eyes and put them through all their paces. The men, bless them, worked like blacks – did everything at the jump, without a mistake. Then the Old Man said, 'That'll do, corporal,' and I eased them off, panting and sweating, and fell back into the ranks.

It was a nervous experience but apparently satisfactory for when I went to him again in the evening he signed like a bird, and gave me a note for the Brigadier as well.

Next morning I went down to the Brigade Office and called upon the

Brigadier.[32] (A brigade is 4 battalions, so the Brigadier is a no-end big pot, and could have old Conyngham blown from the guns at dawn if he wanted; just as he himself could be crucified by the General to whom my application finally goes.) He was an immense old sport, and asked me how I liked life in the ranks; whether I played games or not (they're rather keen on athletic subalterns, and he was quite braced when I said I got colours at Charterhouse and could shoot as well), and all sorts of questions. We got on frightfully well together! At last he wrote 'Very strongly recommended' on the form, and added his signature, and said he would send it off to General Parsons[33] at once, who is a great friend of his and with whom the decision finally rests.

So that's how the thing stands at present, and I may be a gaudy officer yet when I come home on Christmas furlough! (I said I wanted to stick to the Connaughts if possible, and he said it was quite possible I might be gazetted to their about-to-be-formed 7th Battalion.)

[. . .] We had a fearful mutiny last week. The prisoners in the guardroom and cells (50 men, all drunk) rose again – this is not the row I was telling you about last time, but another – and got possession of the place and smashed it to splinters, and then sallied out armed with bayonets upon the crowd outside. For about a quarter of an hour there was all hell loose: bayonets going and bricks flying, until they could get the fire-hose limbered up and turned on to them. That settled them; but there were six men lying unconscious, and many more bleeding from small wounds. Two subsequently died in hospital, one from a stick of a bayonet and one from a bang of a brick over the heart. We had a frightful kick-up over it next day; they brought the General over from Mallow to curse us. I missed it all, because I was away in the town that night, but I got recouped the next night by a scrap in our own lines, when two men went whiskeymad and ran amuck. The sergeant-major was knocked down twice in the scuffle, and two other corporals got beautiful black eyes. I got a bang in the mouth from a boot that hurt rather, but we got them overpowered and taken away to the clink at last.

I told that sergeant-major about the Whitby men refusing to launch the lifeboat, one evening when we were sitting over the fire in his quarters. 'Be damn,' said he, reflectively cleaning his ears with a pin, 'but that was black cowardice, so it was.'

I must tell you how I got snubbed a day or two ago. We were marching out through the town to go to the race-course, with our rifles over our shoulders. Now, you can see that for a soldier to salute in the ordinary way with a rifle over his shoulder would be clumsy and ugly; so military custom says that a man with a rifle shall salute by bringing the free hand over with a slap upon the butt of the rifle. Very well; it's a small point, but there it is. Well, there was a wee girl, less than Mornie's age[34] and size, standing on the pavement as we went by, and she saluted us very gravely with a grubby little hand. I was bringing up the rear of the company, and as I passed by I returned her salute by raising my hand in the conventional way. But not a bit of it; she was on to it like a bird! 'Ye haven't the right of it,' says she, as smart as you please, in a tone of the deepest disgust. I felt properly brought low.

I think the only other news is that I was inoculated against typhoid last week. I had a bit of a stiff arm next day, but not enough to knock off parade. Some of the fellows were very bad, though. Just now I've got a rotten feverish cold; the weather has been beastly and I haven't had dry feet for a week.

They've added another hour-and-a-half to our drill for night-work now (that's outposts, sentries, and picket-work in the dark), and when the day is done I'm just too tired to do anything but go straight to bed, else I should have found time to write before.

All my shirts, etc., are doing well. We get them washed here. Thanks very much for the housewife;[35] I wanted something of the sort badly. I can live comfortably on my pay, so I want nothing except things to eat. When you only get a piece of bread-and-butter for tea between dinner one day and breakfast the next, you have a healthy appetite for almost anything!

P.S. We get up by moonlight now, which is an amazingly cheerless custom!

Fermoy, 12 November 1914
Transferred, pending commission, to join O.T.C. [Officer Training Corps] attached to C Company of the Leinsters. No time for more at present. Address J.M. Staniforth Esqre., O.T.C. C Coy 7th Leinsters, Old Barracks, Fermoy.

Chapter 2

'The time of my life': Order and Orders, November 1914 to March 1915

When an enlisted man became an officer it was usual for him to move battalions, though often within the same regiment. In the early stages of the war, there were rarely battalions of the same regiment in the same brigade (with the Ulster Division being a notable exception) and so a new officer would usually find himself moving brigades, if not divisions. Staniforth's promotion saw him switch regiments but remain in the same brigade, moving from the 6/Connaughts to the 7/Leinsters within 47 Brigade.

As a consequence of remaining in 47 Brigade, Staniforth's time at the front would be spent in close proximity to the men with whom he had first served. In other ways, however, promotion meant that the nature of his service became markedly different to that of the private soldier. His focus in training now turned on how to lead men in battle. Before then, instead of being one of the men, Staniforth would have to learn how to maintain order in the ranks. Discipline had already been a problem in the 6/Connaughts, but was even more marked in units which Staniforth saw less of, in 49 Brigade.[1]

Old Barracks, Fermoy, 6 November 1914
I'm so pleased with the wrist-watch; it puts my brother-officers in the shade absolutely. All my thanks and love for it.

I've been here a week now, and I'm having the time of my life. (I've said that before, of course, but each change seems better than the last.) The Mess are a delightful set, and we get on very well together. There's W. J. Cullen, the Oxford and Monkstown fly-half, who came up to the Varsity a year after I did, and chucked up Honour Mods[2] to come out here. He is a scholar of Pembroke, a fair-haired boy of 19 (20 to-morrow; but still 19 as yet!). We have 16 sub[altern]s,[3] all young and very keen. There is a humorous side in seeing them on parade in the morning, each with a squad of about 20 men, driving them for all they're worth, tremendously serious, and lecturing them on 'soldierly spirit,' 'esprit de corps,' 'discipline,' 'smartness' and all the rest (the subs being any age from 19 to 25, the men from 20 to 50-odd and taking it all meekly), and then ten minutes later in the mess-room ragging like schoolboys. There's something tremendously attractive about the average officer; I think because he has always to be setting an example to the men, and that phrase means a lot more here, somehow, than it did at school or elsewhere. The men are always watching, and you wouldn't believe the number of little things, quite ordinary, that one refrains from doing under their scrutiny. And of course you can't afford to be the smallest bit careless of your personal appearance: a shave twice a day if necessary, hands washed every hour, boots always clean, buttons always shining till you can see your face in them – in fact, up to concert pitch always. It's very trying, but it produces very fine results.

Mess in the evening is a parade, and as such compulsory. Clean white collars, black ties, khaki trousers, and pumps is the attire, with the ordinary khaki tunic. The Colonel sits at the head[,] the major beside him, then the captains, the senior sub, and all the snotties[4] in order down to myself. The King's toast is rather a stirring minute at the end; somehow it appeals to me. Then over the coffee and cigarettes the pipers come in (the Leinsters are one of the pipe regiments) and march round and round the table playing, and it's all very fine. Then the C.O. goes out, and everybody rises to their feet respectfully, and in some curious manner it all gets at one – the whole atmosphere – most indescribably.

The most dramatic moment, I think, is always at church. After the last hymn the organ strikes up the National Anthem, and every soldier in the church comes to attention with a click, from the grey-haired Colonel lean and stiffly straight as a poker, down through the boy-lieutenants (lots of them are no more than that) to the most drunken and thoughtless of Tommies in a back pew. It's a moving sight.

Is it any wonder, when we have all these traditions and grandeur to share among ourselves, that they say we despise civilians? There's so much they lose. I feel much prouder of saying 'I'm in the Army' than I did of saying 'I am at Christ Church . . . or Charterhouse' – and yet they are as great in their way. But the Army is a *man's* work so emphatically, and I suppose that's why one is proud of doing one's little bit. It gives you self-respect.

Now I can study military books (and God knows we have enough reading to do) with a hundred times more enjoyment than I ever did classics or philosophy. They were interesting enough, it's true, but this work is so damn practical. I can see in a moment exactly *why* such-and-such a lesson is laid down, simply because it's the best possible way of doing things, and I realise at once, with a gasp of admiration, that it is the best, of course, and that I should never have got at it by myself in a week of Sundays. And then I never forget it; one *can't* forget it, once it's been shown. There are dozens of small instances of this. For example, it would not occur to me that troops advancing steadily across the open under effective enemy fire suffer less than they would if they were lying down even under moderately good cover – *because of the constant alteration of the range*, as well as the moral effect on the enemy, of course. Again, under direct frontal artillery fire, you get your men out in small shallow columns *on an irregular front*, so that the range from the enemy's guns is different in each case. They're small points, but they were wise men who thought of them.

When I first joined, there were no quarters for me; they were all full up, and I had to billet myself for a couple of nights in the town. After that one of the other junior subs offered me a half-share in his quarters, so I doubled in with him, and we doss together very comfortably. We share the servant, who is not the least of wonders in the Army. Every single thing you could want, or fancy you wanted, he procures in some mysterious way of his own, and the room is kept as tidy and clean as a corner of Paradise. All the kit we need at various times for different parades and messes is laid out and warmed ready; all the uniforms are kept clean and pressed; and in fact for the first time have a first-class valet. Unlike the Oxford scout, he is, incidentally, as honest as they make them, and as willing as can be.

It used to make me laugh at first when I was solemnly saluted by all the old sweats, sergeant-majors with 30 years' service and the like, but one gets used to it. By the way, the two-inch raising of one finger in acknowledgement is heavily discouraged in this regiment; you must return the courtesy of an inferior most scrupulously. And quite rightly; I known myself how much ill-feeling is bred by an officer who takes no notice of your saluting.

The increase of pay you were referring to applies to us, most certainly; so I shall be quite comfortably off when I get it. Unlike Oxford, the Army offers you very few temptations to spend money. Upon being gazetted (did you see mine in last Thursday's Times?) you write to Cox & Co. of Charing Cross, and they send you a lot of forms to be signed, and after that you get a cheque-book to be honoured in any bank, and you draw cheques as you need them at the local bank wherever you are stationed.

Now it's time I stopped. I'm enclosing a few Leinster buttons and a bit of regimental ribbon (2d an inch; I paid 6d for this scrap!).

Old Barracks, Fermoy, 19 December 1914

[. . .] I'm afraid I have bad news for you, so it's as well to get done with it. There was only a limited – a very limited – number of Christmas leaves going in this battalion, and they were all snapped up long before they got down among the subs. It's just possible I may get five days days or so later on in January – if I don't it won't be for want of trying – but one never knows. There's a wild rumour that we are for Egypt after the New Year, but of course these things aren't published till just before, so it probably isn't true. However, this is going to break the record of Christmasses at home; I hope it will be the last, as well as the first.

Your wrist-watch has been invaluable for night work; I'm so grateful for it. If you are still knitting, there are a couple of things I want rather badly. One is a pair of gloves, also for night work; I lost one of my first pair last time we were out – and don't forget the elastic loop; it doubles the value of them. The other pair served me very well; I could just slip them on my wrist, and they were safely out of harm's way. Also they were beautifully warm.

The other is a curious thing for you to try your hand on. I want again something (again for night work, of which we are doing a lot and going to do still more) to go *over* my boots, for quiet walking. It's almost impossible to go noiselessly over roads with big nails in one's boots, short of crawling literally on your stomach, and that isn't pleasant in this weather. I've ruined a couple of pairs of socks that way; torn them to rags; and cloths bound over the boots aren't very satisfactory. I should imagine a kind of big bedsock would meet the purpose, perhaps with a loofah-sole inside, but that's for your own invention. But gloves are the more important; duplicate if you like, for my brother officers are very glad of a loan now and then.

There isn't much news; one day telleth another, and one night certifieth another as they did in the Psalmist's days. We progress slowly with our raw material; we have advanced from Squad Drill (little bodies of a dozen or twenty men, for individual instruction) to Company Drill (a completely different and more complicated set of manoeuvres, for the whole Company of 150 men or so), and in due time we shall reach Battalion Drill, I suppose. Also we have started route-marching: short easy-going marches of six or eight miles to start with, until we work up to the full thirty miles a day in heavy marching order.

I had an amusing experience the other day. We had a free afternoon, and I had a horse out for the day (I'm getting a devil of a horseman now).

We were trotting easily past the gate of the New Barracks when my great beast suddenly gave a yaw to the east and tore in under the arch into the barrack square. Several companies of the Connaughts were drilling there, and the square was hopping with majors and captains, when in comes a second-lieutenant at the canter, rockets helplessly round the square nearly annihilating several companies, and shoots out again!

I was casually examining a sword in the ante-room of the Mess yesterday, when somebody innocently suggested, 'Let's have a look at the blade.' I pulled it out of the scabbard without thinking, and the next thing was gleeful shouts from everybody of 'Drinks all round!' and was gently informed that the penalty for baring steel in the Mess was champagne all round at dinner. However, everyone generously professed teetotalism for one night only; which was very nice of them.

We had a spell of trench-digging the other day, and sweated like navvies for several hours in heavy clay. A trench is no end of a scientific business: 2 ft. wide, 10 ft. deep, with all sorts of traverses,[5] revetements,[6] recessing, drainage, parapets[7] and other delights; not at all the sort of simple hole in the ground you would imagine.

I think that's all for the present. I'm still happy and bright, and enormously interested in my work; but the more you learn, the more you see how much there is in it, and how unfit we are to go to the front for months and months to come. [. . .]

Old Barracks, Fermoy, 25 December 1914
It's a queer experience to be dating a letter to you 'Christmas Day,' and I don't like it. Still, it's in a good cause; there's some consolation to be drawn from that. One of the toasts drunk in the Mess last night was, 'To our next Christmas – in Berlin or heaven!' But, better still, it may be in Hinderwell; and then, please God, it'll be a long time before we have another apart. [. . .]

We celebrate as best we can in barracks, and we contrive to give the place a fairly festive look. There are almost sure to be one or two professional decorators in each company, and the rooms are a mass of coloured paper, in festoons and chains and patterns and artificial flowers. A favourite idea is a brown blanket stretched on the wall with lettering cut out of gold paper and pasted on it in appropriate legends: 'Success to Colonel Wood and the Officers of the Leinsters,' 'Good luck to the Irish Brigade,' etc., and one for each subaltern, 'A Happy New Year to Lieutenant Staniforth,' and all the rest. The men get turkey and plum pudding, with a pint of beer each and oranges and nuts and what extras their company officers like to give them in the way of cigarettes, cigars, port and the like; so they don't do too badly.

As a secret between ourselves, I must tell you of an episode that occurred after dinner. The men get their dinners at a quarter to 1, and at 1 o'clock all the officers visit their companies and drink their health while the C.O.[8] goes round the lot (drinking en route even more than you [Staniforth's father, a doctor] do on a Christmas morning round). We got back to our Mess about 1.30, and of course the men were finished and out of their barrack-rooms before we were half-way through. Well, what did they do but come howling round the Officers Mess, giving three cheers for the Colonel and the rest of us, and all that sort of thing. The C.O. at once ordered the doors to be locked; and there we sat within, like French aristocrats in the revolution, while the mob surged and roared outside the windows. The geography of the Mess is like this:

with folding doors into the billiard room, which also opens directly on the square at the door A. Suddenly we heard a fearful crash beyond the folding doors, and a mob of B and C Company men poured in from the billiard room and violated the sanctuary of the Mess itself, where we were all sitting at dinner. The B fellows made straight for one of their own subs, Johnstone,[9] and the C's came for me. They laid violent hands upon us and tore us out of our chairs, under the scandalised eyes of the C.O., and before we knew where we were, we were out of the Mess and riding round the square. We were taken to the barrack-rooms and stuck up on the table among the remains of the dinner and made to orate to them before they would take us back to the Mess. Of course it was very kindly meant, but fearfully out of order, and we didn't in the least know what the C.O. would say when we crawled rather sheepishly back into the dining-room, considerably heated and dishevelled. However he was at his third glass of port by that time, so he only cursed us a bit for not having our men better in hand.

The afternoon we spent in various rags: cock-fighting on the floor, dancing, tug-of-war, blindfold boxing, intervals of snooker for the less inebriated, and so forth. In the evening I was asked down to a dinner the cadets (O.T.C.) were holding in the hotel. It was no end of a show: champagne flowing like water, and speeches of all degrees of eloquence and coherence, and lasted till midnight. Then I came home and sat up in Billy Cullen's rooms drinking coffee and talking Oxford till 3 or so in the morning. Then we went back to the Mess and found a handful of very drunken subalterns, and had a couple of rounds with them, and then rolled off to bed. And bathed, shaved, breakfasted, and on parade by 8 o'clock this morning (Boxing Day) as fresh as paint! So much for the Army training. But it was a very wet night.

The funniest thing was when two or three of us visited the sergeants' mess, before I went down to dinner. They were just beginning their evening [. . .] and a more bleary, fishy-eyed, solemn set of old owls I never saw. They climbed very slowly and carefully to their feet when we came in, and one of them contrived to bring in a round of glasses and a bottle of John Jamieson[10] on a tray, very much at the slope, and they crowded round, very dazed and muddled and incoherent, and made us drink while they sang to us: strange, dolorous songs of love and death and farewell, in minor keys with hiccoughs to mark the time.

And that was how I spent Christmas. It wasn't bad, but I'd rather have been at home.

Old Barracks, Fermoy, 21 January 1915
We've had a terrible time since I came back. The man who shares rooms with me went away to Cork on twenty-four hours' leave, stayed away five days, and returned last Sunday in incipient delirium tremens.[11] On Monday evening he raved for a couple of hours on the bed in our rooms, disclosing the fact that he was a deserter from the Canadian army, and had been tried for murder in South America, and fought in the Mexican war[12] (all of which he subsequently acknowledged to be true), and later on he sobered up and broke down completely – nerves – and I had to sit up with him all that night. At times he was sobbing in arms, and at other times he was asking for drink and threatening to shoot himself or me. I had to get the revolver away from him, or I believe he would have done.

Next day he was placed under open arrest, but broke it and went down town for more drink. He was discovered and brought back under close arrest, pending court-martial. So now every time I go to my quarters there is an armed sentry outside the door, on guard over a brother officer. It's horrible. The C–M comes off on Monday; I shall have to be chief witness. Poor silly devil; I'm afraid he'll be cashiered.[13] It's rotten for the regiment.
[. . .]

Old Barracks, Fermoy, 26 January 1915

At last the move has been sprung upon us; quite suddenly, of course. The whole battalion, transport, supply, and ammunition column, moves out to Kilworth Camp[14] tomorrow. We got the orders yesterday, just after several companies had been inoculated and were prepared to lie up for three or four days! So now we're in the middle of all the preparations for a flit; overhauling equipments, making up deficiencies, packing up goods, and all the rest of it.

After to-morrow my address will be 7th Leinsters, Kilworth Camp, Fermoy Station.

Thanks very much for the mittens and things. I distributed them to C Company, who were properly grateful, especially as we've just started 7 a.m. parades and it's very cold on a dark January morning. Thank you for my own, too; the leather gauntlet things are fine. [. . .]

Another yarn from Salisbury Plain. 'Halt! Who goes there?' 'Grenadier Guard.' 'Pass, Grenadier Guard; all's well.' 'Halt! Who goes there?' 'Scots Guard.' 'Pass, Scots Guard; all's well.' 'Halt! Who goes there?' 'What blank, blank business is it of yours?' 'Pass, Canadian; all's well.'

Rather nice, don't you think?

Kilworth Camp, Fermoy, 5 February 1915

At last we are here and fairly well settled down. We had a grand march out; the day was perfect; bright, hard, and frosty; and the battalion was a very imposing sight. For the first time we paraded at full strength: servants, cooks, orderlies and all, in full marching order with greatcoats, straps, haversacks, water-bottles, mess-tins, rifles, belts, bayonets and the whole of the British infantryman's Christmas-tree. The Connaughts sent their band to play us out for the first mile, and after that we had our own pipes, fifes and drums. Nearly half a mile of road we took, and every time it curved we caught sight of the line stretching away ahead, just as one does in a long train. We made a great impression coming up through the glens, with those fierce little Irish war-pipes they have screeling and echoing among the hills, and the long column winding up the mountain-side after them.

This is very much like the ordinary hill-station: just a wind-swept collection of huts up among the fells, and one hotel. It's a grand place for field-training, and the views are superb (we are on the lower peaks of the Galtees; Galteemore itself is quite close, and looks fine in the windy red sunsets we get), but the weather has been vile since the first day: rain continually, and sometimes snow and hail, with a wind that would shave the beard off a mouse.

All the other officers have gone into the hotel, and have their Mess there, but I got an empty hut just outside the camp to myself, and live by myself like a hermit until dinner-time, when I go down and spend the evening with the rest. It's better than being in a room in a crowded hotel, and also it's nearer, for the inn is a quarter of a mile away: a consideration on a wet day. The hut is an old wooden drying-shed, so it's warm and dry, and has a topping stove. It's austerely furnished, of course, but very cosy. I call it Tipperary Villa, because it's a hell of a long way – from the others! [. . .]

Kilworth Camp, Fermoy, 14 February 1915
[. . .] We have started company field-training now. The company is struck off all garrison duties – guards, picquets,[15] fatigues, orderly duties, etc. – and we spend every day skirmishing over the Kilworth hills, practising attacks delivered over a two-mile approach, or entrenching, or fortifying small posts, and things like that.

What happens is this. We parade in full marching order, the men carrying picks, shovels, and rifles as well as the usual hardware-shop which is hung about them – as it might be, in the field outside the Anchorage. The captain says, 'The enemy is posted 1400 yards beyond the ridge 500 yards S.W. of ROXBY CHURCH.[16] From here to that ridge we are under his long-range artillery fire. When the ridge is reached we come for the first time within his distant rifle-fire. The company will advance in shallow columns on an irregular front for the first two miles, making every use of the ground, and will extend before reaching the crest of the ridge.' Then the four platoons spread out into a line, about 500 yards apart – say, one at the Anchorage, one beyond the Long Row, one at Far Rosedale, and one in the fields west of the Burning Rock – and we make as straight as we can for the moors inland, avoiding all roads and conspicuous landmarks likely to be range-marks for the guns. It being impossible to damage the enemy with rifles, all we want is to press forward as fast, and suffer as little, as possible. So we curse and threaten and encourage and harry the poor beggars forward, leaping ditches, bursting through hedges, splashing into bog-holes, crowding through gaps (though gaps are avoided as much as possible), endeavouring to keep the men together and preserve some sort of straight line across country and keep in touch with the neighbouring platoons. In 'dead ground' (i.e. hollows invisible from the enemy's position) we pause to regain breath and formations; and finally the platoons explode from the middle suddenly into a long thin line of men ten paces apart, over a frontage of a mile or so, and advance cautiously behind scouts over the crest of the ridge.

Then we do it all over again backwards.

This is called The First Stage of the Attack, and very tiring it is in the rain over this soaked and hilly country. It has rained *every day* since we came here, except when it snowed. I thought Hinderwell could be pretty bad, and Oxford worse, but I never dreamed that God had made any spot like this. Also, in a newly constructed camp, there are no roads, only trampled mud cut up by the builders' traction-engines; and your Dirty Lane pales its ineffectual fires beside them. I have soaked and frozen feet all day and every day, but I'm none the worse so far, though always drenched to the skin.

Kilworth Camp, 29 February 1915
We are still here, but there are all kinds of rumours of impending departure in the air. One says we are to go out to France in April. Another says a selected battalion is to be made up of picked companies and officers from all the regiments in the Irish Brigade and sent out. There are various reasons for them: the 10th Division went out last week and we come next, for one thing. Also we have received two slightly wounded officers back from the front, and they have been 'stiffening' all the regiments this way just before they send them out. Meanwhile, we are still here in the rain, carrying on with the company training.

We had quite a score the other day. The company was on outpost duty at night, and the C.O. was to come round and inspect its dispositions. Now, an outpost company which is protecting a large bivouac divides itself up into several little sections posted at strategic points along the outpost line and called piquets; and each piquet in turn, after making its own self-contained domestic arrangement for defence, cooking, communications, etc., pushes out two or three small sentry-groups along its front. The sentry, on being surprised, falls back upon the piquet, which at once prepares for a desperate resistance in its protected position, thus giving the main body in the bivouac behind it time to get ready for action – and that is how outposts are worked.

I and my command (No. 10 Platoon) were No. 1 Piquet. Piquets are numbered from the right of the outpost line; in other words, we held the flank, No. 11 Platoon were the 2nd piquet, on our left, No. 12 the 3rd, further to our left, and No. 9 was a reserve in position to the rear. Platoons

are numbered consecutively through the battalion, four to a company. So
C Company comprises Nos. 9-12 Platoons, of which No. 10 is my private
and independent command.

I had told my men before that in night-work a sentry sticks to the
bayonet as far as possible, as rifle-fire may give away his position. So all
sentries were lying very close, and the piquet-line was still as the grave.
Then we heard the C.O. coming along on a horse over the moor, and we
saw him against the stars. Two of my sentries he passed at arm's length
in the dark, and then he walked on right across the front of the piquet-
trench. As soon as he was out of sight I sent an orderly back at once to
Capt. Phillips in the rear with a message giving the time he passed us, a
description of him, and a claim to have put him out of action three times.

Well, it seems the C.O.[17] went back to Pipps[18] in a deuce of a rage and
began to give him hell for leaving the right flank unguarded. 'I was over
the ground myself,' says he, 'and not a sentry was there there.' So Pipps
says nothing, but shows him our message, and explains that the right flank
wasn't so unguarded at all. Then he came back and made us show him all
our sentries again, and complimented us on their posting and good behaviour.

There is a great recruiting scheme on. A selected platoon is to be
dressed in khaki and equipped properly, and tour the south of Ireland
with a band and a banner, 'Flock to the Irish Brigade'[.] I don't envy the
officer put in charge of it. There is altogether too much politics in this
Irish Brigade business; if there were less politics and more soldiering we
might see the front sooner. We have Kettle[19] and Gwynne[20] already, and
Willie Redmond[21] arrived the other day in the cadet corps, so they have
what Smith (my servant) calls a 'click' now.

Smith's very funny sometimes. Said I to him the other day, 'Smith, is
it raining outside?' ''Tis, then,' says he, 'and what's more, there's a strong
weighty drop leppin' this minyit on yer own hearth-stone, so there is.'
(And so there was, indeed; I had to put a bottle under it to catch it.)
Another time he wanted leave off parades, and I told him to ask the C.O.
'I will not,' says he, 'I ast him one time and he ate the head off me. Roarin'
mad he was, like a wet hen.' The idea of our C.O. in the least resembling
a wet hen, and also of a wet hen 'roarin' was too much for me. [. . .]

Kilworth Camp, 16 March 1915
Your parcel of 'comforts for the troops' was very acceptable; it was the
best parcel I've had yet. And thank you particularly for the identity
disc;[22] I'm wearing it always and thinking of you.

They have sent all our C Coy officers except two away on courses of instruction, so we've had a very strenuous time for the past fortnight; one of us to look after the company's domestic affairs (pay, messing, crimes and prisoners, furlough, correspondence, etc.), and the other to look after it on parade. We take it in turns, and I don't know which is the more wearing job. Also, as they do in the Army, when I could least be spared they sent me into Fermoy for four days to attend a series of tactical lectures, and left poor Purcell[23] to run the whole show on his own.

I think it's time you knew my brother officers in the company. Let me introduce them. First, there's Capt. Phillips[24] who commands us: a new captain, only promoted since the New Year; a Canadian, aged 28, with a round fat face and thick lips like a negro's – there you have him in a nutshell. Capital fellow, and works like a black. He's making the company very efficient.

Noel Purcell is our second-in-command: the kind of Chap who lives in Norfolk jackets with a pipe, you'd say. Very square-shouldered, a topping swimmer and Rugger player, fair-haired and square-jawed, and T.C.D. – that's him. One of the best.

Then we come to the platoon commanders. No. 9 is run by Studholme,[25] 2nd Lt. I think probably you'd like him almost best. He's an old House[26] man, aged 29, dark, and very quiet – almost timid. Very shy, but very-thoroughbred and very fine-natured. I believe he owns half the town of Birr, and his hobbies are daffodils and kittens. Yes, certainly you'd like him.

No. 10 Platoon is my own. No. 11 is little Wilmot's.[27] You'd like him immensely, too. Just a wee little fellow with spectacles, thin ratty hair and a head like a coconut; a mathematical honours graduate of T.C.D., portentously learned, frightfully serious, and very simple and good-natured. He's getting a transfer into the Engineers, where he rightfully belongs.

Charlie Denroche[28] runs No. 12, about our most popular subaltern, and certainly the one that knows his job best. He's dark and handsome, stroked the Trinity boat at Henley, and played Rugger for them as well. Scouting is his speciality; he's training the company scouts as well as his own platoon's. Another of the best.

So you see I'm in luck's way, as far as the men I have to work with. We're admitted to have the best officers, and we're supposed to be the friendliest company; all the others have their little feuds and splits except us.

There's a course I'm trying very hard to get sent on just now; it's a course of signalling at Waterford. Signalling is my speciality, just as scouting is Charlie's, and I look after the company signal section (also, I've applied to be battalion signal officer). A course at Waterford with semaphore, Morse, helio29 lamps, and wireless to the ships in the harbour would suit me down to the ground. It's the most interesting side-show of military work, I think; though it's also a bit dangerous at times unfortunately.

To-morrow is Patrick's Day, and the G.O.C.[30] has closed all the pubs within 30 miles of Fermoy. We have no parades, of course; the band plays for an hour after reveille (6 to 7; chilly work!), the morning is free except for a C.O.'s parade with music, and there is a long programme of sports in the afternoon. In the evening I'm going to Fermoy to a big banquet given by my ex-comrades the cadets. It's all very frivolous, and when God will be good enough to let us see the front, only He knows.

Kilworth Camp, 25 March 1915

We had a great show yesterday. Parsons (G.O.C. the 16th Division, including the famous Irish Brigade) ordered a grand review and march-past of the Brigade, so that he could judge of its progress up to date. (We had just one day to practise it in.) The order was to parade on Race Course in Fermoy; which was all very well for the Connaughts and Royal Irish, who are quartered in Fermoy, but rather rough on the Leinsters who had an eight-mile walk down from the mountains. However, we foot-slogged in and arrived very muddy but in good condition, and well on time. In a few minutes the other two battalions rendezvoused up. The Brigade formed up in 'brigade column of mass,' facing the saluting base, like this:

The letters are companies, and the numbers platoons. The fourth battalion of the Brigade, the 8th Munster Fusiliers, are lying in Templemore, so they couldn't come. Old Miles, the Brigadier

(Brig.–Gen. J. Miles, Cmdg. 47th Inf. Bde.), sat upon his horse at the front (about where the first 'e' is in 'Leinsters') with a galaxy of scarlett [sic] -hatted staff-captains and A.D.C.s about him. The Brigade looked meekly down its noses behind him. Presently the General arrived on his charger, a meek little man, like Lloyd George; the Brigadier arose in his stirrups and cried 'General Salute!', the bugles pealed out a long note, the 3,000 men presented arms with a clash and a flourish, the officers remained stiffly at the salute, and the massed bands in the rear broke out into a little ruffle of drums and squeal of fifes. For an instant we stood so, then crashed back into immobility again while the rank and fashion of Fermoy burst into volleys of hand-clapping. A very pretty little compliment it was to the General.

After that we marched past in platoons, one by one, the Royal Irish leading ('Right turn!' – then each platoon in succession, 'Left turn! Quick march! Left wheel!' and 'Eyes right!' going past the base; see diagram), formed up again in mass, turned about, and marched-past back again all together in review order. Very imposing. Then the officers were congratulated and photographed. I'll send you a copy.

I'm for a month-or-so signalling course in Fermoy to-morrow, and then perhaps Waterford. Address 'Royal Hotel, Fermoy.' Don't begin to worry yet; we shan't see the firing line before September!

Chapter 3

'Thrills enough to satisfy the most reckless glory-hunters': Signals Training, April to September 1915

Staniforth's time at Kilworth Camp saw him training in the basics of discipline and leading men. In short, he learned how to give orders. He also began to develop a specialism which would give him a crucial role in any action undertaken by his battalion: that of signalling. From April 1915 his training focused on developing that specialism.

It is worth reflecting that over six months into his enlistment, Staniforth had come nowhere near to battle, yet this was not atypical of experiences of enlisted soldiers. The early stages of the war were fought, at least on the British side, largely by regular soldiers and by reservists, men who were not full-time soldiers but had either served previously (many were veterans of the Anglo-Boer War of 1899-1902) or had undergone annual military training.

The training given to those who enlisted in late summer 1914 was lengthy, although there is a vigorous debate among historians over how effective it was in the case of the 16th Division. Among Irish volunteer battalions, those of the 10th (Irish) Division were first into action, but not until August 1915 at Gallipoli. The Ulster Division joined battle on the Western Front in October. When Staniforth began his in-depth signals training in April, his division still had another eight months to go before it would arrive in France. There is a view among some writers, supported by contemporary views, that this was because by the middle of 1915 it was widely held that the 16th Division needed much further training before it could go to the front.[1]

Royal Hotel, Fermoy, 12 April 1915
[. . .] This course is going to last about six weeks, I think. At present we haven't got beyond flags and the buzzer (that's a kind of dummy Morse key and sounder, something like the thing at railway stations). They require every man in the section – that's 26 in each battalion – to read 14 words a minute on the buzzer, and 20 from the officers. As a matter of

fact, that's not as difficult as you might think at first; 25 is the usual Post Office rate of sending, and 32 the expert's absolute limit.

It's interesting work, and I like it immensely. We do two hours' flag-drill in the morning (Morse), and then buzzer and technical lectures; in the afternoon we do station-work in the field. The class is broken up into 'stations' of 3 men, who go out and take up positions so as to form a long chain 3 or 4 miles long, and practise sending messages right through from end to end.

The three men work like this. At a sending terminal one man holds the message and calls it out word by word (the Caller); another sends it as called (the Sender), and the third watches the distant station for the answers (the Answer-Reader). At a receiving terminal the Caller becomes the Writer, taking down the message letter by letter from the Reader, who keeps his glasses fixed always in the distant station. At the end of every word the Reader calls 'Group', the Writer, if satisfied, says 'Yes' to the third man (the Answerer), who accordingly acknowledges. It's very fascinating to watch good station-work, and surprising how smoothly and accurately it can be done. Of course the same system works if we are using telegraph or buzzer.

Later on we shall get to lamps, helios, signalling discs, and field-telephones, but we haven't touched them yet.

There's one thing – I shall always be able to get a job as a telegraphist when the war is over!

I hate to disillusion you, but the Signal Officer doesn't do anything so picturesquely foolish as waving flags on the top of a conspicuous hill between two armies. It makes a good illustration, but it's really not done by the best people. What he does far more often is to crouch in a flooded dug-out controlling a complicated commitator with scores of lines on it, like a girl at the Telephone Exchange, and swearing because the line to Brigade Headquarters leaks in about seven places (what with being laid through pools of water and walked on by men passing up and down the trenches) and the current isn't strong enough to work the key; or cursing the men at a distant station for rotten sending.

On the whole, it's a safe but very responsible and trying job. You see, the Lieutenant of Signals in a battalion is responsible for maintaining communication at all times from his Bn. Hdqrs. to the Brigade, to the component companies of his battalion, and to the units on either flank, and to establish the necessary stations accordingly. A few of his other duties are to know, at all times of the day and night, the position and station-call of the Brigade Headquarters signal section and of all the units of the Force, and of any other unit with which communication might at any time conceivably be required, and the intentions and plans of his Commanding Officer. (2nd Lieut, to Colonel: 'I must request you, Sir, to explain all your private intentions in full to me at once.' Colonel: '?!!??!!' Tableau.) He must also keep the Brigade Signal Officer informed as to the movements of his own battalion or when any particular line of communication breaks down, and any other useful information.

So you see it's a responsible job, which might at any time suddenly become all-important. 'The Signal Service,' as the book rather pompously says, 'is the nerves of an army, without which activity is impossible.' On the whole, as I say, it's a safe job (from its very importance, it has to be protected), though quite exciting. Occasionally, of course, it emerges from a kind of underground safety and obscurity right into the limelight; then it's 'some job,' and gets thrills enough to satisfy the most reckless glory-hunters. Laying a fresh cable between outpost positions under fire, for instance, can be a ticklish enough bit of work, or when your insulation fails (as it often does in the exposed conditions in which cables lie) and you have to go out and repair it, or worse still have to take to flags and come right out into the open. Still, they tell us that a flag has hardly been seen at the front yet; it's all buzzer and field-telephone work.

Did you hear of the woman in Suffolk who, being congratulated by the Rector on her son's enlistment, said, 'Well, sir, 'twas only to be expected; for after all what does the Scripture say but, "Train up a child, and away he do go."'

I've heard unofficially that I'm up before Headquarters for a second star and a full lieutenancy; I hope it'll make good. Watch the 'Times' in about a month's time. If I'm gazetted I'll apply for a month's leave on the spot!

Royal Hotel, Fermoy, 26 April 1915
[. . .] I must tell you a story about our doctor. It's rather obscene, but a good side-light on Army methods. J. Murphy O'Connor is his name (yes, you're right; not a Scotchman); he was qualified about six months ago; a raw Cork fellow, you know the kind. Well, we'd been having an awful lot of men shamming diarrhoea to get off parades; it's [a] favourite stunt, because it's so difficult to disprove. (A man of mine, though, was more naif and original; 'ye see, sorr,' said he, 'it's this way; in the

barrack-room I have me health grand, but the minyit [sic] I hear the Fall-In goin', I do be gettin' that light an' dizzy in the head.') However, my brave Murphy O'Connor made light of difficulties. Four heroes came up to him one morning when there was a long route-march on for the battalion, all pleading fierce, though intermittent, diarrhoea. So what does he do but sends over to the A.S.C. depot for four plain white utensils of domestic earthenware. 'Now,' says he, 'ye sit on these pots till the rigiment [sic] comes back, me buckoes, and then we'll have a look at your diarrhoea.' And begad, he marched them over to the guard-room, each with his little white pot under his arm; and there in the cells these four great ruffians sat for three hours while a sentry mounted guard over them with a fixed bayonet. And at the end of three hours, when the battalion returned, there wasn't as much as would cover a farthing in any one of the pots!

We've had no more malingerers on that tack since.

Our C.O. has been chucked by the medical board for active service. He left us on Saturday, I believe to get a brigadier-generalship somewhere. They say the leave-taking was most impressive. He's a perfect type of the traditional 'officer and gentleman,' you know; a very upright and stately old aristocrat. (He frightened me [. . .]; I always used to drive my platoon round a corner when he strolled out on the parade-ground.) He formed up the whole battalion on Saturday, and addressed them something like this:- 'Officers, warrant officers, non-commissioned officers, and men. They have told me I am not fit to go on active service with you, so I have ordered you here this morning to bid you farewell. I wish to thank you for your help and cheerful obedience to my orders; we have worked together for six months now, and I think we may say we have made something out of nothing. I have no more to say, except that I am confident that when you get your chance in the great game you will carry on the traditions of our 1st and 2nd Battalions. Dismiss the parade, please, Mr Adjutant.'

Then he mounted his horse and rode slowly down the road out of our lives, as the stories say. Everyone wept like children. It was a great speech, wasn't it? No sentimentality or heroics; just plain and soldierly like himself.

Last week-end I went to Cork for the first time. We played the Connaughts up at Kilworth in the afternoon – hockey – (we drew, 3 all; I scored for us), and afterwards Charlie Denroche said he would take me to Cork in his side-car if I'd come. So I put a pair of pyjamas in my great-coat pocket, with a toothbrush and comb, and we started off, just like that. Of course we broke down half-way, miles from anywhere by the roadside, but we patched her up with a piece of wire we found in the road (!), and finished the journey very gingerly with a bit of rusty wire between us and ruin. We went to a music-hall that night, slept together in the last remaining bed at the Metropole, went to a Turkish bath on Sunday morning, and returned in the evening.

They say Cork is the coming city of Ireland (Dublin was, Belfast is, Cork will be), but I didn't think much of it, except the river-view, which is pretty and rather continental: white houses clustering on wooded slopes both sides of the river. We heard 'the bells of Shandon sounding so grand on the pleasant waters of the river Lee,' but unlike Father Prout[2] we thought the girls of Cork horrid. Still, it was something to get into civilisation again, with electric trams and cafes and plate-glass windows and theatres, after Kilworth Camp.

The signalling goes on fairly well, though the men are a bit slow. Lamp and buzzer work is what we do all day long now.

Royal Hotel, Fermoy, 4 May 1915

[. . .] The only news I have for you is that the fourth regiment in our Brigade has now been marched over from Templemore and settled down under canvas beside us in Kilworth Camp; that's the 8th Munsters. So now we have the whole 47th Brigade quartered in or around Fermoy: Connaughts, Leinsters, Royal Irish and Munsters. I suppose that means there'll be some hard Brigade field days two or three times a week now. However, the signalling class goes serenely on, and is near its conclusion now as it was five weeks ago.

Most of our officers are away just now: Billy Cullen is on a week's leave, Studholme on sick leave, Phillips in hospital (mumps!), one away on a transport course, another at Dollymount on a machine-gun ditto, another at Chelsea on a general Officers Training Course, and myself away signalling.

The new C.O. has arrived, but I haven't seen him yet. Beyond that he's 'a very big man' and has been promoted temporary Lt.-Col. from plain captain and named Buckley,[3] I've heard nothing about him.

There is a lad here, back wounded from Neuve Chapelle,[4] who was four years at Charterhouse with me. He lives here, apparently; which his name it is Brooke [sic], of Hodgsonites.[5] He says there is one officer besides himself left alive in the 1st Battalion of the Connaughts. Stiff, isn't it. The Leinsters have been getting rather cut up just lately, too.

Royal Hotel, Fermoy, 23 May 1915

We have been 'in action' for the first time now! – just returned from a week's Brigade training. It was a capital week, too; packed with interest and not a dull moment from cover to cover, as the reviewers say.

We and the Rangers (Brown Force) were opposed to the Royal Irish and the Munsters (White Force). On the first day we marched out with our allies to the 'theatre of war,' 19 miles from here among the mountains and bogs. We were a most imposing column on the road: first the band – fifes, drums and pipes – then the signallers, then the scouts, then main body: four full companies of very dusty Tommies in full marching order (packs, straps, bandoliers, water-bottles, greatcoats, mess-tins, and rifles and bayonets: the whole Christmas-tree); then the machine-gun section with their spidery little guns and spidery little officer, then the transport – three majestic G.S. wagons with four horses and a driver apiece, and a couple of little limbered wagons with officers' transport and rations – and finally the baggage-guard and stretcher-bearers. We took up about three-quarters of a mile all told. A state of war did not exist till midnight, so we had no need to adopt precautions on the line of march.

At 6 o'clock in the evening we reached the bivouac-ground: an open field in the middle of heathery waste, at the top of a slope. For half a mile the ground dropped away southward, down to a little stream with wooded banks (the BRIDE), and rose again on the other side to a ridge of hills. (Imagine us camped above the Quarry behind the Anchorage, with the ground falling away past the railway-bridge over the STAITHES road to the beck, and then rising again through OAKRIDGE Wood up to the moorland ridge beyond, and you have some idea of the position.) A road ran down out of the bivouac to the river, and made a T-piece with the road that ran along the river bank. Half a mile west of this T-piece was a bridge over the river.

The battalion closed up into mass-formation in the field, and the order was 'sleep where you stand.' (The Connaughts were there before us, and had their arrangements already complete.) The men took off their packs and rolled out their blankets and got ready their sleeping arrange-ments, and then fell out for the evening. The cooks arrived with their field-kitchen smoking, and supper was soon going round. Fires were lit, and in the twilight we began to look quite like the picturesque idea of an army round its camp-fires.

Headquarters were under a couple of pine-trees just outside the field, where the two colonels and their staff were quartered. That was my place, of course, as I was responsible for the communications. I had a detachment of 25 signallers under me, whom I told off four to each company, and eight to headquarters with their sergeant and myself. I had also four cyclist orderlies whom I kept in my own hands. These, and my 8 headquarters section, I brought over to where I could lay my hands on them in the night; the rest slept with the battalion.

After I had made these arrangements and seen the men get their supper, and got my own, and explained to them just where every company officer, adjutant, colonel, etc., was to be found in the dark, it was 11 o'clock, and most people had turned in except the sentries. Hostilities didn't commence till midnight, so I rolled into my flea-bag for an hour's sleep. It was raining softly at the time, so I was thankful for it (the flea-bag).

At 12 o'clock the outposts moved off to take up their positions: two companies of the Rangers. I went with them. We put piquets along the river front wherever the enemy might cross, and a sentry-post at the bridge. For communication, we laid a cable from the Headquarters at the bivouac down the road to the T-piece and along the river bank to the headquarters of the O.C. Outposts. Between him and the units of his command (piquets, etc.) we had a chain of orderlies on foot or cycles, as the roads were good and the woods too thick for any sort of visual signalling.

By the time the piquets were all posted and communication established from end to end of the outpost line, it was close on three o'clock, and the reliefs were not due till six; so I walked back to the sleeping camp and had another two hours in the flea-bag. At five the reliefs paraded, and I went down again to the river with them to see them into position and explain the communications to them. This time they were A and D Coys of the Leinsters.

After they were in position the regiments breakfasted, packed up their transport, and got ready to move. About seven o'clock the enemy, who had made no sign up to now, got into touch with the outposts, and we heard a few scattered shots down by the river. Then messages began to come in over the wire. They had come down in strength and forced the passage of the river; the outposts were being driven in; supports needed, etc. (This, by the way, was all part of the General Idea; we were to fight a rearguard action as we retired; the G.O.C. wanted to test White Force's offensive and Brown Force's defensive powers.)

So we threw out three companies widely to hold the enemy all along his line (his front was then about a mile and half), and the outposts fell back through them and had their breakfast behind the firing-line.

By this time we had fallen back clear of the woods along the river, and all the signalling staff were working at high pressure, with flags twinkling all over the landscape from behind hedges and walls and houses and everything. I had a steadily-mounting sheaf of message-forms under my hand, and the C.O. was licking 'em up like a cat lapping milk and asking for more. We had reeled in the cables as the firing-line withdrew, and there wasn't much more than a quarter of a mile of it now. The sappers had *their* wire laid back to the G.O.C., a mile or so further away in the rear, and I think he kept fairly hot too, with messages to the C.O.

All that day we retired and fought, clinging to every hill or ridge that could be held, and tramping doggedly along the roads when there weren't any, with shots going on behind us where our firing-line was holding up the enemies advance to let us get back safely to the next position. It was beastly hot, too. The signalling was rather difficult, what with every unit on the move all the time.

At nightfall we halted about five or six miles to the rear of our previous bivouac. We were amongst mountains by this time; little hills and kopjes all over the shop. Battalion Headquarters were in a deserted cottage that night, and I was on the roof working the lamp-key to the outposts on the hills around. There was what the papers call 'a certain liveliness' all night, but on the whole we scored. Plenty of messages came through. 'Enemy attempted to rush piquet here; we captured three,' my operator at No. 1 Outpost Coy would say, from a hill a quarter of a mile away to the left; and just as his flash died out in the dark, another would blaze out on the right, 'Cheero, nine more prisoners!', trying to send it in such a hurry that his letters tumbled over each other like an excited messenger stammering. Lamps and telegraphs are very human; they respond in an awfully sensitive way to the man behind them. I could tell from my cottage-roof every time the operator was relieved at the other end, just from the difference in the sending.

It was a long night, and rather cold, but two incidents broke it agreeably. Once when a sergeant brought me hot tea and biscuits – that was about one o'clock – and again an hour later when an orderly came back from the outposts to me with a captured signalling-lamp and telephone of the enemy's, which made a valuable addition to our equipment. It seemed the subaltern of that particular piquet had got tired of sitting in the dark, so he took out a patrol and went skirmishing on his own among the enemy's lines. The first thing he stumbled on was their advanced signal station, busily signalling back progress to their headquarters; and when they looked up from their work, they were prisoners! They said it was not playing the game for an outpost, which is essentially a thing that sits still on the defensive, to turn itself into a dangerous wandering thing like a patrol, which bloweth where it listeth.

Altogether that night we got 68 rank and file, 5 non-coms, and 2 officers prisoners, all for meddling with our piquets.

From that time on, we retired slowly all day and every day, 'disputing every inch of the way.' (The retreat from Mons was nothing to us.) At night we slept for an hour or two in ditches, and generally woke up to retire some more at about two in the morning. And retiring a battalion with all its gear across trackless hills in the dark is a fairly good test of soldiering. There were three incidents, from my point of view, during the show. One was when the transport mules, picketed just behind my ditch, stampeded from their lines at midnight and came gambolling round me with flaming eyes in the dark. They were more clumsy and inquisitive even than Kipling's commissariat camels.

The second was when we came across White Force's cable laid across the field and tapped into it with a buzzer which translated several of their messages for us. Later they spotted this somehow, and we had to content ourselves with putting wet fingers on the line and reading the long and short shocks; which sounds awfully *Boys' Friend*-ish,[6] but is quite commonplace really.

Well, the end of it was all beautiful. We were retiring at two in the morning slowly across the hills, with the enemy about half a mile after us; and we fell back into a lovely little cup in a hill: just a tiny round amphitheatre with heather-covered sides. We were posted here, on the far slope, in three successive tiers like the pit, balcony, and gallery in a theatre, each tier well under cover in a ditch; so:

Then we put one company of the Rangers on the top of a hill well to the right of our position. They were to be seen as the sun rose (about three o'clock) hurriedly digging themselves trenches as though to make a last stand on that hill. The other three companies of the Rangers, who were contesting the enemy's advance, were to retire obliquely across our front, from left to right, as if falling back on their comrades on the hill – taking no notice whatever of us as they passed across our lines, and drawing on the pursuing enemy right under our rifles.

Well, for some God-given reason it all fell out just so. We juked[7] down in our heather ditches before dawn, and you could have walked right over us and sworn there wasn't a sign of life for miles around. Then, as the dawn broke, we saw the little black figures of the Rangers silhouetted against the sky, digging for dear life. It was really very theatrical, just like a recruiting poster. We lay close, and the shots in front of us got nearer and nearer, and then over the skyline to our left came a little stream of tumbling, running toy soldiers in pell-mell retreat. And oh, they did it beautifully! Right across our front they passed, while not a man moved an eyelash as they ran by under our very muzzles. A little pause, and then after them came the enemy: wee white-capped figures pouring down the slope after them. It was awfully difficult to keep our men's heads down in their excitement, but they behaved splendidly, and not a man showed up or loosed off a single round before the moment.

We let them get right down to the bottom of the cup, about 30 yards from the muzzles of our front rank, absolutely unsuspecting, and then there came three great blasts from the Colonel's whistle and the whole hillside burst into flame. Three tiers, one above the other – 1,000 rifles – ten rounds of rapid fire from each man – and the enemy huddled up not fifty yards away. It wasn't battle, it was massacre. Not one of them had an earthly chance of course.

After that we fraternised, and marched our nineteen miles back again, and arrived home at lunch-time. And that's all. We all enjoyed it immensely, and learnt a lot.

The signalling course is now over, and I'm back at Kilworth starting another to-day for sixteen new recruits. They believe in one earning one's pay, I think. However, the C.O. told me to-day my second star has received the General's approval, so it's only a day two before it's published in Orders now; and that's cheerful news.

Oh, I forgot to say we spoofed a flag-message through to the Munsters on the second day (some spark discovered their code-call) ordering them to suspend operations till the arrival of the umpires; which they did, and got several kinds of particular hell for it. That was rather funny.

I'm getting another officer as my second-in-command for signalling. The humorous thing is that he's really my senior officer otherwise, and doesn't like it a bit.

I'm sorry this letter is all about myself, but there's nothing else here to talk about.

What do you think of the enclosed?

Sir owing to letters received by me for the past month I see that it is impossible for me to get on here any longer as I cannot leave my mind to the work I have to do.

So I ask you sir if you could possibly get me a pass if it was but for three days to take my wife from the party that is trying to separate us and leave her in another town as her mother and the remainder of her friends are doing their best against me for enlisting. Sir if possible kindly oblige

Your obedient servant

James Kerrigan

The overleaf postscript proved irresistible. I got it for him.[8]

Sir if you can grant me this favour I promise to repay you as far as it is in my power and if need be even on the battlefield.

Kilworth Camp, Fermoy, 12 June 1915

[. . .] Thank you for your telegram of congratulation.[9] It was the first intimation I got, do you know. I got so sick of waiting for the thing that I had given up looking in the Gazette. By the way, I'm still 'Esq[ui]re.' on an envelope, though, and not 'Lieut.' Still a subaltern, you see, (though a senior one now), and therefore still very small potatoes, and nothing to swank about. Only one shilling a day extra, too.

I'm up to my eyes in work just now. The battalion signallers are increased to 53 instead of 16 (they're getting very important in this war), and I have only one competent N.C.O. under me as yet. They're divided up into four different classes of proficiency, from the oldest lot I had at the beginning down to the latest and absolutely ignorant class I started last week, and I have to dash round from one to the other all day. From 6.45 till 7.30 the whole lot do the flag-drill together (which is like a musician doing his half-hour's scales every day); from 8.45 till 9.15 I sit in judgement upon their crimes (of which there are very few), their sicknesses, pay, clothing, and other private troubles; then till 12.30 we work, some laying telegraph-cables, some doing buzzer work, some more flag-drill, etc., with a lecture to the infants' class. In the afternoon we put them out to station-work with flags around the countryside from 2 till 4.30.

From 5 to 7 I look after their shooting on the range and train the special team for the Signalling Competition at the big Brigade Sports next month. And from 10 till 11 every night we do lamp-work. So at the end of a day I don't feel up to much.

They are giving me another subaltern as an assistant instructor, who is now away at Mallow on a course. When he comes back and I have put him in the way of things, and the latest class is able to feel its feet a bit, I shall try to put in a fortnight's leave and come home for a rest-cure. I'll try to work that round about July 31st [his mother's birthday] if I can.

Fortunately all but a very few of the men are quite keen, and that makes the job much easier. I had them out for a couple of nights last week, after I had shown them how to make tents of their blankets and tree-branches, and we had quite a good time. We marched out by map and compass to a place about four miles away over the hills and camped there, cooking our rations in mess-tins, doing flag-work in the daytime and lamps at night. The only drawback was the weather, which was too hot for words.

And that reminds me; if you can find any of my old cellular shirts around, I'd be very glad if you would send them out. These heavy khaki things are impossible with a tightly buttoned tunic in this weather. The same remark applies to white flannel trousers for the (rare) spare moments, together with white socks and shoes.

Kilworth Camp, Fermoy, 27 June 1915
[. . .] The C.O. says we are going to move to Seaford for a short while before going overseas. I fancy it's a small place on the Sussex Coast somewhere near Brighton, though I never heard of it before. But I don't think he knows anymore about it than we do, anyway. Still, I hope we go. I think the regiment would be better out of Ireland. They're very fretful at being kept here so long, as it is. And of course it would be easy to get to London now and then. You'd have to come down and stay in town.

My birthday [23rd June] was a great glad day all right, but it resembled a Mess guest-night rather, in that the night before was heaven, and the morning after (when I awoke in a pile of letters as high as a hat-box, all needing to be acknowledged) was the other place.

The enclosed is a précis of the Orderly Officer's work in a day, exclusive of ordinary parades and duties. I thought it might interest you.

7th (SERVICE) BATTALION LEINSTER REGIMENT.

REPORT OF ORDERLY OFFICER FOR THE DAY.

Kilworth Camp

_6/15_ 1915.

As Orderly Officer I performed the following duties:—

1. I inspected the Guard at Guard Mounting at _9.0_ a.m. The men were clean and well turned out.

2. I inspected the Old Guard before dismounting at _9.15 a.m._ all were correct.

3. I attended the issue of rations at _7.0_, _8.45_, _12.30_, _4.0_. The meat and bread were of good quality and in proper quantity.

4. I turned out the Guard at _10.30_ by day, and at _11.30_ by night. All were present, alert and regular.

The Sentries were acquainted with their orders. I visited the prisoners in the Detention Room The Room was clean. The men had no complaints.

5. I visited the Hospital at _11.0 a.m._ The patients have no complaints.

6. I visited the Canteen and Grocery Bar at _12.30 p.m._ and found all correct.

7. I inspected the meat for the following day's issue at 12 noon, it was of good quality.

8. I visited the Cook-houses and Wash-houses at _11.30 a.m._ and found them clean and regular.

9. I collected the Reports at Tattoo. _Seventeen_ Men were reported absent

10. I saw "Lights Out" at _9.45_ p.m.

11. I did not quit the Camp during my tour of duty.

John H. M. Staniforth Lieut,

7th (Service) Battalion Leinster Regiment.

Staniforth was at home on leave between his letters of 27th June and 18th July.
He returned to Fermoy with his bull terrier, Finn.

Kilworth Camp, Fermoy, 18 July 1915
[. . .] We had a good crossing and reached Fermoy very tired at 9 in the
morning; so I had a bath in the hotel and went to bed till the evening,
before I went on up to the camp. Finn was very fed up with trains and
boats and strange people, but he is settling down quite well now, and is
very healthy and very much loved.

We are moving to Salisbury Plain as a Division. The guns go on the
29th, but we don't follow till August 16th. It's a pity it isn't Aldershot;
much nearer London.

I found the Brigade Office had mysteriously presented us with two
magnificent telephone sets in my absence. The only difficulty was that
they were the new Ericsson pattern instead of the old ones, and no one
had dared take them out of their cases for fear of smashing them!

I was talking to a snot[10] back from the Front on the boat. He was lying
at the point of death, gassed and all but unconscious, with just enough
energy to beckon feebly to a chaplain, who came doubling up to shrive
him before he passed. The padre bent over to listen, and a faint whisper
came, 'Sergeant, tell our . . . . .s to keep a . . . . Sharp look-out for
those German . . . . . . .s over there.' Collapse of zealous chaplain.

[To his mother only]
Kilworth Camp, 30 July 1915
To-morrow is your birthday, and soon after that it will be the War's. It
is a year of anniversaries. They say that savages and women do not
observe birthdays, but I'm writing on spec for all that.

But after all, what shall one say? We have known each other for a score
of years and more; one feels a little more every year, but I think perhaps
one says (and needs to say) a little less.

It's true that in these days anniversaries acquire a certain poignant
significance; to resolve to appreciate that significance is as futile as to
clutch desperately at a fleeting moment on a summer's evening and say,
'I will enjoy this hour to the full, simply because it will never happen
again.' Efforts at complete realisation and the attempt to ensnare an
emotion are destined to failure, I think.

The sun is sinking early in clear green skies, and far away to westward
over the hills a singing west-wind is crying the heartache of the expiring
day, and I'm just feeling that it's not much good trying to do anything,

after all. Work all wrong, misunderstood by one's best friend[11] – toute la boutique.[12] Hence this decadent letter. [. . .]

The Divisional Signal Company of the R.E. has just been ordered to France, so we are left without any professional signallers. To fill the gap they are going to make a temporary 'coalition company' selected from the battalion signallers of each regiment. This they have ordered me to take charge of. It's a compliment, of course, to be selected from so many men, but like most compliments from headquarters there's a lot of extra work 'in the heel of it.'

Kilworth Camp, Fermoy, 8 August 1915
[. . .] You do jump at conclusions, little mother, don't you. There's a big difference between the O.C. Divisional Signal Company, who is a captain in the Royal Engineers responsible for the communications of 18,000 men, and an O. i/c Brigade Signal Section with only 4800 men to look after. And even the last is a bigger job than the regimental Signal Officer, responsible only for communication inside his own battalion of 1200 men.

So far we haven't had any manoeuvres since my new appointment, so it's been a sinecure as yet.

Finn[13] lay very quiet for a week or so. Then he sat up and took notice – of the other camp dogs. As a consequence he is now convalescent, with gaping wounds in his throat, back and shoulders. I got zinc ointment from the doctor and washed him and dressed him (not the doctor; Finn), and he's getting on very nicely now, thank you. I think he enjoyed it all immensely, though. He nearly killed one mangy old bitch; fortunately it seemed that no one owned her. He also got run over by a motor car; no harm done, though.

Kilworth Camp, Fermoy, 15 August 1915
[. . .] we vacillate between Aldershot and Salisbury Plain. Of course I'll let you know when we come over. But before that we're going to have the deuce and all of a function. On Wednesday next we all go to be inspected by the Lord Lieutenant[14] and Lady Wimborne at Fermoy; the whole Division, horse, foot and guns; and next day all the officers go to a garden party to meet Their Excellencies at Adare Manor in Limerick, where they're staying with the Dunravens. We have the privilege of paying for a special train there, and I suppose about another fifty guineas for a diminutive cup of tea and Garden-of-Eden cake, and the pleasure of walking through the grounds at Adare in fiercely defensive little

groups, taking cover behind the rhododendrons from anything that looks like a host or hostess.

Last week I had my first show as Brigade Signal Officer. We were doing a retirement: two battalions retreating before the onslaught of a third, with the fourth behind as general reserve. Brigade HQ of course retired also, some distance behind the main body. It's difficult to keep any sort of communication with units all on the move, but the Brigadier was pleased to express approval at the subsequent pow-wow; the joke being of course that nobody except myself knew quite how badly we had done, and I had the sense to keep my mouth shut.

Finn is in very rigorous confinement now; under close arrest, in fact, with a month's C.B. He broke out last week and made a fearful mess of himself again, scrapping; came home in such a state that you wouldn't have known him, but thoroughly happy and impenitent. I think he's learning to fight now, which he never did at Hinderwell. I sent over to the M.O. for some carbolised Vaseline, and my servant produced a 'field dressing' from somewhere, and we washed, anointed, and bandaged him; and now he's chained to the stove in my quarters for convalescence, and very unhappy about it.

I am spending all my days in the saddle now, either riding round signal stations in the mornings, or joy-riding about the country with Billy in the afternoons. He's got an old lady's hunter (I mean a lady's old hunter) from the transport officer, and Bucephalus (mine) is the adjutant's old charger, so we get on very well. I'll send you a snapshot[15] of us both when they're developed.

I'd like you to know Billy; you'd like him enormously. When I send my things home and you see three big photographs of him signed 'Billy Cullen' remember who it is. Funny we never knew one another at Oxford; rooms opposite each other (Pembroke and Ch. Ch.[16]) and both members of the Paddy Club.[17] Such is life.

Kilworth Camp, Fermoy, 22 August 1915
We have our official notice to quit now – at least, we have our destination, though not the date. The whole of this Division is to go to LARKHILL, which I think is somewhere in the middle of Salisbury Plain, though I can't find it on the map.

Well, the Lord Lieutenant held his inspection last week. For full details see my earlier letter of a former inspection. This one was exactly the same, down to the smallest details. Afterwards His Excellency said a few kind words of encouragement, and told us he had obtained the leave of the

Secretary of State to make a definite public statement to the effect that we were shortly going to England for a brief period! Anti-climax.

Then the battalion walked back to Kilworth (the show was held at Fermoy), and Billy and I stayed behind. The beauty of being a departmental officer is that on these occasions they take all your men from you to swell the ranks of their companies, and you are left without a job. So the Scouts Officer and the Signal Officer remained in Fermoy and spent a thoroughly enjoyable day, while the others marched back in the heat. We were invited to lunch in the Munsters' Mess, and a very nice lunch too. Afterwards we took a boat on the river, and bathed (a priceless bathe, the best I've had for months) and rowed back slowly in time for tea. In the evening we went to the cinema. It was a topping show, featuring Charlie Chaplin (have you seen him? A little idiot with a wee bowler, rather like an Italian ice-cream man) and we both laughed ourselves sick. At night we were given a lift home and had a nightcap in my room. Altogether an enjoyable day.

On Tuesday Their Excellencies gave a garden party at Adare. Billy and I went, and a couple of the Leinster subalterns, and of course the C.O. and Adjutant, with one captain, so we were fairly well represented.

Adare is the Dunravens' model village, a few miles from Limerick, where the Adare Cigarette Company is that makes those abominable Irish weeds. Adare Manor itself is the most glorious place I've ever been in. There is a very keen gardener, and there is every kind of tree, shrub, and plant you can think of from all over the world, acres and acres of them.

We were both presented, of course, and then we cut away from the 'gaily dressed and fashionable throng on the terrace' (see following day's Press) and went off to explore the grounds. We stayed two hours and it didn't seem longer than ten minutes! I can't tell you much about the party itself, because I didn't see any of it, but it was the usual crowd of top-hats, frock-coats, uniforms and Paris fashions that you see in pictures of Vice-regal fêtes. Tea in a big marquee (we gave it a miss), the band of the 3rd Leinsters on the tennis lawn, and all that sort of thing.

We left at 6.15, arrived home at 6.40, dined at the hotel in Fermoy, and drove up very tired to bed; and none as glad as I then.

And the next day we rode into Fermoy again, making three successive days.

The snapshots of Billy on Peter and myself on Bucephalus came back from the developer this morning, but the silly goat sent no prints, only the negatives, so until they're printed I can't send you any.

We've had no more Brigade shows this week; I hope they're too busy arranging our move to bother about them. [. . .]

Kilworth Camp, Fermoy, 3 September 1915
I should have written last Sunday but we were in Cork. Billy and I decided it was worth spending money to get out of Kilworth for a few hours, as we don't need to get formal leave for Saturday night and Sunday.

So we cast pyjamas and a toothbrush into a suit-case and departed by the 12.20 on Saturday morning and got to Cork by 1. We rushed straight to the Picture House and sat through the matinee of a most amazingly rubbishy piece called 'Love and Laughter.' It was so bad that it was good, and we were so glad to be away from the camp that we enjoyed it heartily. Then we went to the Imperial Hotel and booked a bedroom and drank tea. After tea we went for what we had really set our hearts on – a Turkish bath. After it, feeling very much cleaner than when we came in, we returned for dinner and went to a music hall, where we saw quite a good show, and so to bed; though I think it was about 1 in the morning before we finished talking and went to sleep. Clean sheets, real beds instead of Army beds, big fat pillows, a room where one could turn round – it made a fine time, to be enjoyed to the full.

Next morning we went down to breakfast at 11, after a very hot bath and a shower, and lazed about Cork in the sunshine till lunch, which we had at the club, even though non-members.

In the afternoon we hired a motor car and drove out to Queenstown, about 17 miles. It was a priceless day, and the drive was beautiful. We had tea there, and wandered around taking photographs and things. We heroically resisted battleships and destroyers; not from lack of observation, but because we didn't want the camera confiscated. And then we drove back in the evening, with a glorious sunset over the hills.

We slept the night again in our rooms, and caught an early train back in time for parade on Monday morning.

Of course it cost us some money, but we enjoyed every minute of it, and felt so much better after it that we both agreed it was thoroughly well worth it.

We have gone halves in a camera, which gives us both much delight; but as we're too lazy to do the developing ourselves, we send the films away to be developed, which saves a heap of trouble. I'm enclosing some of the first-fruits; there aren't any of Billy, because of course we split the results and each keep our own, but I'm having some more printed and I'll send them on, so you can see what he's like – if, as I suppose, you're desirous to know; you must have heard so much about him.

We're moving at last; all in a rush as usual. The advance party goes to-morrow, and we follow shortly. Apparently it's *not* to Larkhill, but to Blackdown (South Camp, Aldershot), thank God. The only thing that makes me doubtful is that we'd all *like* to go to Aldershot, and usually they pick out the worse possible place to send us.

If I don't write on Sunday, don't worry. I expect we shall all be working hard packing up the battalion.

We had a priceless day yesterday, being a half-holiday. The first part of the day we spent in the river in Fermoy, and the evening at the pictures (Charlie Chaplin again). We drove up to the camp about 11, and supped in my rooms. The weather was gorgeous; it often is in September here, after a wet sunrise.

Kilworth Camp (for the last time), Fermoy, 5 September 1915
The general atmosphere here now is very end-of-termish. The advance party has already gone, and the battalion goes on Tuesday morning. There are no parades, and everybody is up to the eyes in cleaning and packing. No parades; weird mixtures of uniforms and shirt-sleeves; straw and packing-cases everywhere; big A.S.C. wagons and horses loading up all over the place, and the whole camp in disorder.

Billy and I are being left behind in charge of the rear party. That means that for two or three days after the main body has cleared out we shall be going round with inventory lists as long as a wet Sunday 'handing over' to the newcomers, as an outgoing guard hands over to its relief. It's a long job, of course; every blessed thing has to be checked, from the camp build-ings down to the key of the cupboard where they keep the toilet-paper. And of course we have to see that every barrack-room, guard-room, offi-cers' mess, canteen, sergeants' mess, officers' quarters, wash-house, bath-house, hospital, transport stables, miniature range and every possible hut or shanty has been scrubbed, washed, swept and garnished exactly as it was when we came in here – a battalion in nine months leaves quite a lot of dirt and damage.

On the other hand, we have certain advantages. We don't have to sleep on the floor without blankets for one night at the end, as the other offi-cers will have to, and we have a quiet journey across instead of being herded over in droves in troop-trains and transport-ships.

So it will probably be the end of the week before we get across. The address will be Dettingen Barracks, Blackdown, Aldershot, Surrey.

Chapter 4

'The sun slipping west over the snowy fields': England, September to December 1915

The final phase of training for the 16th Division offered the permanent facilities of the British Army centred on Aldershot. During their stay in the area the division was made welcome by local Catholic organisations and Irish residents who ran social events for the officers and men.[1] In preparation for the Western Front, rifle training was a particular focus, fine-tuning soldiers' abilities before they arrived in France. However, before the entire division could arrive at Aldershot, Kilworth Camp had to be cleaned and made ready for new soldiers. Staniforth found himself in command of the 'Rear Party' carrying out this work.

Kilworth Camp, Fermoy, 7 September 1915
The battalion has gone at last, after making this place its home for the better part of a year; and Billy and I are left behind with a handful of men to sweep and garnish it ready for seven other devils worse than the first.

They marched out at about 7 this morning, each man loaded to the eyes with all his Lares and Penates.[2] As soon as the last of the column passed the camp boundary, we dug in. Hercules and the Augean stables had nothing on us this journey. Say, it sure was some dirt! And the things they left behind smelt foul. In two hours, we had collected 32 lbs of bread, 11 2-lb pots of jam, 73 tins of bully beef, 140 lbs of tinned peas (yesterday's rations) and about a cwt[3] of Army biscuit. And they talk of waste. Anyway, we mounted a couple of military police and picketed the camp approaches all the morning – we could see ass-carts loaded with 'unconsidered trifles' belonging to H.M. Government and driven by innocent women in black shawls who 'didn't think we were doing any harm, God save yer honour.' Then we told off a party into fatigues and set them to work collecting stores, swabbing out rooms, burning refuse, and a hundred and one other jobs. Now the worst is over at last, and we have got to get the whole barracks as neat and clean as a new pin, and we are resting on our oars, having caused *no* blade of grass to grow where two grew before.[4]

We have come together to-night, among the remains of our joint furniture, into my room. I know I ought to say I am writing this by the light of a candle stuck in a whiskey bottle, sitting on corded packing-cases, but in actual fact we are very cosy with a fire (out of coal left behind), two big lamps, easy chairs, a bed with cushions (from the Mess!) on it, gorged with a hot supper brought from the Soldiers Home ready cooked – God bless them – and surrounded with much good tobacco. So we've no complaints, thank you; at least, I haven't, and Billy looks quite happy too, writing opposite me.

To-morrow we hope to get the actual handing-over done in the morning if the A.S.C. and R.E. representatives show up punctually. Then we shall get loaded up about 9, march to Fermoy, entrain, embark at — — (deleted by censor),[5] land at —— (erased by Press Bureau), entrain, arrive at —— (suppressed by G.P.O.), and run down to Aldershot in time for breakfast.

We had rather a funny experience this afternoon. We were inspecting the guard-room and cells after our party had cleaned them, and in looking behind the door of one cell we banged it shut thoughtlessly, and of course the beastly thing had a confounded spring lock on it, and there were we, the only two officers in the place, confined together like a couple of criminals in a solitary cell! Fortunately we managed to prise it open again with our knives, and got out none the worse.

Seeing that we've been up since 7 this morning. I'll finish this now by daylight.

Later I've unpacked this again, at the other end of our journey, since when I've received two of your letters, but no telegram. I couldn't telegraph to you our date of crossing or any other particulars, as you asked. As a matter of fact I was in charge of the postal arrangements myself (signalling officer again), with express instructions to censor just that kind of telegram, along with any other information, however general, of our movements; so it wouldn't have looked well to have set the example myself.

Well, we finished up our handing-over in great style, down to the last 'poker, soldier's, one' in the last barrack-room. (Did you know that a 'poker, soldier's' is quite a different article from a 'poker, married soldier's'? It is, though; and it's not the least good trying to palm off one for the other on an unsuspecting Ordnance official, oh no.) We got all clear at about 12 midday, telephoned for an A.S.C. 5-ton lorry to take the men's kit into Fermoy and for a bakery van to meet us at the station with their travelling ration, and for extra coaches on the train. We paraded the whole crowd left in the camp, and found we were rather richer by this time by two new recruits come to join their regiment, five men recalled from furlough too late to go with the battalion, and three Royal Irishmen who had missed their crowd when it went out the day before. We gave them each sixpence as travelling allowance, and started them off down the road under an N.C.O. Then we finished packing our own kit, telephoned for a motor, paid one last visit to all the barrack-rooms and camp buildings, and went to get a 'biting-on' at our old friend the Soldiers Home.

When the car came we whizzed down into Fermoy, arriving of course before the men, and arranged with the station-master about carriages, and also got the 40-odd portions of bread from the baker ready for distributing. We went to the Fermoy Soldiers Home as well and arranged for a last meal for them at 3d a head. By the time we had done this they were just arriving, so we paraded them on the platform, counted heads, stacked their gear and mounted a baggage-guard over it, and packed them off to eat their last Irish meal.

Twenty minutes before train-time we fished them back, told them off to their compartments, and got them entrained, each man with all his kit, eight to a carriage, and turned the key on them. We wired to Mallow that we had a detachment for the Dublin mail, and instructed them to have extra coaches in readiness there; we wired to the Railway Transport Officer at Kingstown[6] to arrange for embarcation [sic] on the steamer; we wired to the battalion at Aldershot to notify them of our intended departure (telegrams are cheap On His Majesty's Service), and despatched a written message to Divisional headquarters stating that all instructions as to handing-over had been carried out and giving particulars of the steps we had taken to consign things left behind and instructions as to their disposal.

Then at last we took our seats in the train, feeling we had done all things man could do (even to the buying a sufficiency of cigarettes) – and found we hadn't a match between us.

We hustled the men across at Mallow and into their coach, which was hooked on to the Dublin mail when it arrived, and we sent one more wire to Maryborough[7] for the portable troop-water-wagon to be brought alongside for the men to fill their water-bottles, and then we separated ourselves from half-a-crown for the benefit of the head-waiter and secured a table for two in the dining-car and disposed ourselves in luxury for the journey up. At Maryborough we got out and superintended the water-work, at Ballybrophy we strolled down to see if the men were all right – which they were – otherwise we played cards in comfort, and I took just enough off Billy to pay for our teas and dinners, so that was all right.

At Kingstown we had our only mishap. The men of course were locked in; but while the N.C.O. in charge of one compartment was leaning out talking to a porter on the platform two of them did a dive out of the other window, which was open, and cut stick for the town (both Dublin men, of course), and we haven't seen them since. They'll be brought back in a few days, no doubt, but all the same it was a pity. Otherwise we lost no more from the draft all the way across.

At Kingstown Billy had some of his people to see him off (he lives at Bray, by the way), so I took charge of the party and got them marched on board. They had a special gangway ready for us, and we checked each man as they filed along it with their kitbags and equipment. Then I showed them their deck-space and posted an N.C.O. over the kitbags (our own personal baggage was stowed in two berths for us, which in fact we never used), and ordered supper. I was introduced to Billy's people when I went to look for him, and we chatted for a minute or two, and then we slipped our moorings and pushed off. The boat, by the way, was the *Munster*, which I think you have both travelled by.

At Holyhead we drove them off the ship and packed them into the Irish Mail. They didn't beetle off this time, for they had a corridor and could go along and see their pals. (Also the sanitary problem wasn't so pressing.) We wired to Euston to have breakfast ready for them, and to Crewe for another water-wagon, and then we had just time to capture our seats in a first-class compartment before she pulled out.

We had an uneventful run up to town, sleeping most of the way (and please, Mother, I *was* good to Billy, 'cos I gave him my great coat to sleep under as well as his own), and arrived in Euston about 6 in the morning. The men turned out rather dirty and dishevelled, but all present and no kits missing; but we found that a big draft of Navy men had preceded us with the breakfast order, so there was none for us. Fortunately, however, we had stated in our telegram that we were en route for Aldershot (you may be generous with your information when you have such a small party) and someone had 'phoned on to Waterloo and our breakfast was waiting there.

So Billy said he would collect our own things and run them across in a taxi and see about the breakfast, as well as arranging about the train to Aldershot, if I would bring the men round.

I led them down into the Tube station (we went down in two lifts, and I just managed to herd back the other half from rushing away to a train for Shepherds Bush or the Elephant & Castle or somewhere at the back of God's world) and explained to them that the trains here were not exactly the kind of easy-going Irish affairs they had been used to, which would wait half-an-hour for them to get leisurely on board. Apparently they took this to heart, for when the train pulled in there was a stampede and they nipped in for their lives like a lot of bunnies going to earth when a man comes round the corner with a gun. In a couple of seconds there wasn't a trace of them to be seen. They made themselves awful unpopular with their stampede, too, because the train was very crowded with folk going to work, and these 50 men who surged in all stuck out a couple of feet all round with their rifles and tins and blankets and kit-bags.

At Waterloo we saw their breakfast, and gave them a packet of Woodbines each; and then, as we couldn't get a train down till 10.30, we turned them loose on the platform for a smoke and a rest and went to see about our own breakfast. First of all we had a gorgeous hot bath in a princely bathroom with big sponges and taps that roared like the Atlantic ocean and shiny nickel fittings and showers and warmed Turkish towels and scented soap (different from a bath in the distressful country, I'm afraid) and then, after having our hair cut and shampooed, our faces shaved, our boots polished, and putting on clean underclothes and socks, we felt real good, and went in to order all the things we can't get in the Mess, and ate a breakfast that scandalised even the head waiter.

Shining with soap and repletion, we came out at last, and strolled heavily across to put the men in the train for the last lap, and despatched a final telegram ahead to order a transport wagon from the regiment to meet us at the station.

It was a slow train, and it wasn't until twelve o'clock that we reached Frimley. Here we tumbled out, loaded up all our stuff into the wagon, and started to march the two or three miles up to Blackdown Camp.

We got here about half-past one, and handed over our reports, accounts, and marching-in roll to the C.O., and dismissed the men with a profound feeling of thankfulness and wrote 'finis' to the show. I couldn't help thinking how differently the men behaved from the first draft that came down from Galway.

I haven't seen enough of this place to describe it yet, but we're messing in one of those pretentious little houses that stand in the middle of about 5 acres of trees, so common in Surrey. Billy and I share a decent enough room at the top with a priceless view and an electric fire in the fire-place, so we might be a lot worse off.[8] He was at Christ's Hospital, which is at Horsham; I was at Charterhouse, which is at Godalming; we are now at Blackdown, not 20 miles from either – *voilà tout*. He came over to Charterhouse to play cricket for C.H. against our Maniacs[9] once, by the way.

Finn travelled over quite all right with me. He came as a recruit, so I didn't pay a penny for him. I had something else to do than bother about dog-tickets.

Blackdown, 10 November 1915
I have been doing musketry for the past four weeks, and finished at last, D.G.[10] Musketry duty is divided into two parts, butt duty and firing-point duty. There is only one thing worse than the butts, and that is the firing-point.

In the butts you cower in a brick-lined trench immediately behind the targets and mark the score. There are three ranges at Pirbright, each with 24 targets. An officer controls six targets simultaneously, each worked by two men. At the blast of a whistle the men haul up the targets with chains, and you wait and listen for the bullets. The whistle goes again, and they haul down the targets. Then No.1 finds the bullet-holes and signals back to the firing-point by showing various coloured discs above the trench while No.2 pastes up the holes and calls them to the officer, who checks them and enters each shot in its proper column on an elaborate form called a butt-register. And then da capo.[11]

Well, firing begins at 8 sharp and goes on till 4.30, with a quarter of an hour for sandwiches at lunch. You don't move from your trench all day; you haven't an idea who is shooting at the other end; it is possibly raining, probably blowing, and certainly cold; there are thousands of shots fired in a day, each of which means a figure to be entered somewhere and totted up somewhere else in a total; and there is no possible variety.

So much for butt-duty.

At the firing-point you control groups of probably about six men by turns. You see that they are present when their turn comes, that they don't load before ordered, that they remember all that has been drilled into them in previous weeks of preliminary training, and that they don't leave the ground with a round still in the magazine. Each 'detail' of six men takes about five minutes from first to last, and then you start over again. The only relief is that when the whole 250 men have fired you have a brief five minutes with the rifle yourself. It's like fielding all day for the sake of your own innings and then coming out in the first over. And it's even colder than in the butts, for there isn't even a trench.

However, the whole Division has at last fired its course, and now we're back at ordinary work and normal hours.

By the way, I'm back with the Company again now. The signallers know all there is to teach them, and the sergeant is quite competent to carry on with them, so I'm taking a platoon again (my old No. 10) before I forget how to.

Thanks so much for the photos of Mornie. I didn't notice them, you know, in the parcel at first, and they lay for a couple of days in the drawer with the socks, until Billy drew my attention to them. I think they're absolutely priceless; the best I've ever seen. [. . .]

Finn is temporarily mislaid. I'm afraid he's living in sin with some other regiment in the garrison.

[To his mother only]
Blackdown, 28 November 1915
This is a timeless November afternoon; nothing moves except the sun slipping west over the snowy fields; and you sit alone in your room and listen to the wind-crying round the corners of the house, full of memories of dead years, just as I have sat in the Anchorage and heard it; and just as you are perhaps sitting now by the hearthstone and listening to it crying down from the moors. An afternoon when all time is annihilated, and the heart of all the Past is in the long, long hours of wind and sunshine.

So I lit a pipe and called the dog and went over to see our trenches after writing the last bit. They are two miles away across the moor, constructed by the whole Brigade since it came from Ireland; and as we are to occupy them for forty-eight hours sometime this week, I wanted to see about my arrangements for wiring them up for the telephones between the various dug-outs. On the way back I stepped into a frozen bog well up to my knees and had to change everything. I resume after the interlude.

Well, little mother, we're on the move at last; on December 12 we 'proceed overseas,' as the orders have it. All our stores are drawn at last (3 tons of ammunition we drew last week), all our leave is cancelled except the final 48 hours; all the men have their identity discs, field dressings, and Testaments; all the musketry is finished; everything, whether personnel or equipment, that we are not taking on service has been disposed of, and we are now *en état de partir*. The poor old 49th Brigade, the runt of the Division; has been washed out and replaced by a Brigade of South Africans;[12] and General Parsons, who is too old to take us out, has been replaced by a Major-General Hickey [Hickie][13], of whom I don't know anything.

I'm going to apply for my two days' leave next Monday and Tuesday. Mark the subtlety; my leave begins at reveille on Monday morning so there's no reason why I shouldn't fade away on Saturday, as I'm not required over the week-end. And then, if I can square my company commander about Saturday morning parade, there is again no reason why I shouldn't go on Friday night. So if all goes well I shall catch the midnight train on Friday and be with you from Saturday morning till Tuesday afternoon, take the midnight train back to London, and catch a train back here in time for Wednesday's parade.

I was out on a rather strenuous scheme last week. I received orders on Tuesday night (after doing a fifteen-mile route march) to take six of my best signallers and rendezvous at Sindlesham on Wednesday. I searched the map, going round and round in wider circles from Blackdown with growing apprehension, till I found Sindlesham right on the outskirts of the map, fifteen miles further off. We were to take two days' rations in our haversacks. Well, of course, that meant Army biscuits and bully beef, and I didn't see us doing a scheme which began with a fifteen-mile walk on that if I could help it. So I called my sergeant and gave him a chit to the master-cook and certain words of counsel. When he was fairly established in the cook-house I sent urgently for the master-cook and detained him in conversation while O'Riordan whipped out two kit-bags and grabbed right, left and centre. (It may interest you to know how far we 'supplemented' our haversack rations: 5 lb. of undercut for the signallers' mess, 1 stone of potatoes, 4 loaves of bread, 3 pots of jam, 3 pots of apricots, 2 large cakes, onions, tomatoes, tea, butter, milk, sugar, salt, pepper, and mustard! Not bad.) I borrowed a limber[14] from the Transport Officer to carry it, but subsequently washed that out and dumped the stuff on the Rangers' wagon (which saved me having to provide forage for the horses). At 9 o'clock on Wednesday we set out, carrying arms, full pack and equipment, 2 blankets per man, and our instruments and cables. We started off heel and toe, halting ten minutes every hour; and at Sindlesham, which we reached at 2, we found the Engineers – our bosses – established, with orders directing us to take up our first position at the corner of a wood 1½ miles further on, and establish communication with them as soon as possible. So we pushed off again and hunted up this position on the map. Luckily it wasn't far from a cottage inhabited by an old wife [. . .] I made love to her and got leave for the men to use her kitchen range and to sleep by her kitchen fire instead of in a ditch by the roadside. We got the cable laid, and one of our first messages was to the effect that we should advance just after dark (it was then 4 o'clock), and that therefore it was of no use starting to cook the men's dinners until after the move. (By the way, I had established my office in the old woman's kitchen, which was better than keeping two operators out in the cold all the time.) So we gave Mrs Englefield – that was her name – some of our tea, and she boiled water and we had a drink and a smoke and waited for dark. The old body thought I was a sergeant for some time, and was profusely apologetic when I told her I was only an officer.

At 5 we got orders over the wire to move on to our advanced position, but it was explained that probably this would become untenable later and we should fall back again to the place we were now occupying. So we pushed off to our new spot in the dark, laying cable as we went, over unknown country with no lights and no noise. We got fixed up by 8 o'clock, and they kept us there till 11, when we got a message to fall back again. Reeling up the cable and reaching Mother Englefield's about half-an-hour after midnight, we received permission to cook our dinners at last, which kept us occupied till after 2. At half-past two I sent them all to bed except the operators; but at 4 we got orders to pack up and report to headquarters by 5.

There we found instructions to push on to Wokingham for breakfast: a small town about 7 miles away, which we reached shortly after 8 and where we spent the morning laying cable along the streets and fastening it up the sides of the houses. At 2 we were told to move to Easthampstead and proceed with dinners, and wait for the Sappers to follow us – Easthampstead was 6 miles from Wokingham. We got there about a quarter past four and lit fires and put on the dixies, when a D.R. came up on a horse with a chit saying the Sappers had found the hour unexpectedly late and pushed off home, leaving us to follow as best we could!

By the time we had finished the dinners it was pitch dark and rain falling, and we were 15 miles from home without the vaguest idea which road to follow – and all dead beat. Cheery situation.

However, we, consulted maps and compasses and things, and struck off southwards over a blasted heath, plunged into a forest, and in ten minutes lost ourselves completely and absolutely.

The rest of the story is, as they say, nothing but a 'confused nightmare.' I remember roads where no roads should be, and precipitous descents where we had to brake the wagons down, and more arduous ascents where we had to shove them up, and one place where we pulled five large fallen trees out of the road, and other vague incidents, but mostly it was Kipling's 'Boots . . . boots . . . boots . . . boots . . . movin' up an' down again.'[15] I know we didn't halt at all during the last 7 miles, because we knew we should never start again if we did.

At 11 p.m. we rolled into barracks, having done, all told, just under 55 miles in three days with no sleep and only the food we carried, bearing all our equipment, blankets, and signal gear. But nobody came out with a brass band; nobody said, 'Oh, the heroes!' or anything; would you believe it? Billy said, 'Hullo, John, you back?' when I came in, and cursed me for shaking wet clothes about. Unappreciative beggar. By the way, my feet gave out for the first time after that, and I had to be carried upstairs. I was all right next morning, though.

In September, Staniforth's parents had been in London and met their son, along with his friend, Billy Cullen. Dr Staniforth also visited Blackdown and saw mock trenches. In early December, Staniforth visited home for his farewell leave. Mrs Staniforth was obviously stoical as they parted, as her son reflected in his next letter.

[To his mother only]
Blackdown, 12 December 1915
You were very brave about it all, weren't you? Poor wee thing, and do you think I didn't know what you were suffering? But never a word out of you at all; a smile and brave face to the end. You're a proud little person, you know.

Now I'll tell you something to take the sting away. You can set your mind at rest until April. We saw General Hickey the day before yesterday, and he blamed other Divisions very much for sending their men up into the firing-line right away before they got used to new conditions and Boche habits. He intends to keep us in French billets for a month, to acclimatize us, far away from the war zone. Then a month somewhere behind the lines, taking up officers and men gradually bit by bit for a day or so each, for instructional purposes. Then a month with the whole Division in the trenches; not to take part in attacks, you understand, but to accustom the men to trench life and all that sort of thing.

So you see we are to be blooded very gradually. Does that please you?

I have got myself a big long oilskin macintosh, coarse, heavy, ugly, and utterly waterproof, like the fishermen's. The man at first said he had nothing but pretty yellow cobwebs of Shantung silk, 'a smart garment for officers, sir.' So I pulled out a price-list of the firm across the street, and then he hurriedly remembered this. Also I got a pair of big Wellington gumboots, up to the knee, and a pair of long ordinary boots as well which I am having armour-plated with nails. I have an order for a revolver (Colt .45, one of the big man-killers), but I haven't got it yet; and I got a second oiled ground-sheet.

The advance parties have gone. I still don't know when we shall push off; quite possibly not till the end of the week, it seems. Anyway, I'll wire you.

I caught all my connexions quite easily. The London train was fortunately 15 minutes late at York, so I had no rush. When it came in I got a comfortable table in the dining-car (although it was very crowded), and I sat there after dinner right into London. We were only five minutes late into King's Cross.

The company got caught in the rain yesterday, filling in those trenches which I took Dad to see. I was three hours standing in the drench without a coat or shelter of any sort, and when I raced back to this beautiful Mess afterwards there wasn't a drop of hot water in the house, nor coal for a fire anywhere. So I have a glorious cold to-day. *Mess-management*, isn't it?

Chapter 5

'Greyish ashen squalor of filthy humanity': First Impressions of Trenches, December 1915 to February 1916

With training at Blackdown complete, the 7/Leinsters departed for France on 17 December 1915, around midday on trains from Farnborough.[1] At 5pm, the battalion sailed from Southampton on three transport ships, the SS Bellerophon, *SS* La Marguerite *and SS* Empress Queen, *arriving at Le Havre around 5am the next day. The strength of the battalion was twenty-seven officers and 950 other ranks. They brought with them sixty-four horses and mules, twenty-two wagons and nine bicycles. After a long and slow train journey through northern France over the night of 18 December, and much of the next day, the battalion arrived at Gosnay, a village near Béthune, just a few miles from the front line.*

By this stage of the war, there was little movement along the front. After the line had stabilized towards the end of 1914 there was little movement in 1915. The British gained Neuve Chapelle in March, but the Germans failed to take much of the Ypres Salient in April. French attacks in Artois and Champagne made little progress; nor did the British have much success at Loos in September to October 1915. By the time the 16th Division arrived, the lines were well and truly set for the winter.

As Staniforth suggests in his letters, the commander of the 16th Division wanted men to stay in billets as long as possible without being placed at the front. However, there was a rapid introduction to fighting for some. The 7/Leinsters were first into the trenches, with six officers and eighteen non-commissioned officers attached on 23 December to the 1/6th (City of London) Battalion (Rifles), the London Regiment, for instruction. Staniforth was one of the six and he described his experiences in detail to his parents.

From this point, letters sent to the Staniforths from the front could only include vague indications of locations. Precise details from the battalion war diary have been added in the text and at the start of each letter.

Gosnay, 29 December 1915

The enclosed is a souvenir of an attempt at a Christmas dinner.[2] Will you keep it for me, please. (Stephanie is the demoiselle de logement.[3])

You'll wonder why I haven't written before; it's because I've been in the trenches. Just for a couple of days and nights, for instructional purposes, but I wouldn't have missed it for the world. It was like this.

We paraded early in the morning, about a score of officers and sergeants, with all our kit and trench-boots festooned about us like a Christmas tree, and crowded up on an old Camberwell Green L.G. [London General] Omnibus which rattled and jolted us over five miles of the most villainous pave[4] into the remains of a village whose name you would probably recognize if I were allowed to mention it. It has seen more fighting than any other village probably, having been taken and re-taken seven times in the last few months; and not a house in it is now anything more than a blackened shell. Here the bus stopped, and we climbed down and were met by a lance-corporal from the battalion in the trenches. He guided us about three-quarters of a mile further up the road before we came to the opening of the trenches. On the road we watched the guns chasing a Taube[5] just overhead. You could see the plane dodging and turning in the air, but making her reconnaissance all the time, and the little bursts of flame against the dark clouds round her, and then the stain of white smoke hanging like a mushroom – then another, and another, and another, as fast as the gunners could register. But they never got her, and she continued her observations, ringed all round by the shrapnel-bursts, until she finished and slid away gracefully to her own lines unharmed. It was the most fascinating duel you could see.

Later we passed the guns in action. Just one battery: six 18-pounders in a row, in byres and barns and pig-styes, all covered with sods and straw. It was a lovely picture; the gunners stripped and sweating, each crew working like a machine, the swing and smack of the breech-block as clean and sweet as a kiss, and then a six-foot stream of crimson flame from the muzzle, a thunderclap of sound, and away tore the shell over the hills to the Boche trenches 5000 yards away.

At the end of the road – a poplar-fringed, dead-straight highway just like Hobbema's 'Avenue' – we left it, crossed into the fields on the right, and plunged into the opening of the mile-long communication trench. Up this we moved in single file: just a seven-foot-deep cutting, with steep sides two feet apart and with wooden gratings underfoot, twisting and turning like a broken-backed snake: until at last we came to the suburbs of the underground city.

I was told off to the headquarters dug-out, which of course was in the third or rearmost line about 500 yards behind the fire-trench. You bent your back and scrambled down a flight of wooden steps. The dug-out itself, which was twenty feet below the surface, gave one the impression of being in a coal-mine. There were the same enormous pit-props shoring up the roof, the same eternal drip, drip, drip from the ceiling, and the same heavy atmosphere, and absolute silence. It was about as big as your bathroom, and six of us slept there: one on the table, one under it, the Colonel on his bed (a hospital stretcher, raised on two trestles), another under that, and two of us side by side on the floor.

After I had dumped my things down; I went out to explore the front line. The water in some places was up to the thighs, and nowhere under the ankles; the wet walls of the trench smeared one all over as you pushed along between them; so you can believe that when men come out after four days on duty there is absolutely nothing to be seen of man, uniform, cap, equipment, face, or rifle. And the mud is of every consistency, from thin gravel that is half water to the stiff gluey clay that pulls the boots off your legs.

And the front trench – that firing-line that every tub-thumper refers to glibly. Imagine a garbage-heap covered with all the refuse of six months: rags, tins, bottles, bits of paper, all sifted over with the indescribable greyish ashen squalor of filthy humanity. It is peopled with gaunt, hollow-eyed tattered creatures who crawl and swarm about upon it and eye you suspiciously as you pass; men whose nerves are absolutely gone; unshaven, half-human things moving about in a stench of corruption – oh, I can't describe it. And they're the men who are doing the work for you. They're rather fine, don't you think? Because there's no romance in it, oh, no; just squalor and sordid beastliness past all describing. However, I mustn't say this, lest it should 'prejudice recruiting' – good Lord!

Well, I had my share of experiences. The Boche lobbed over a trench-mortar shell beautifully, which fell just a traverse away from where I was standing. One poor devil was sponged out quite, we couldn't find enough of him even to bury, and another had his head blown off. Do you know, although I was standing not half-a-dozen yards away, and of course I'd never seen anything like it before, I have absolutely no emotions of any sort to record. It just seemed part of the life there. That's curious, isn't it?

And of course we got sniped at. It's remarkable how soon one gets used to the 'wop' of a bullet in a sand-bag beside one's ear. I wonder very much if you'll think this is 'swank.' But it isn't. As in the case of the shell, I couldn't honestly discover any emotion of any sort, either fear or excitement or anything else, even though at the time I was vaguely annoyed with myself for not feeling some kind of appropriate sentiments.

Early in the morning, before it was light, we crawled out from the furthest sap over no-man's-land. (Don't worry; it's quite safe in the dark.) We crawled all among corpses lying just as they had fallen in the attack of September 25th,[6] poor devils, and studied the Hun lines about 30 or 40 yards away. When a star-shell or flare goes up, you lie still and pretend to be one of the corpses.

The Boche is a poisonous blighter. They have got hold of a dead Scotsman, propped him up with his backside towards us, and turned up his kilt in mockery; and there he stands, with one of their sentries beside him so that we can't get at him, though we try night and day. Ugh!

The people I have conceived a thorough dislike for are our own heavy gunners, though. They have a hearty lunch in their princely chateau about six miles behind the lines, and then stroll out smoking big cigars. On the velvet lawn they catch sight of their elephant gun. 'Oh, I say,' says someone, 'this jolly old gun, what?' 'Suppose we let off the bally thing, dear old chaps?' suggests another. So they whistle up a fellow and order a couple of fine old crusted shells, and ram them in and poop them off, and go back to finish their cigars. Then for about five hours the infuriated Hun hammers our front trench madly in revenge, and a fat blooming gunner asleep in an arm-chair hears the strafing, cocks a drowsy eye, and remarks lazily, 'Poor old gravel-pushers; comin' in for some more hate, what?' and off he goes to sleep again . . .

At least, that's how I picture it.

Their heavy shells make a fine noise coming over, though; just like a railway train, pounding along through the sky quite slowly, very different from the venomous scream of the shrapnel, or the whizz-*bang* of the little high-velocity shell, or the shattering thunder of a trench-mortar bomb. In the foreground from our trench rise two twin towers, probably as familiar to the British public as to us (now then, Sherlock!),[7] and we watch the gunners shelling them, miles and miles away behind the German lines, and we love 'em like brothers. For although *we* can't do much except sit in the wet and hate just at present, the guns strafe away day and night and put the fear of God into the Hun, who only replies now and then. You needn't be out there five minutes before you realise the superiority of our artillery.

And the keynote of the whole thing is boredom and weariness, utter and absolute. You sit in a dug-out and read or play cards from morning till night, and your nerves get worn out with watching against Hun attacks which never come, and with shoring up parapets that crumble-in even as you dig, and pumping out water that fills up again as fast as you get it out.

It's not a rosy picture, and I'm not pretending it is, even when you see it with the spice of novelty as I did. Yet they stick it, and I suppose it might be worse.

Before I forget, could you get me a small half-crown air-pillow, the sort that you blow up with a valve, and keep in your waistcoat pocket when you're not using it? They're invaluable for sleeping on the floor, and I want one badly.

I only saw one Hun, and loosed off my revolver at him, but 'there was nothing to report, and the situation was unchanged.'

When we got back to billets it took us about two days to get clean again. I had a bath in the only wooden tub on the premises, and slept for hours in a real bed again.

Goodbye, and all good wishes for the New Year to you all. I wish I could see it in with you. Think of me as the clock strikes.

Love from us both[8] – well and happy.

[Enclosure]
C Coy Officers' Mess
Christmas Eve 1915. 'Somewhere in France.'

(Signatures)

After Dinner	Before Dinner
John	John H. M. Staniforth
Noel	Noel M. Purcell
Paddy	P. S. Lynch
Pipps	W.E. Phillips
Ghirnam	P. J. Aherne (Hon. Member)
Lancelot	Studholme
	Jas. P. Roche
The young 'un	J. J. Kelly
	Stephanie

Menu
——

Dinde à la Stephanie
Plum-poudinge 'Daily-News'
——

Vin de Graves.   Mandarines.   Juice de Lime.
Café. Biscuits. Curaçoa [sic].
Fromage du Divisional-Train.

Toasts
——

'Bachelordom'	Mr Purcell	(married 15/12/1915)
'The Entente Cordiale'	Capt. Phillips	('Stephanie')
'Our Ordnance' . . .	Mr Aherne	(Quartermaster)
'Cocoa'	Mr Kelly	(Cocoa Press)
'The British Grenadiers'	Mr Lynch	(Bomb Officer)
'The Ladies'	Mr Studholme	(a misogynist)
'Absent Friends'	Mr Staniforth	?

Music
——

Capt. Phillips will sing 'Put Me Among the Girls'
Mr Studholme will tell stories in the manner of Mr George Robey
Mr Lynch will sing (?) 'Won't You Come Back to Bomb-Bomb-Bay'
Mr Aherne will recite Kipling's poem, 'Boots'
Mr Kelly will sing 'I like your Old French Bonnet' after the casualties have been removed.
Mr Purcell will perform 'The Turkey Trot' (being full of his subject)
Mr Staniforth, being speechless, will play Ballyhooley on the tin whistle*
* (An impertinent addition of Noel's, to which no importance whatever need be attached.)

Gosnay, 30 December 1915
Just a line in a spare moment, though there is no news. We received orders to move to other billets a few hours ago, and are just packed up for the night and waiting to move off first thing in the morning. We are going back a few miles further away from the front for a spell; I don't know why.

The signed menu card mentioned in Staniforth's letter of 29 December 1915.

There has been a lot of hate going on to-day. The Huns were shelling a village a mile to our right quite heavily (they broke a few windows here), and I'm told they tried a push in the front line this morning but were repulsed. Certainly we were concentrating artillery, for the guns passed through here in the small hours of last night. [. . .]

It's very dull in billets here. All I have done to-day to make the world a better and a nobler place is to take out a party in the rain and build a princely row of latrines in Madame's orchard. We took a pride in our work; we sodded them, we fixed up seats by lashing tree-trunks along, we added a spurious air of decency by fixing up a screen of brushwood hurdles and we topped it off by improvising a dozen little shovels made of biscuit-tins – and now we vacate the billets to-night, and lo, another reapeth where we have sown. A hard world. Hand me the office harp:-

'What did *you* do in the Great War, Dad?'
'I dug latrines – for others, my lad.'

I can't write any more just now, because our last dinner is on the table and the bread-and-cheese is getting cold. It's rather tragic to think of the poor men trying to keep body and soul together on nothing but roast beef and hot soup and jam pudding while the bloated officers banquet on biscuit and cheese rations, isn't it? Mostly you can define our meals as a minute bunch of crumbs entirely surrounded by booze.

Laires, 6 January 1916
[. . .] Our former billets were quiet enough, being near to a town which diverted most of the Hun's hate. Brer Boche's motto seems to be, 'It is a fine morning. There is nothing in the trenches doing. We abundant ammunition have. Let us a little frightfulness into the town pump.' So he pumps. Which doesn't hurt us, and pleases him.

At the same time, we do get a touch of the real thing now and again. They brought one of 'Minnie's' victims here to bury, the other day. Minnie (the German Minenwerfer, or Heavy Trench Mortar) is alto-gether horrid. Her modus operandi is to come right up into the [German] front trench (she has only an extreme range of 200 yards) and let slip a disgusting cylindrical bomb, which sails very slowly through the air, describing somersaults as it goes, and falls with a soft thud on your parapet. There, after an interval of ten seconds or so, it explodes; and as Minnie's offspring contains 30lb of dynamite, no dug-out or parapet can stand against her.

Again. There is a tree at a cross-roads in the village here. Some months ago a Uhlan[9] patrol passed this way, with a wounded British prisoner. They crucified him to this tree, and stood around watching him until he died. He was a long time dying.

Some of us had not heard of Uhlans previously. These have now noted the name for reference – and future action.[10]

Now listen to a comedy of Staff work – the Practical Joke Department of the Staff, that is.

The day before yesterday this regiment was lying happily in barns and stables (the best billets for tired men) in a village which we will call Staithes[11] [Laires], though it was by no means as big. Came, at 7 o'clock of a grey and weeping morning, a message over the wires:- 'The battalion will leave at once for Mickleby [Verchin]; dinners to be served on arrival.' So there were alarms and excursions; harassed caterers concluded yet another demoralising bargain with ruthless tradesmen; stores were swept into carts and limbers somehow; and we fell in breathlessly just as the clock was striking ten, and set off.

After an hour and a half's marching we halted in a village square, and were met by our own advance party, returning baffled with the news that Mickleby was already occupied by French troops to the number of 850.

To go on was foolish. To go back was disobedience to orders. So the Colonel went to lunch with the mayor; eleven hundred fighting men stood dripping in the square because it was too wet to sit down, and a galloper rode back to the Brigade Office, where he found the Staff in full bloom. He reported that a round thousand men were at large on French soil. The Staff smiled winningly. 'What rotten luck,' said they. 'And by Jove, it's raining too, isn't it?'

Ultimately we were instructed to push forward and try Ugthorpe [Luby], Mickleby Howe [Coupelle-Vieille], and any other villages on the map.

So the eleven hundred fighting men, with four stone upon their backs, took the road again; and six officers with nothing on their backs rode up and down the column and exhorted it to endurance.

The rain fell – our spirits fell – night fell – and still we traversed the pleasant land of France.

At ten o'clock we found a forgotten, rat-ridden hamlet [Coupelle-Neuve], hitherto avoided by troops because of the unpleasant number of scarlet-fever corpses that lay in the houses, and were rammed into it 'by fifties and fifties.' Studholme and I rolled in our blankets on the floor of an estaminet kitchen, and slept off our hunger.

Next morning the Practical Joke Department said to itself, 'The regiment has now been faithfully dealt with; now's the hour and now's the minute for a Ceremonial Review by the Army Corps Commander.'

And, believe it or not, it was so; and the A.C.C. in his subsequent criticisms 'noted with displeasure that certain units had failed to polish their buttons.' This, however, by the way. The cream of the joke is that owing to a misreading of dates by the Staff in question, we were removed from Staithes three days too soon, and should really have stayed in our comfortable barns and stables while the French leisurely evacuated Mickleby for us.

So after the Review we marched back again to Staithes!

I have only one complaint about my billets there, and that is my little bedfellows. The first night there was great joy. 'Come along,' they cried, 'pass the word around,' and they fetched their uncles and aunts and cousins and friends, and Grandpapa hobbled out of his corner, and Grandmamma woke from her winter sleep and tottered along, and there was great feasting entirely. But next night Pharaoh hardened his heart and wrought a frightfulness in the land. I bought a tin of powerful parasiticide, and concealed it from them when I went to bed. In half-an hour the bed was warm, and they had mobilised in massed battalions. Then with great suddenness I sprang swiftly out of bed, lit a candle, and dealt sweeping destruction till the land was utterly laid waste.

Now I sleep in peace in that hut.

Laires, 12 January 1916
There's as usual no news of any importance to chronicle. I can only fall back on description, and give you a few impressions that may help your imagination of An Evening in Billets.

The shadows were gathering in the corners of the old kitchen, and the rain streamed on the windows outside as the short day drew to its close. All day it had rained, and all the day before, and for more days than they could remember . . .

The younger of the two subalterns threw down an old *Bystander*[13] and stretched himself. 'It's too damned dark to read,' he grumbled, 'and it's two hours till supper. What a life!'

The elder, who was cleaning a revolver by the fire, made no remark; and the other grumbler lit a cigarette and sat down to criticise operations.

The outer door slammed, and a third occupant of the room came in, dripping and muddy. He removed his oilskins and long gumboots, peeled off his tunic, and sat down in shirt-sleeves and stockinged feet in imitation of the others. Not the slightest notice was taken of his arrival; they had all learnt a certain economy in their intercourse by this time.

'Any post?' queried the youngest of the three, pitching away his cigarette.

'No,' said the newcomer, 'not till tomorrow. They never sent the post-corporal for it . . . That makes four days since we had one,' he added dispassionately.

An orderly came in and lit the pretentious oil-lamp that swung in its cradle of chains over the table, and replenished the tin box-stove; and the three drew up their chairs and settled down to pipes in the daily routine of rolls and returns.

'This Fighting Strength Return[14] gives me the fair hump,' remarked one scribe plaintively. 'What the deuce is the sense in showing that old ruin Macdonald on the fighting strength, when everyone knows he's on his back in hospital, and never likely to rise up again in this world?'

The fourth of the small community entered noisily at this moment, bringing a gust of wind and rain with him. Like the others, he proceeded to take off his soaked garments and dry his socks at the stove.

'Where have you been, J.J.?' queried the Boy, lifting his head for a moment from his bewildering Fighting Strength.

'Rounds, darling,' explained the latest arrival laconically, struggling with a boot-lace. 'Plenty fellow making one first-chop tea, allee-same top-side hotel.[15] It was the first time the poor devils had had a pukka meal since we came into this God-forsaken hamlet. Lend me your knife, Boy; there's a black knot on this you wouldn't loosen in a week.'

A knock sounded on the door, and a sergeant stood in the opening. 'Letters, sir,' he intimated with a salute, and laid a bundle of open envelopes on the table.

'Fall in, the Censor-squad,' sighed No. 4, hoisting himself wearily out of the one arm-chairs in the room and helping himself to a handful of the letters. 'Give me a pencil, someone. All right, sergeant; you needn't wait. Look in again in half-an-hour.'

'Very good, sir.' The sergeant saluted again and withdrew noiselessly, and the four fell to work on the heap of correspondence. The task had long since lost its novelty. Though there were letters of all sorts, humorous, pathetic, tragic, amorous and indignant, no one commented on them. Each was ripped out of its envelope, skimmed rapidly through, a few erasures and amendments were made here and there, and it was slipped back into the envelope, initialled, and tossed on the growing pile on the table.

As the last letter dropped on its fellows, the orderly entered again to lay the table for supper. A tin mug, a tin plate, and a coarse knife and fork were laid on the oilcloth opposite each place, and salt, pepper and mustard in small pots were placed in the centre. The meal itself consisted of the inevitable ration-beef and mashed potatoes, with tinned apricots as a sweet. They drank Graves[16] in their tin mugs, and subsequently tea, hot, strong, and red.

'One short pipe,' yawned the Boy sleepily, 'and then I think bed is indicated.' He put down his empty mug, and felt in his pockets for a pipe.

'Carried nem. con.,'[17] murmured someone; and while the smoke floated up to the blackened rafters, and the conversation flitted in a desultory manner from one topic to another – pantomimes, the latest dancer, gossip from Dublin, shreds of the day's work, and a dozen other subjects. Meanwhile each officer's servant removed his master's crockery from the table and proceeded to make up his bed. The Boy slept on the table, the other three on the floor around the stove, and their preparations were of the simplest. Each man pulled off his boots (if he had not already done so) and breeches, rolled himself in his blanket, put the discarded garments under his head for a pillow, and settled himself for the night.

'Dirty night,' commented No.4 as he snuggled comfortably into his blanket. 'Thank God I'm warm at last. Put out the light, Boy.'

Before the other could comply there was a tap at the door, and an orderly entered. 'Beg pardon, sir; the officer on duty is wanted at No. 10's billets. There's some misunderstanding with the woman there.' He smiled as he delivered the message to the four recumbent bundles of blankets; it was certainly a very dirty night. But No.4' s feelings were beyond expression. 'Hell!' he said simply and with fervour; 'all right, corporal, I'm coming.' He struggled out of bed, laced up his boots, shrugged into his wet oilskins with a little shudder of disgust, caught up his hat, and disappeared.

Incuriously they watched him go . . .

And that's how we live. It's not much to write home about, is it? Seldom in the one spot for three days together (that's to teach us 'mobility') and smoking our pipes in every farm kitchen in France, like Brigadier Gerard.[18] Always the same farmer's wife in the billets; always a barn for the men and a kitchen for the officers; always the same scene on the second day – the agitated and voluble dame interrupting us at dinner with the usual complaint.

'Pardon, m'sieu. Les soldats . . . '[19]

'Oui, madame, les soldats . . . ? Continuez, madame,'[20] we prompt her, knowing exactly what is to come.

'Ils font toujours pipi sur le blé.'[21]

'Vraiment? C'est bien méchant, ça,' we agree gravely. 'Mais sans doute M. le capitaine arrangera tout,' we assure her.[22]

'Ah, bon, alors. Merci, m'sieu.. merci bien, m'sieu . . . pardon, m'sieu,'[23] and she curtsies herself out backwards.

It's a grave offence, of course, and bad for the young crops. But on a dark night . . . and the latrine far away . . . human nature is weak sometimes.

Your conjectures quite correct. Have numbered as requested.[24]

Throughout January and early February 1916, much of the work carried out by the 7th Leinsters was laborious. However, parts of the battalion also spent periods at the front attached to the 47th (London) Division in trenches in the Loos Sector. The 7/Leinsters' first casualties were at Les Brebis. There, on 16 January, two companies were shelled while assembling in the church square. Ten were wounded. Staniforth described what happened.

Maroc sector, 20 January 1916

Well, we have had many exciting times since my last letter. We started on a three days' trek from our last billets just after I wrote, to come down by easy stages to a portion of the firing-line. The first night we walked into a village occupied by a battalion of Highlanders, and Billy and I each ran into an old schoolfellow among the officers, so we had a free dinner and a festive evening among the kilts. That night I was with C Coy, and we slept 7 in a kitchen, with nothing but the blankets we carried in our packs. Next day we walked some more, and fetched up in a mud-camp; and I slept in a tent. The third day we were halting for lunch by the roadside when word came back from the advance party that the rest of the road was under heavy shell-fire, and that the billets they had selected for us that morning were no longer in existence. So we halted there in a field till after dark, watching the chimneys and houses falling in the town in front of us; and after dark we pushed on into the town and hesitated there while fresh arrangements were made. Unfortunately we chose the main square to halt, and it was there we got our first taste.

I was just chatting to Billy, with the signallers and machine-gunners round us, all sitting, or standing around the square smoking and chaffing, when there was a whizz-zz-zz-zz-*BANG*!!! (I can't describe it any other way: a rushing scream, growing louder and louder, then a blinding flash and a deafening roar, and lastly the patter of stones and earth and splinters.) The battalion picked itself up and shook itself and proceeded to count heads. I mayn't tell you how many casualties, of course, but it was a satisfactorily small number on the whole. You'll see it for yourselves in the papers, I suppose. Considering that the shell (it was an 18-pounder) dropped right in the centre of a massed battalion, it did wonderfully little damage. Personally I lost my last box of matches, that was all. The men behaved splendidly (we have been collectively mentioned in despatches by the Divisional commander since, for 'steady behaviour in trying circumstances'!), seeing that it was their baptism of fire.

Then the divil happened – from my point of view. We were dispersed in small bodies and told to go down side-streets and alleys and await orders. So I did, and got no orders, and half-an-hour later sent to enquire, and found the battalion had pushed on and left us – destination unknown. There was I, left with signallers, pioneers, quarter-guard, transport, bombers, and a handful of other stragglers, after dark, in the shell-zone, and no way of finding which way the battalion had gone. I made enquiries here, there, and everywhere, and at last found a doubtful Frenchman who mentioned a certain village two miles away. I collected my little column and we shoved off into the unknown, spacing out the files and skirting along the side of the road, which was pitted with shell-holes. Ahead we could see the flares and star-shells going up from the front line, and hear the bombs and rifle-grenades. And of course our own batteries were all around us.

Eventually we came to a big pair of ornamental iron gates. The village used to be a kind of model garden-city for the miners, though nothing is left now but cellars and blackened shells of buildings. The battalion of course had gone to ground; and to find a subterranean regiment in the cellars of a ruined town like Kipling's Cold Lairs[25] is no easy matter. I got the men under cover as best I could, and sent out scouts to draw the coverts. And we waited for over two hours while they searched. A good many shells and sniper's bullets were buzzing round, but none so near as the first. At last a guide came back, and set out to lead us home. Unfortunately he lost his way, as is the universal custom of Army guides, and we were another three-quarters of an hour before we got in. I got all the men safely into cellars, and then reported to the C.O. He cheerfully suggested that I should occupy the rest of the night laying telephone wires! That's what the Bible calls asking for bread and receiving a stone, I suppose. However, I told him I hadn't any instruments yet . . . it wasn't true, of course.

Since then we have lived here. It's a queer life. Imagine the Germans holding the railway line at the bottom of your garden, running parallel to Hinderwell village, and our own line running opposite to it between you and the railway, and the British forces (except those actually holding the line) living in the cellars of every house in Hinderwell, and you have a fairly exact picture of our bit of the line. The difference is that this village is on a 'forward slope' – i.e. like the cemetery at Hinderwell, it can be seen from the German lines – and therefore the main village street is *not* in this case invisible from the enemy. So the place is a network of deep trenches, to enable you to get from one house to another in the daytime. Of course you can't have trenches everywhere, and the inhabitants of a few of the cellars have to make a sporting dash over open country for the last dozen yards or so of their journey, which adds a stimulus to life. At night the whole population rises silently and hosts of dim ghostly figures appear above ground like stokers coming up to breathe on deck. It's then that all our working parties do their jobs: mending shell-torn trenches, bringing up rations, water, ammunition and other stuff, relieving the trench garrison, sandbagging more cellars, and all that kind of thing. Then Fritz sends up a flight of star-shells, and we all drop flat and try to hide under a cobblestone till the limelight goes out, and the Boche machine-gunner looses off a belt just to tickle us up. Then he has snipers, who build fixed rifles into their parapets in the daytime to cover a certain mark or sweep a certain street, and at night he poops them off every five minutes or so, just on spec. And, of course, shells, more shells, and always shells. They drop on our houses, in our gardens, in the trenches – everywhere. Our solitary shell in the market-place the other day seems very far away now. But as not one in a hundred does anything but landscape-gardening, so to speak, and as our batteries (hidden in cellars all over the place) send over three to every one of Fritz's, nobody bothers about them. In spite of star-shells,[26] shrapnel, whizz-bangs (a high-velocity, low-trajectory 18-pdr.), pip-squeaks (6-pdrs.), bombs and snipers, the trenches are practically deserted at night, and everyone walks about above ground.

I, being now established at Headquarters[27] (I think they appreciate the importance of communications now), am fortunately exempt from trench-duty and working parties. So I sit here in this cellar with Billy most of the day, except for wandering round my four company offices in the morning and dropping across to Headquarters for meals over the way; and when the night cometh when no man can sleep, I take out the section and we overhaul all our wires, mend the broken ones, reel up any abandoned cable lying about for a rainy day, and lay any new wires that may be required, and get back to bed about 2 or 3 in the morning. The job no one likes is mending wires. Imagine me shinning up a little ornamental tree in some garden to get at a wire at the top, and Fritz putting up a star-shell, and the wretched Signal Officer freezing like a bear at the Zoo on top of his pole (and a most inadequate pole) while the Boche machine-gunner turns loose his bi-hourly belt. Also I hate ransacking deserted rooms for material (wood for poles, drums, nails, staples and that kind of thing) and hearing a devastating bellow right under my feet, and finding that I have strayed over a cellar where one of our 9" howitzers has chosen to embowel itself. Unfortunately we have a howitzer in the next cellar to ours, and though I have printed a large notice saying STREET NOISES FORBIDDEN and hung it up in the trench outside, it doesn't seem to touch the spot. Gunners are a notoriously inconsiderate crush.

The cellar, cleared of cobwebs, straw, bottles, and other litter, and embellished with a bed (great stunt; I stole it from the Major 's dug-out the first night, before he knew it was there), table, chairs, shelf, books, pictures, and so on, makes a most commodious habitation. You have to be a good – shall we say, 'procurer' – to look after yourself in these times, but we've fixed ourselves up quite adequately. Listen to our prospectus: – 'CAHERDRINNEY CASTLE. An exceptionally airy and well-ventilated bijou maisonette, with roomy basement accommodation; patronised by Jack Johnston[28] and other notorieties; extensive snipe-shooting within two mins.; one min. from Underground, Outer Circle; free firing; coal-box[29] in every bedroom; gas laid on free of charge, and good service of Elevators.' How's that for ducal living?

Seriously, I'm perfectly safe, as you'd realise in a moment if you were here, though I admit it doesn't sound so – and incredibly content. Your parcels are exactly what we want. (The potted meat, by the way, was in excellent condition.) Sweets and literature (stray magazines, or old seven pennies) are always in demand, and above all *candles*, which we can't get here except in rations of one a day. If pastry or honey could be packed safely . . . but these are idle dreams. Give Jane[30] my love, and tell her she would be the darling of twelve battalions, six batteries of guns, a squadron of idle horse, and many engineers and Red Cross men, if she could arrive out here and make those tarts and lemon curd. [. . .]

Livossart, 30 January 1916
We left the trenches at 8 in the morning on Tuesday; that is, myself and half the Signal Section. The idea was that we should go on in advance to

the town where our billets were, two miles behind the line, and get telephone wires put up from HQ to the companies before the battalion came down in the evening. We marched down after the men had had their breakfast (I hadn't had more than a cup of tea, in the hurry of packing suddenly), and had a fairly quiet march, though Fritz shelled the road a little. When we got in, we found that a certain Brigade Headquarters preferred our billets to their own, which were in rather an unhealthy part of the town (in point of fact, in the church square where we got our first shell a fortnight ago), and had just annexed them. We were told we must find temporary billets for that night, and next morning could move into their old place (not safe enough for a Brigade, but quite good enough for a battalion, you see). So before I could get out any lines I had to wait for the billeting party to select new headquarters; which they didn't do till two o'clock. At 2.30 I started four lines simultaneously from the four company offices, converging on Hqrs. At 3.30 those four lines arrived at Hqrs, and were told that I was again changed, as the billet didn't suit the Adjutant's fancy. I waited till 5.30, but received no notification of his new choice; so I said, 'Damn the Adjutant,' and finished my wires and opened the office in the room of my original choice. Immediately I had connected the last instrument I received advice of his new Hqrs – half a mile away. Then the battalion began to arrive out of nowhere in the dark, by single sections and platoons; and the usual chaos of billeting after dark in a strange town began. My diary for the evening runs something like this:

8.30. Reported to HQ; no one there. Billeted signallers and M.G. section, whom I met in the dark with Billy.

9.30. Reported to HQ; no one there. Billeted self and Billy. Closed down company offices, being manifestly useless.

11.0. Reported to HQ; no one there. Came home to supper. (It was then that your parcel, which had come along with the battalion, was opened, and saved two young lives from extinction – the first food we had had that day. We made love to the old lady, and she heated coffee for us and gave us butter for the scones. I think we finished every scrap that was in that parcel then and there, and blessed you with every mouthful.)

12.0. Went to bed.

12.30. Called up by Adjutant to report at HQ. Dressed, went out, came back, undressed, back to bed.

1.30. Woken by Adjt's orderly to explain position of Signal Office. Dressed, went out, came back, undressed, back to bed.

3.0. Called out by arrival of Brigade cable-laying section with wire.

Fixed them up, opened office for Brigade messages, kicked up operators and linesmen, reported to Adjt.

4.0. Back to bed.

Next day Billy went sick; feverish, chills, temperature 102°. I packed him off to bed, gave him a Dover's Powder,[31] and reported to the orderly-room that I had taken over temporary command of the M.G. section. The following day we were to move off early in the morning again, so I got the doctor to see Billy and give him a chit to ride in the ambulance while I brought along his section, and I gave instructions to my baggage-guard (who bring along all the gear on lorries, and consequently arrive several hours before the foot-slogging battalion) to see him straight into bed at the other end and get his valise unpacked at once. That day we padded along about eight miles, and camped at a filthy half-way house. Luckily my baggage-guard had worked for once, and I found Billy safely asleep and his stuff unpacked. I went away and billeted our respective men (they're always together, as signallers and machine-gunners are both headquarters personnel, so it was no more difficult than looking after my own Section alone), saw to their food and my own, and returned to the billet to find him awake and hungry and much better. So I made him undress and get into my pyjamas (of course he had gone to bed in his boots), and bought three eggs at fabulous prices from some old horse-leech's daughter in a filthy farm somewhere in the town, and commandeered our landlady's kitchen (she suffered, by the way, from an ingenious combination of quinsy and goitre, which made her an unpleasing conversationalist, had primitive notions of sanitation, and suckled a perpetual infant – altogether a charming household to be sick in), and concocted a biting-on of poached eggs on toast and coffee, which appeared to satisfy him.

Next day we pushed on another seventeen miles over villainous roads. Billy was all right again, but rode in the lorry for luck. In the evening we arrived in our real billets; back billets, that is. Billets are of three kinds: front billets, such as we have been in just now, when the battalion is in the trenches (these are usually cellars, of course); reserve billets where the battalion waits between reliefs (these are usually in a village a mile or so behind the line, and are thoroughly disgusting, because they have no cellars but are almost as frequently shelled as the others); and rest billets, where it goes for a month at a time between spells. So we are here for four or six weeks now probably, about twenty miles behind the lines as the crow flies. Speaking for Billy and myself, we have fallen on our feet, and don't care how long we stay. They are the best billets we have struck yet:

two small bedrooms opening off the mess-room itself, instead of having a three-minutes walk in the mud to get to meals. We sleep in one, and use the other as a dressing-room – swank! – and of course use the mess-room fire and lamps in the evening after the others have departed to their billets. Also there is a little room opening off the orderly-room (which is in a neighbouring farm) which makes a perfect little Signal Office, which I can keep perfectly private for my own wires, instruments, clerks, files, etc., instead of having them crowded out by other people and gear. Altogether a thoroughly cushy billet.

We have got rather a bad name in the English Division to which we were attached in the trenches,[32] because the men would not keep under cover in the daytime, and we had to put the sergeant-major with a rifle loaded with candle-grease bullets[33] to keep them in the trenches. However, the Munsters did worse. They had a poor devil killed by a shell one night up there on a working-party (his head was blown clean off), and his pals didn't quite know what was the correct procedure. So they asked a Staff officer who was riding by. He was very fed up with the whole war, having been out about fifteen months; so he said off-handedly (not dreaming they would take him seriously), 'Why, bury him, of course.' And the poor simple folk in all good faith planted the poor headless thing then and there by the wayside, and smeared a heap of road-scrapings over him to hide him, and trotted back to their headquarters well content. There they got several kinds of hell, and were ordered to go back and dig him up and fetch him along for official disposal, which they had to do. But the story of the Irish regiment alternately burying and digging up a headless corpse in road-scrapings by furtive glimpses of somebody's electric flashlight has gone all round the Division.

Well, as this isn't a book I suppose I'd better stop. I've broken my pipe and am smoking one of Billy's at present; so if you could get a medium-sized large-bore flush-mouthpiece silver-banded half-crown English briar, I'd be very grateful. *Not* a Peterson patent mouthpiece: I can't abide 'em. [. . .]

Livossart, 6 February 1916
Your last parcel arrived last night: the one with the honey, I mean. The other portion of the same parcel reached me three days ago. The bacon-and-egg travelled well, and served us for breakfast in a hurry this morning, before we moved off. My experience is that the larger pastries survive the journey quite well, but the smaller ones – cakes and buns and

things – are apt to get rather battered. The honey was quite all right, not leaked at all; and very good honey too.

I think perhaps the best parcel is one that contains something that will do for the mess: the pasty, for example, or a cake, or a tin of fruit (apricots always barred) – you see, the small headquarter mess subsists largely on private contributions – and then the sort of thing that Billy and I consume in the secrecy of our own apartment, as it were. Just the things we don't get out here, I mean: sweets particularly (say a shillings worth of mixed sweets and chocolates, like we used to get at home sometimes), or toffee. And of course stinkers.[34]

I feel a pig demanding things like this, but you did ask to know, didn't you? and if you knew how much more than their weight in gold those small things are worth out here, you'd understand. You see, it just makes the difference between the little luxury that makes you happy, and the rather hopeless existence without much to look forward to that one sometimes gets to believe in. However, I'm sure you understand, don't you?

This is not a proper letter, only a biting-on. We were dug out of our back billets by a telegram last night, and ordered to proceed to the trenches for more instruction. So we're on the road again, going up by easy stages. This is written in the evening in the farm kitchen of our first half-way house. To-morrow we shall be somewhere about ten miles further up, the next night another seven or so, and the next night in the front line again. This makes our thirteenth move in six weeks. I wish they'd let us alone for a bit.

Poor Billy is doing a temporary understudy of the billeting officer, and moves perpetually ahead of us like a cloud by day and a pillar of fire by night. He doesn't like it a bit, having to find homes for a thousand men every day, and I'm rather lonesome trailing along behind with his Section and kit as well as my own. I'm afraid we depend rather too much on each other; it's not altogether a good thing, I suppose. He made me promise to be his best man last night, by the way. I brutally told him to go to sleep.

Chapter 6

'Covered with fresh blood':
Cambrin, February to March 1916

The 7/Leinsters went into the trenches for the first time as a whole battalion on 11 and 12 February in trenches at Annequin and La Bassée attached to the 19th and 20th battalions, The Royal Fusiliers, and the 1st and 1/5th battalions, The Cameronians (Scottish Rifles).

During this time, one of the battalion's former INVs, Sergeant John Tierney, won the Distinguished Conduct Medal. A Belfast man, Tierney rescued a Corporal Murphy, who was trying to bring barbed wire back to the lines, and had a hand blown off. When asked by a journalist why he had saved the man, Tierney said, 'I wasn't going to look at the poor fellow lying there without doing something. No man with a heart could do that'. Tierney added, 'His hand was swinging by the skin from his arm' and 'well, I just brought him in. That's all.' As for Murphy, there was some excited newspaper speculation that he had been recommended for the Victoria Cross for the initial expedition, but he did not receive it.[1]

Staniforth was not part of the operations on 11 and 12 February, but did enter the trenches on 14 February when the battalion relieved the 18th Battalion, The Royal Fusiliers, at Cambrin, taking over a portion of front line for the first time.

Béthune, 11 February 1916

We are in reserve billets just now; that is, the four companies are up in the front line for 48 hours, while the HQ staff is behind in a town. Billy and I are on velvet for a spell; all our men are distributed among the trenches, so we have for the moment no responsibilities, and we are billeted for the first time on record in a real town with shops and lights and people and even a theatre. We share a decent enough little room above the HQ mess, and spend the time having baths in turn at 2 francs a head – or rather a body – above a chemist's shop. It's the first bath I've seen in France yet. Formerly we've had to borrow the farmer's wooden tub wherever we've been. So God is very good.

To-morrow the men come out, and after a day's rest go in again, and we go with them. It's a quiet part of the line just now, though a bit wet and muddy, ('You *have* heard there is mud in France?' as Punch says), so I don't suppose we'll have any trouble.

When I went up to see the men in, I made the acquaintance of the German Flammenwerfer[2] for the first time, Fritz's latest toy. It's a cylinder containing oil and compressed nitrogen, which is carried on a man's back. The compressed gas is used to force out the oil, which inflames at the jet and spreads out in a broad cone of flame and smoke. This covers 6 yards of front when stationary, and has an extreme range of only 30 yards and a duration of about a minute. The smoke is very dense and black, the flames are yellowish red, and there is a loud roaring noise; so altogether, until the men understand its limitations, it's quite a good example of Boche frightfulness. The upward current of air, caused by the heat, prevents them directing the jet downwards, so a man crouching on the fire-step or just inside a dug-out is perfectly safe.

I'm writing this in the dining-room of M. Somebody-or-Other, which we have taken over as an orderly-room; Monsieur himself having left for the good of his health. His taste in furniture is abominable. A gilt-Cupid clock under a glass case (it isn't going, of course; they never do), flanked by polished steel vases; sham me'ogany sideboard, oilcloth on a round table, a gigantic hanging paraffin-lamp, and the rest all drab paint and china door-knobs. Can't you see it? And the noise is worse than the trenches. All the town streets are paved; and there is an endless procession of motor ambulances (coming down full, or going up empty), motor lorries, transport wagons, guns and limbers, and strings of every kind of horse and mule going up and down outside all day and night.

I'm writing a dictionary of French for Tommy. Here is the first page:-

I have none	)	
Thou hast not any	)	
We have none	)	
There is none left	)	
We are out of it	)	
He is wounded	)	Nah poo
They have been killed	)	
The ration-boxes are empty	)	
There are no letters for you	)	
Leave is cancelled	)	
No -nobody -nothing – nowhere – never	)	

The senior major asked me if you could instruct B. & W.[3] to send him a medicine-case exactly like mine, with the same drugs inside. He says it's the best selection he's seen yet. If you could do this, I should be very glad, because he's been good to me once or twice. Address Major E.W.C. Monro, 7th Leinsters, B.E.F.

Staniforth sent his parents a postcard from Béthune on 13 February, simply signed and dated, to show them where he was.

Cambrin, 16 February 1916
[. . .] Well, we're holding a bit of front line [. . .]. It's a cushy bit of trench; at least, it's drier than most, and the dug-outs are quite waterproof. I wonder if the scheme of a battalion's day in the trenches would interest you? Anyway, it works something like this, as we did it.

A battalion holds about 800 to 1000 yards of front-line trench, as a rule (that is, supposing it to be up to full strength), and of course is also responsible for the depth behind the front line. A sector of trench is rather like this:

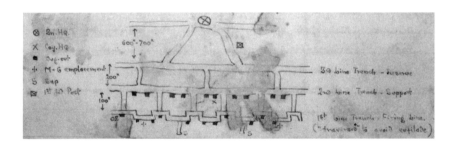

You must understand that it is in reality nothing so regular as this; the 'communications trenches,' for instance, connecting up the different lines, it would be madness to dig as straight as I have shown, as a sniper would shoot right down the length of them. They are also much more numerous; and in addition there are lots of little blind alleys for latrines, and old disused trenches and things.

Three of the battalion's four companies hold a section each of the front line – Right, Centre and Left companies – and they usually select a dug-out in the Support Trench for their headquarters. The fourth company goes in reserve, right back somewhere near Battalion HQ. In the same way the four platoons in each company dispose themselves: three in the firing-line, and one behind them in support. The front line is garrisoned as

thinly as possible, to avoid shell-casualties: a few men in each fire-bay
with rifles and periscopes, and the rest of the garrison in their dug-outs,
where they can be called out instantly – leaving their rifles loaded standing
on the parapet all ready. The saps (projecting short trenches running out
towards the enemy) are garrisoned with bombers as well as riflemen. And
at intervals along the front line are carefully sandbagged emplacements
for machine-guns. (The point I have marked 'O.P.' is an artillery
Observation Post, where the gunners send an officer to control the fire of
their battery somewhere away behind a hill, to which he is connected by
telephone.)

Away back, a thousand yards or so, is a collection of superior wooden
dug-outs at Battalion HQ; one perhaps for the C.O. and Adjutant, one for
the 2nd-in-Command and Doctor, one for the Signal Office, one for the
Orderly Room, and so on. (Personally, I double in with the Doctor.)

About half-way between HQ and the front line is a big dug-out for the
Regimental Aid Post, where the stretcher-bearers bring the wounded.
The serious cases wait there till nightfall, and are then carried back out of
the trenches to the Field Ambulance, which is usually a big house in a
village somewhere close behind the lines. They pass him on, if sufficiently
serious, by motor ambulance to a C.C.S. (Casualty Clearing Station) in a
town still further back, out of shell-range; and his next step is the base
hospital at Rouen or Havre, by a hospital train. If his wound keeps him
more than a fortnight there, he is earmarked for 'blighty' and shipped
home.

My section lays four lines down the trenches to the four company headquarters and establishes an office in each of them, and a big Central at
Battalion HQ, where the lines from Brigade and Artillery also come in.
Consequently I live in the HQ mess, as my work lies in the Signal Office;
Billy, on the other hand, has his four machine-guns all in the firing line,
of course, so he naturally makes his headquarters in whichever company
suits him best, and while the battalion is in the trenches we never see him
in the mess. The same applies to the Bombing Officer, who is normally
an HQ member.

As for routine, I work in shifts with my sergeant. He takes control from
2 to 6 in the morning while I sleep, and then sleeps himself till midday.
After midday we are both on the job together. My servant brings me some
tea in the morning and fishes me out of 'bed' (you may not remove more
than your boots in the trenches when sleeping – the flea-bag is invaluable), and I walk down miles of sticky wet slippery communication-trench
and spend the morning overhauling the lines and inspecting the company

offices, etc., and then wander back to HQ in time for lunch, where I feed outrageously. The afternoon I generally spend in the Signal Office checking the files and testing the lines and that sort of thing or tinkering with defective apparatus, until dusk, when I go round the companies again, and send out fatigue parties to collect disused wire and various odd jobs of the kind. That is the 'recreation hour,' so to speak; one drops into company dug-outs for drinks and chat, and borrows rifles here and there along the parapet and takes an odd snipe at the Boche, in the intervals of one's own work.

The night, of course, is everybody's busy time. There are working parties everywhere, repairing broken parapets, improving the barbed wire out in front, scraping and draining trenches, or going down to the village to fetch up the next day's rations and water from the transport dump. (The Quartermaster and Transport Officer live right back in the town, each afternoon they draw the rations and mail from the A.S.C. and drive it up to the dump – that is, the nearest point behind the lines where carts are allowed – and we send down carrying parties after dark to fetch it up. The men cook their rations as they want them on braziers of charcoal in the open trench.)

All along the firing-line there are empty shell-cases hung up; and at the first sign of a gas attack every sentry hammers hell out of his gong with a bayonet, and men come tumbling up out of dug-outs everywhere, and every rifle and machine-gun opens up at its top capacity; we telephone through to the batteries, and the artillery 'barrages on its night-lines.' (That simply means firing battery-fire at 5-second intervals – battery-fire is when the four guns of the battery fire in order, 1-2-3-4, 1-2-3-4, and so on – at the target the guns are normally laid on at night, which need-less to say is the enemy's front-line trench. They thus form a 'barrage' – pronounced French-fashion – or solid curtain of dropping shells, which troops cannot pass through. Sometimes you barrage Fritz's second-line trenches while you do something particularly poisonous with his front line; like stopping a rabbit's bolt-hole before you send in a ferret. Talking of pronounciation [sic], by the way, the place you asked about is a mono-syllable rhyming with the noun (not the verb) 'abuse;' [Loos] and the place that suggests a telescope rhymes with Mons [Lens]. I'm afraid I can't be more explicit.) [. . .]

Two days later. Rather a bad time since I wrote last. The Prussians relieved the Bavarians in our little bit, and started in right away with a bouquet of rifle-grenades. (A rifle-grenade is exactly like a rocket to look at: a head and a stick: the stick is inserted in the barrel of a rifle on a light tripod-mounting on the parapet and the grenade discharged neatly into the opposing trenches, where it explodes with considerable unnecessary violence.) They started handing them over about 10 in the morning, damn them, just when I was going round the front trenches. You hear a soft phut as the thing starts, a whistle in the air and a warning shout from the sentry, and everyone throws themselves flat in the mud at the bottom of the trench and waits for an agonizing eternity for the burst. Then you get up and shake yourself and pick up the pieces. Well, we were garrisoning rather thickly that morning, unfortunately, and we got it in the neck. One poor devil was blown into the next world just as I came along, and the same explosion shattered my wires. So I had to mend them – all covered with fresh blood – and you should have seen me kneeling there under the parapet, working for dear life with pliers and insulating tape and smoking a feverish cigarette while the stretcher-bearers carried off the bits of poor Commiskey[4] – trying hard to forget that rifle-grenades are fired from a fixed tripod and at the same range, and that they would probably send over two or three more into the same place in the next few seconds! I never quaked so much or prayed so hard in my life before.

When I went back later, after communication was re-established, you ought to have seen the Dressing-Station in full blast. The doc was working by candlelight in a shirt and trousers only, with his sleeves rolled up to his elbows and his arms all crimson; working like a fiend from the pit, with stretchers crowding the dug-out all round, and the whole place a reek of blood and iodine and bandages, with the candle casting flickering shadows on the low mud roof and pit-props. It was rather a wonderful sight.

We rang down to the battery when those grenades got really troublesome; and asked for help; and then the battery got busy and there was hell to pay. Of course Fritz turned on his field-guns too, and we countered with howitzers, and they replied, and at last we played the trump, 15-inch 'Grandmother,' three miles to the rear, and Fritz gave it up as a bad job and subsided into a sulky silence. Meanwhile the poor infantrymen, having called in their big brothers, sat tight in their dug-outs and listened to the storm. They started with pip-squeaks – that's the little 12-pounder shell similar to our own Horse Gunners' – and whizzbangs (the ordinary field-gun, corresponding to the 18-pdr of our R.F.A., but a bit smaller), and then the big howitzers, 4.2's and 4.9's and 6-ins and 9.2's, came in, with a noise like a train rumbling over in the sky and a deafening roar as they burst. Altogether it was a very windy morning, and I didn't like going up and down the trenches a bit. Our wires were smashed to blazes, of course.

We got word that the 15-inch was going to do a turn some time in the afternoon. Now the 15-inch is the biggest of all imaginable big guns, and the number of specimens possessed by the British Army in France tallies with the age of my cousin in Manchester [two]; and her projectile is so big that only one can be carried on an A.S.C. motor lorry. So you can understand that when we heard Grandmother was going to fire one round (which she does about once a week) for our especial benefit, we left our dug-outs and crowded up to see. Sure enough, at about 2.30 there was a muffled thud somewhere away behind the hills to our rear, and the air was filled with a noise like the chariot-wheels of God, and when we looked for the village they were laying for, it simply wasn't there. (I understand now why they say shells never drop in the same place twice; it's because the same place isn't there any more for them to drop into.)

However, we pulled through somehow, and were relieved by Bob Jackson's[5] old regiment, in which I found an old Robinite[6] serving as a private (né Muhlberg, now Millburn!). The relief was complete about 11 p.m., we marched five miles back to the town I sent you a p.c. of (did you ever get it, or was the Base Censor base enough to censor it?), slept for a few hours, pushed off first thing in the morning, marched twenty-five miles, and arrived back here in our old billets – the ones I wrote you approvingly about last week – and very tired we were when we got here.

I must tell you how the wily Hun slipped it across our fellows the other week. In the portion of line we held there was an old shell-ruined house between the opposing trenches. This was of course a sniper's paradise; and every evening at dusk it became a race between the two parties which could occupy it first. Men would wait behind the parapet watching the sun set, and directly the shadows fell a cyclone of machine-gun fire broke out to cover them and away they tore; and once established, they sniped away all night. At last this became a nuisance, and we said to the R.E., 'This is the limit; suppose you blow it up once for all.' The R.E., however, said, 'Not so; suppose you dig a new front-line trench and bring the house within your lines; then you will have it to snipe from in perfect security.' Like this:

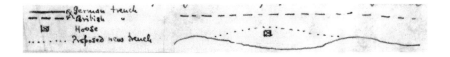

So we thought that was a good idea, and next night we went out and laid down nice white sandbags to mark the proposed new line and guide the diggers, and sat down to wait for a dark night to complete operations. When it came, out went a couple of battalions with picks and shovels and went at it hell-for-leather, digging in the dark and following the line of sandbags, not without a fair number of casualties from rifle and machine-gun fire and bombs which opened up on them.

When dawn broke they stood up in their new trench and surveyed the landscape o'er, and found the house still in front.

The Boche had got there first and shifted the line of sandbags.

So they decided after all to blow it up, and the R.E. put a big demolition-charge in it, and sent round notice of the fireworks to everyone, and at midnight precisely some general probably made a solemn speech and pressed a button – and nothing happened. A couple of officers and a party went out with another big charge to fix it up again, and when they were all safely inside the house Fritz pressed his button – and that was that. There are no flies on the Hun.

On the other hand, we surprised him very much the other night, in a small way. At three minutes to 11 exactly I phoned through to the battery, 'Test X6' (which will do as well as any other trench-number, though guaranteed fictitious). Now, on receipt of this message from the infantry, the battery guarding the particular sector of trench quoted should fire one round from each gun in reply, within 50 seconds from the receipt of the message just to show they are awake and taking notice.

Well, the Bavarians, as it happened, had been very peaceful all that day and evening, and so had we. But at two minutes to 11 exactly, as a freak of fate would have it, one of them said, 'Look here, this is damned slow getting, what?', and he picked up his courage in both hands and scuttled up to his front line and pitched over four rifle-grenades, and then ran like blazes back to his dug-out.

The result of the coincidence was that fifteen seconds after his grenades exploded in our trench, 'boom! – boom! – boom! – boom!' came four large and ponderous shells on his parapet – as it chanced, exactly where the grenades had come from. It was for all the world like a naughty little boy and a big policeman.

In the amazed hush that followed you could almost hear the very-much surprised Hans whispering to the equally-disconcerted Fritz, 'Fritz mein boy, it would better haf been not to do that foolishness,' and Fritz's reply, 'Ach, ja, Hans; der are on der englisch-artillerie not der flies ve did think – ach, nein.' Anyway, it shut them up like an opera hat for the rest of the night.

The 7/Leinsters were withdrawn from the front on 18 February and spent the remainder of February marching, drilling and training. In early March, there was heavy snow but the battalion was in billets. On 17 March, St Patrick's Day, the battalion was given a holiday marked by brigade sports. The shamrock that was presented in the traditional way had been sent by the man whom many of the men regarded as their political leader and who had urged them to join up, John Redmond.

Montcornet, 29 February 1916
This is a queer life, and here is a queer picture for you. The setting is a tiny little room off a French kitchen, in a Godforsaken village twenty miles from anywhere. Time, about one o'clock in the morning; the whole farmhouse sound asleep except the cattle in the byre next door. I can hear the rattle of their halter-blocks and the restless bang and stamp of their feet through the thin plaster of the wall. The only light is a candle-end, shivering in the draught. I am sitting on Billy's bed, writing this with one hand; the other arm is holding him (and has been dead for a dickens of a time, too). He is sleeping restlessly, very flushed and feverish. Outside, the snow is very deep; and the only sounds are the cattle, the stamp and turn of a very drowsy sentry just up the road, and – occasional and very faint – the boom of the far-off guns.

(Strange days for your baby boy, Mother . . . I'm brooding a bit to-night, I think.)

You see, it began with a tooth of his which has been worrying him for several days. To-night it got past bearing, and of course, as would happen, the Doc was five miles away at another village. Poor old Billy – I ransacked the dispensary till I found a hypodermic and injected a drop of cocaine, but that wore off presently, so I bundled him into bed with whisky bottles full of hot water as warming-pans. Cold sheets are no catch this weather, in rooms neither air-tight nor water-tight; and we settled down to wait for the Doc. After endless hours of waiting he came – and had to dash off again almost at once. He had just time to take a particularly wicked pair of forceps and do the deed. It was a big molar, and must have been a devil of a wrench, but there was never a sign out of Billy, plucky beggar. But I think the strain of suppressing it was too much, because the reaction came afterwards. He sat up in my arms for half-an-hour, shivering violently and spitting blood, as white as this paper. Shock. Then I dosed him with morphia (my dears, I handle the most deadly drugs with the assurance of complete ignorance), and he quieted down, after I had talked much nonsense to him. 'Don't go, John,' was the last thing he said, about half-an-hour ago, so here I am, and hence this letter. It probably won't interest you all that much, but I'm scribbling at random to pass the time; and anyway it goes to prove that even in a world-war small things like teeth may be more important than the Kaiser's armies.

And it's all experience. You know, mamma, I've been looking back at myself as I was two years ago, and I think I've changed a good deal. Not necessarily for the better, I mean – in several ways probably not – but I've learnt a heap of Life. I wonder what you'll think when we meet again.

Many thanks for the parcel (the last of February), which arrived today. I got one also from Sheffield: toffee, and dates stoned and dusted with nut-gratings, good but not as good as replacing the stone with a whole nut, I think.

Yes, you were quite right in your conjecture about our billets. The 'village twenty miles back' you wouldn't possibly know even if I told you, and wouldn't find on any map. It's just one of a thousand other country hamlets, about the size of Ellerby. In a week I shall have forgotten the name of it myself.

There's no news. The snow is very deep and wet, and the weather is beastly, which means billet-life is also beastly. The two are intimately connected. But I'm as fit as a horse, and have never been better since I came to France, except during the early days when I was getting acclimatised. I hear we're all to be inoculated again, by the way, as it's more than a year since we were done. [. . .]

Allouagne, 10 March 1916

[. . .] This Division is going to do big things. That isn't a boast. It is. The Boche got it in the neck from the French[7] – he asked for it. He also got it in the neck from the Canadians[8] – he asked for it. But wait and see what he gets from the distressful country – without asking for it.

Our Corporal Chievers was in command of a section in the trenches. Our Corporal Chievers was told to take four men and cast bombs from a sap-head. Our Corporal Chievers knew very little about bombs, but a lot about the duty of setting a good example. So he withdrew the firing-pin and advanced gingerly up the sap, and the four tiptoed behind him, open-mouthed and heart-throbbing. They arrived at the sap-head; Brother Hun a bare score of yards away. Corporal Chievers took a deep breath. 'InthenameoftheFatherandoftheSonandoftheHolyGhost,' said Corporal Chievers, crossing himself wildly, and cast the bomb into space . . .

Rather touching, don't you think.

Allouagne, 19 March 1916

That was a great parcel (2nd of March). The pies were especially good. But just one thing: you forgot the cigarettes. Pies may come and pies may go, but give us this day our daily stinker.

They gave us a little rest to celebrate Paddy's Day, so we played soccer. The Hun, who is an irreligious blighter, shelled somewhat heavily all day. Billy and I bought miner's long blue cotton jeans and cut them off at the knee to make football shorts. Very chick, not to say bazaar.[9]

Just as the game finished, we heard that the Boche had come over his parapet, and we were all expecting to be packed off up to the line at a moment's notice. Sitting down to dinner with gas-helmets and revolvers and all. However, nothing materialised, so we have a few days more peace, I hope.

The weather is beautiful, and we are lazing about all day, with just enough parades to keep our hands in. In the evenings we have impromptu sing-songs on the village green round a bonfire, and you hear all the old Dublin ballad-singers with their weird melancholy songs. It's all very restful and contented.

Fritz's aeroplanes dropped a bouquet of bombs here a couple of nights ago, but all went in the fields and exploded harmlessly. He is a wonderfully bad shot.

The General[10] addressed the regiment before St. Patrick's Day, and exhorted them to behave as St. Patrick would have liked. 'The holy saint's favourite beverage,' says he, 'is well known to have been a good glass of pure sparkling water. Moreover we have it credibly reported that he had a great aversion from Government rum.' Not bad for a brigadier, the regiment decided.

One of our flying officers was killed in the German lines not long ago. Next day a Boche plane flew over and dropped a message. 'Captain So-and-so was buried with full military honours at ——' (giving the exact location of the spot). Rather sporting of them. We dropped an answer thanking them very much, and saying we would do the same for them!

Allouagne, 21 March 1916

[. . .] My leave gets due, failing unforeseen circumstances, on the Glorious First of June. The C.O.'s starts next week, but it takes a lot of time to work down to a subaltern. What a time we'll have! I shall say I'm going to Ireland, and get the extra day (nine altogether), and pay the difference on my warrant from Chester. A white lie in a good cause, don't you think? [. . .]

Chapter 7

'I've had miraculous escapes': Puits 14
Bis and Hulluch, March to May 1916

From late March 1916 the 7/Leinsters continued to be based around Béthune, but moving around different trenches. Some of these were in a terrible condition and regularly under attack from German shell fire. From their arrival in France in late December 1915 until 24 March the battalion lost only five men killed, but it then lost four on just one night (28 March). Over April to May, another twenty-six men were killed or died of wounds.

Even at times of rest, life was far from easy for the battalion. One officer in the 6/Connaughts, Blake O'Sullivan, noted how 'This term "rest" became a standard joke'. He described how due to the 'back-breaking work parties' in which men fetched and carried material from the front line, 'many a tired man welcomed the return to the death-dealing "line".'[1]

Puits 14 Bis, 29 March 1916
These are poor trenches, but might be worse. Yesterday we had rather a bad day. The Boche pushed over rifle grenades on the front line, and heavy stuff from his 4.7's round about HQ, for two or three hours. Unluckily one of his first shells set light to our reserve ammunition store, and we sat in our dug-outs while it burned next door, among the crackle of exploding cartridges. Underneath the cartridge-boxes were seven boxes of grenades, each filled with high explosive. When the fire got to those we knew all about it. So did the Boche, and he jubilated with 9.2's. A trench looks rather sick when it has been saluted with 9.2's. You will understand that this is bad for telephone wires no thicker than a piece of string. We arrived up here the night before last, and I spent that night taking over the cable-system. Then yesterday we had this bean-feast, so I spent last night refitting it. I would now cheerfully sell myself for twopence-halfpenny. Unfortunately there are no takers. Three days and two nights without sleep make Jack a dull boy.

I saw a little tragedy yesterday. A man was blown in at the door of a dug-out, a man belonging to another regiment. We were digging out what was left of him, and there was a little knot of onlookers. At last we recovered him. His arm and shoulder were blown off, and his thigh and leg shattered and horribly burnt, and his neck was mostly blood and fragments, poor chap. We laid him on a trench-board – and one of the bystanders, a kid of 18 or so, burst into tears. 'My brother . . . .' It was rather wretched.

2.4.1916. I haven't had a chance to write any more of this since. We worried through our six days somehow, and are now in reserve billets about five miles behind the lines. Our relief was not complete till 2 in the morning, and then we had to start out and walk two miles in the trenches and three more on the roads with all our gear, as a wind-up. We got in here at six in the morning. Another night's rest gone west!

On the last day I telegraphed urgently for four miles of new cable, as the stuff we had laid down was getting impossible. It came up by special motor lorry from the Division: four big drums weighing a hundredweight each, and we humped them down the trenches and renewed the whole system that afternoon. It was rush work, but worth it; and I handed over the whole lay-out in perfect order to the relief.

Apropos of cables, I dropped a brick the other day. Of course all disused lines, of which there are rather a lot lying about, come under the 'finding's keeping' rule. You take an instrument and tap into the wire, and if there is no answer you thank God and reel it up. (When I came out to France all my signalling equipment was carried in a small box; now I have a transport wagon for it!) So when I struck a beautiful new cable lying on the ground I tapped it at once, and getting no answer promptly reeled in. I walked up 2000 yards of this, pouching it as I went – and ran slap into a battery of French 75's in action, completely cut off from their headquarters! I had to apologize profusely and lay it all down again. They were very nice about it, though.

These billets are a small mining town about the size of Loftus. It is shelled a little, but not much. We have a little room over the mess; I sleep in the bed and Billy on the floor. The people are awfully nice, and mother us most carefully. The man has been twice through the Boche lines to Valenciennes, and has been appointed by his (French) general as guide in charge of all roads and tracks around there. Considering Valenciennes is many miles deep in Boche territory, this is rather cool. The French are a wonderful nation.

They have brought down a couple of aeroplanes here in the last two days, I saw the first one from the trenches. The shrapnel puffs burst all round her for a long time, and then – smash! a direct hit, and she dropped like a shot lark.

The larks here are in full song, by the way. It's funny to wake up in your dug-out and hear one singing overhead at five in the morning with a brilliant blue sky and golden sunshine, and have to walk about in an infernal ditch all day, with Fritz pushing over grenades and mortars and big shells as hard as he can shove.

I'm too tired to write any more. Thank you for the parcel, the last of March. We never tire of dates. 'What, never? – No, never.'

Nouex-les-Mines, 3 April 1916
Only a line to say I'm still AI. The Hun is not working any more fright-fulness at present, and the wind is temporarily in the west. I walked over yesterday to see Billy. He is about three miles away. I found the Boche plastering his lines for a two-hour hate, and had to crawl on my tummy over the blown-in bits of the front line. It wasn't a bit the idle evening stroll I had intended. I found him sitting in a front-trench shelter, with a sheet of tin between him and the 4.9's, arranging his relief. Lucky dog, he went out for a six-day spell last night. I waited until the Hun calmed down a bit, and came back. On my way I met Stephen Gwynn.[2] He has had three dug-outs blown in on him, and his company are beginning to regard him as a mascot.

We have about cleared our trenches of dead now, and they are a bit better. Since they have been removed and buried, we have been able to patch up the broken bits. By the way, they found an officer of the Black Watch gassed after the attack – and he was no Black Watch at all, only a German spy.[3]

Mazingarbe, 22 April 1916
I ought to have written before, but I've been almost worn out for the last sixteen days. (We do sixteen days in the trenches now, and eight in rest. It's too long, really.) In the bit of line we came out of last night, there are ten mine-craters where No-man's-Land used to be, and practically no front line except saps and sandbag breastworks; and the nights are spent by each side in crawling round the lips of the craters, dressed in white (because it's all fresh-turned chalk), with pocketfuls of bombs, until you run into the enemy. With luck, you spot him before he spots you – at about six feet range, on a dark night. Without luck, you don't; and the casualty-lists speak for themselves. It's a sticky bit of line. The wires were all blown to blazes when we came in, and I had to telegraph for

200,000 feet of fresh cable and re-lay the whole system before we could do anything. Even then we were mending breaks all day and all night to keep through to the front-line companies. And the Boche strafed us like hell all the time. However, we came through all right; I don't know why or how.

Billy was relieved the night before us, and when we got out he had a bed and clean sheets for me in the same room as himself, and billets for my men all settled, and heaps of hot water. He had turned out all sorts of people all day long to keep the place for me. It just makes all the difference whether you have to start arranging billets for your men and yourself at the end of a very wet relief, or whether you simply walk in and find somebody has done it all for you.

I don't think I've written one letter since we left our old billets. I simply couldn't. When you're sixteen days without taking off more than your boots, and living underground all the time except when you're slopping about in wet trenches mending wires, you don't feel chatty.[4] And the water for washing is one petrol-can per day between four of us, because every drop has to be fetched up 2½ miles of trench. Still, I'm all right now, except still feeling a bit strained, and shall be ready for another spell after a day or two's rest. It's a great life; I'd like it even more except for one or two of my immediate superiors, who worry us a bit.

Leave has been stopped this last week or so. It always is during what G.H.Q. calls 'periods of activity;' i.e. when we are afraid of a Boche push, or intend making one of our own. However, it is to open again on the 25th, I believe. Of course, though, it puts us all back a bit. There are still six officers to go before me. I suppose a month ought to see them through, unless they close leave again. In any case, if nothing untoward occurs I shall get it just as the Division comes off trench duty and retires into the backwoods for a month's rest. Just my luck.

I've had miraculous escapes this time; shrapnel through my gloves, and a bullet that tore my tunic, and grenades and shells bursting just a few seconds after I had left places where I had been standing for ten or fifteen minutes; but they'll keep till I see you. So far the identity disc you put round my neck has kept me quite safe. It's never been taken off, you know.

I'm most awfully glad I'm not married. This is no place for married men. It spoils their work, and makes them nervous, too, in nine cases out of ten. [. . .]

Mazingarbe, 25 April 1916

This is a place of blessed peace. We are quartered in a chateau with actually a garden. There is a big bed of tulips just coming out, and trees all snowy with cherry-blossom, and bees humming round the currant-flowers, and a big lawn. I'm sitting out-of-doors scribbling this in the sunshine; Billy is at an upper window with a pair of field-glasses alternately watching shell-bursts (the Germans have been putting heavy stuff all day into a row of miners' cottages three or four hundred yards away) and throwing pebbles at me, which interrupts the even tenor of this letter. And the chocolates you sent are very good, and tobacco better, and in a few minutes we shall have tea on the lawn, and Billy and I are together again after sixteen days – so although I haven't had a bath for three weeks, God is very good.

An orderly is coming across the lawn with the post . . . two for me, and three for him . . . it's very difficult to throw letters to an upper window . . . I'm afraid he'll have to come down . . . pause; while I read yours.

[. . .] There is a gas attack expected, and we have to go about with gas helmets unbuttoned and ready day and night. It's an awful shame to spoil a glorious day like this with such foolishness.

Billy and I walked into town (about two miles of hot and dusty road) this morning, and the Boche followed us with shells half the way, dropping about 100 yards or so behind us. It was for all the world as if their heavy gunner were sending £50 shells at two harmless subalterns out for a walk. None of them did any damage at all, that was the funny part. [. . .]

Mazingarbe, 27 April 1916

[. . .] We were to go up into the line again to-day, and Billy and I were luxuriating in our last night in bed. At the unearthly hour of five in the morning we were awoken by a fearsome din; all the guns talking at once. It was like a heavy thunderstorm; the whole sky crashing and rolling; the air full of shells, some light ones leaping from the guns with a long scream and away, just as if they ought to leave a visible streak in the air, and others (heavy) droning along the sky, as some one says, 'thoroughly enjoying the sensations they arouse in the unfortunate humanity underneath.' And an occasional hiccough from Archie[5] the Anti-Aircraft, and a rattle of machine-guns, and fusillades of rifle-fire. We lay in bed and blinked at the sunshine for some time, and still the noise went on, so after a cigarette we thought we might get up and see what was going on. There was a blizzard of shells in the street, all smashing on a cross-roads at the end. When we got to HQ there was a telegram from Division ordering all ranks to stand-to, and a warning of a possible attack. So we climbed into harness and had a bit of breakfast and waited.

Then it came. First thin broken wisps of greenish film[6] in the sunlight, and then stronger whiffs, until our eyes were all bloodshot and dripping. (Of course we are a mile behind the line in billets here, so we only got the after-taste of it.)

Right through that came the guns and limbers, hell-for-leather; full gallop down the street they thundered, like a London fire-engine racing for a fire. A German shell smashed down by the wheel of one limber; fortunately it was a dud and didn't explode, but the limber canted right up on its tail, hung for a moment, and smashed down again. The gunner was hurled off his seat and fell on his hands and knees in the road; no sooner had he touched the ground than he was up again, made one leap at his horse, and was into the saddle again – God knows how he did it – and they were off round the corner, their eyes pouring tears and the whips rising and falling in a cloud of dust till they were out of sight. I never saw the guns go into action like that before. It was magnificent.

After that the ambulances began to roll back; and men on stretchers; some with their faces covered. And still we waited.

About 9 o'clock we heard that the Boche had taken the first two lines of trenches in the sector we came out of last week, where I wrote my last trench-letter to you. And about an hour later we heard that we had launched a counter-attack and pushed them out again, with enormous losses (to them);[7] and we were allowed to stand down and climb out of our harness. At present we are waiting to watch a big batch of German prisoners come down. It's rotten being so close behind and yet not knowing what is happening. The only tangible score for us is that our relief-orders are cancelled pending further instructions, so we'll get another night in bed – unless of course we are hauled out and rushed up suddenly at midnight.

Later. I've been talking to a lance-corporal just down, who was through it. He says that at about 6.30 this morning the Germans released their gas. It hung for quite a long time over their own trenches before the wind (very slight) began to carry it over to ours. They came out behind it; only their feet were visible under the cloud. Half-way over they lay down to form up; and as soon as they got up again we opened everything on them: rifles, bombs, trench-mortars, machine-guns and all. In spite of that they cleared us out of the front line (which is only very lightly held. Retirement is better than the expense of 'prevention' in rotten trenches like these. I mean, either side can at any time walk over into the other fellow's front line, but they can't stay there. As the drillbook says, 'A trench may be lost, but a system of trenches never.'), and got a foothold in the second line, twenty or thirty yards behind. Then we collected bombers and things, and booted him out. And that's that; quite an exciting day.

Over Easter 1916 public attention in Britain and Ireland was gripped by fighting not on the Western Front but on the streets of Dublin. Between 24 and 30 April 1916, 450 people were killed in the Easter Rising as rebels sought to win an independent Ireland through a popular uprising. Of the dead, 116 were military, sixteen were police, and the remaining 318 rebels and civilians. In the official figures no distinction was made between rebels and civilians, but it is likely that only sixty-four were rebels.[8] News of the Rising filtered through to the public and serving soldiers gradually. Staniforth certainly knew of it by 28 April when he wrote 'Poor old Dublin. Always in the wars.' News of the Rising would come through in detail over the next few days, sometimes in the form of taunts from German trenches, as Staniforth's May Day letter describes.

Mazingarbe, 28 April 1916
Just a line to say all quieted down after my letter of yesterday, and we're still sitting in the sunshine among the tulips. I expect we shall go up in the ordinary way to-morrow. Oh lord, another sixteen days in this heat! Billy is probably going up to-night; he always takes over his gun-positions a day before us, you know. Sixteen days in – eight days out – and then, about half-way through the next sixteen, I ought to be getting due for leave. Only they'll probably stop it again just before that. Blessed is he who expecteth nothing, for he shall not be disappointed.

Poor old Dublin. Always in the wars.

Hulluch, 1 May 1916
[. . .] Well, we moved up, just after my last letter, into advanced billets in the remains of a hamlet just behind the trenches, as the battalion in reserve. We booked our rooms and unpacked all our kit, and sat down to a meal of sorts. (Personally I gave it a miss and went to bed instead, misfortunately.) We were just stretching our legs after the march when a despatch-rider came up with urgent orders. The brigade [49th] on our left was so weakened by the gas and the fighting that we were to be lent to them, and were to relieve one of their battalions [the 8th Inniskillings] in the front line at once, before dark. So the meal was swept away, and

the kits bundled back into packs, and the packs strapped on, and off we trudged. By the way, it is no longer the custom, when a battalion is suddenly and unexpectedly sent up to the line, for the bugles to ring out an imperious summons and the regiment to fall in on a massed parade in the village street. It folds its tents like the Arabs and silently steals away by single platoons, without paying p.p.c.[9] calls or staying to tip the servants. In that manner we came to the trenches. I don't know how to describe them. The bombardment of the last three days had flattened them into mere hummocks and morasses, and has also prevented the evacuation of casualties. Everywhere we picked our way over dead and dying, all gassed. Up to the present we have evacuated 440 men killed by gas. It's a nightmare of a job; the expressions of men caught suddenly and choked aren't pretty.

About an hour after we had got in, there was more gas. This time we were on the alert – the poor devils who died had left us that legacy, at least – and we had our gas-helmets on in no time. Over it came, in the same slow rolling cloud, and the usual hell broke out: everything turned on to its full capacity on both sides. However, this time the Boche didn't follow it up with an attack as we expected, though we were standing to all night.

The worst of gas is that it ruins everything it touches, even if it doesn't harm you yourself. Every rifle, machine gun, cartridge, bandolier, telephone wire, and metal of any sort turns a dull arsenic green, with a corroding film, and has to be cleaned at once. To give you an instance, I was hunting over the whole system all last night and this morning for some mysterious fault that was bothering us; and when we ran it to earth it was a tiny bare joint hidden under a sandbag, that had been gassed and was holding up all current. Imagine a string running from you to Ellerby two miles away, all zig-zag across country, in company with twenty or thirty other strings, sometimes wide apart, sometimes clotting together for half-a-mile in a confused crowd; take a pitch-dark night, and season it with a few shells, mines, gas clouds, rifle grenades, mortars and machine guns, and then go and try to find a knot placed somewhere between you and the Ellerby Inn and return in a minimum time. That will give you some idea of how my linesmen work. They're magnificent.

The thing that is engrossing all our attention and conversation just now is the weather. You don't know what it is like to pray for rain when your trenches are full of corpses and the Hun is using gas. (Rain dissipates a gas-cloud and makes it useless.) And every day the dawn breaks out of a cloudless brassy sky with a blazing sun. All day and all night there are little knots of men clustering around the little wooden weather-cocks that

The 'Great uproar in Ireland' placard referred to by Staniforth on 1 May 1916, now held at the Imperial War Museum. (Photo © Imperial War Museum FEQ 310.)

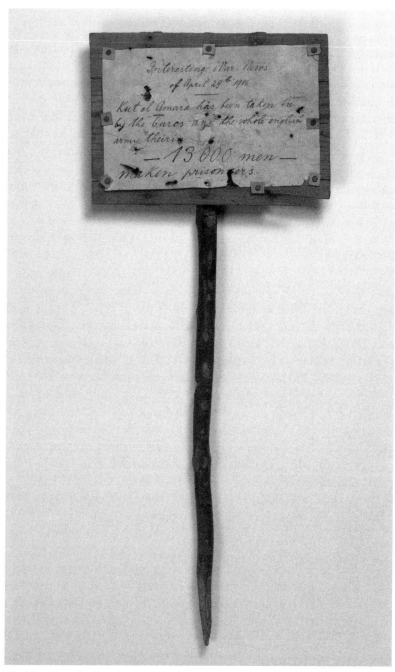

The Kut placard referred to by Staniforth, now held at the Imperial War Museum.
(Photo © Imperial War Museum FEQ 172.)

are erected in every trench to give warning of a gas-wind, and every little flicker is watched and noted, just as every speck of haze that might be a rain-cloud is watched in the sky. And still the wind hangs in the east. It's the most tantalising of winds: fickle summer airs that back and veer all round between N-by-E and S-by-E, but never work round to the west. We watch it like the Ancient Mariner; and every now and again the Hun puts up a smoke-bomb from his front trench to test it, and the smoke drifts across into our lines, and everyone bustles for his gas-helmet. Everyone except the dead. I think their complete and beautiful indifference to all the tumult is very striking. They lie in rows, and we surge backwards and forwards all day long past them, and shells drop beside them, and guns bang in their ears, but they never heed it. They've done their job and finished it, and they just lie there.

The Germans put up three large placards this morning. One said, 'IRISHMEN. GREAT UPROAR IN IRELAND. ENGLISH GUNS ARE FIRING ON YOUR WIFES AND CHILDREN.' Another said, 'KUT CAPTURED. 13,000 ENGLISH PRISONERS.' The third and largest said: 'ENGLISH GUNS FIRING ON YOUR WIFES AND CHILDERN. ENGLISH DREADNOUGHT SUNK: ENGLISH MILITARY BILL REFUSED. SIR ROGER CASEMENT PERSECUTED. THROW YOUR ARMS AWAY. WE WILL GIVE YOU A HEARTY WELCOME' Aren't they impudent devils? We played Rule Britannia and lots of Irish airs on a melodeon in the front trench to show them we weren't exactly downhearted. It was a company commander who played, and he stuck to it for an hour, although they pushed over all sorts of stuff at him. We also stuck up a notice which annoyed them so much that they threw rifle-grenades at it till they destroyed it 'PLEASE TELL YOUR DESERTERS TO COME OVER SINGLY NEXT TIME, AS THE LAST SIX WERE TAKEN FOR A PATROL AND UNFORTUNATELY FIRED UPON,' which was a fact.

Your telegram has just reached me. I'm afraid it's not much use wiring; you see, all Army stuff comes over the wires, and a private telegram simply waits for a quiet moment. Yours was apparently despatched on the 29th, and this is the 2nd, so a letter would really be quicker. And anyway, always remember that no news is good news. If I were wounded or killed, you'd know from the War Office probably within 24 hours; so if I cannot write (and it's sometimes impossible), you may conclude with absolute certainty that I'm all right. And anyway I'm a great believer in my star. If I were going to be killed I'd have been killed long ago; and as for a nice jammy wound – why, the sooner it comes the better! Walking about trenches all day long hand-in-hand with death, you can't help becoming a fatalist. That sounds bombastic, but it isn't meant to be. What I mean is that it's no use calculating chances; if you stand still, the shell you hear coming may drop on your head, if you hurry on you may run right into it, and if you go back they may be shelling the place you've just come from and you'll wish you hadn't; so the only thing to do is to go on and finish your job and come back.

Philosophe East, 6 May 1916
All is very quiet; there's a summer sun shining, and a west wind blowing, and nothing much doing except to swot the bluebottles and watch aeroplanes. The heat is stewing, and everybody is going about in shirtsleeves. Some battalions have even been issued with 'Gallipoli shorts,' and run about bare-legged. If there were more water to wash in we'd be happier, but the labour of fetching it up is immense. I wonder if you're having the same kind of weather, or your usual May of rain and storm?

I've been doing Intelligence Officer for a bit while the pukka I.O. was in hospital; so what with that and my own job, and running the Headquarters Mess, I'm fed up with the 'ole bloomin' war, I am. Of all the three I hate the last, which they stuck me with about three months ago. Thinking about food and drink all day is bad enough (I'm no Mrs Beeton), and collecting mess-bills is worse. And no mess-cook ever dreams of coming in to say there's nothing for dinner before 7.25. Troubles of being the junior member of the mess. [. . .]

Philosophe East, 10 May 1916
Thank you for your letter of this morning. Hardly a week seems to pass without a Zepp[elin] raid at Hinderwell now. I don't like it at all. I think I must bring home a platoon and reinforce your defenders; how would that be?

I wish you could come out here just for a flying visit and see what things are like. It's impossible to describe half the unforgettable things one sees. You'd have a long, long journey in a crawling train up to railhead, and you'd tumble out at midnight into something like a big goods-yard, with crates and bales of every sort, under a brilliant white light from the arc-lamps. Very faint and far away you'd hear a dull, heavy thump; that's the guns firing, ten or fifteen miles away. Then you'd climb on an old Putney or Cricklewood bus,[10] painted battleship-grey, with all her windows boarded up, and she'd go rocking away into the night along the country roads, swinging on two wheels round corners and skidding past shell-holes, with the guns in front getting louder every mile. Then you'd turn into one of the French *routes nationales*; one of the straight paved avenues of poplar trees that lead up to the crash and flame of war itself. Every minute the traffic would get thicker: strings of motor convoys, rumbling transport wagons, ambulances going up (empty) and down (not always), lorries, limbers, staff cars, and everywhere the despatch-rider snaking his motor-bicycle in and out of everything; for this is one of the big highways to the front.

Then the bus would come to a few blackened shells that were once a village, and you would be told it was unsafe to drive any further, and you'd have to get down and walk. Before very long you'd top a little rise, and then stand and catch your breath with the whole Front spread out before your feet. Imagine a vast semi-circle of lights: a cross between the lights of the Embankment and the lights of the Fleet far out at sea; only instead of fixed yellow lamps they are powerful white flares, sailing up every minute, and burning for twenty or thirty seconds, and then fizzling out like a rocket – each one visible at ten miles distant, and each lighting up every man, tree and bush within half-a-mile. Besides these you will see a slim shaft swinging round and round among the stars, hunting an invisible aeroplane; and every instant a ruddy-glow flashes in the sky like the opening of a furnace-door and there is a clap of thunder from the unseen 'heavies'. The whole makes a magnificent panorama on a clear night.

Then you'd step down into a trench, and that would be your last breath of open country for sixteen days, if you were staying in with us. The rest of your time would be spent in a world of moles, burrowing always deeper and deeper to get away from the high explosives: an underground city with avenues, lanes, streets, crescents, alleys and cross-roads, all named and labelled and connected by telegraph and telephone. 'No. 3 Posen Alley' was my last address, and you reach it via 'Piccadilly,' 'Victoria Station,' and 'Sackville Street.' After you've wandered for perhaps two hours in the maze you'll see a hole at your feet with a mass of wires of all sizes and colours running along the ground and disappearing into it. Go down twenty or thirty feet, down mud steps, and you come into a low, long cave, lit by candles stuck in bottles and a swinging hurricane lamp. At a table at one side are a row of men sitting at telephones and telegraph instruments. On the floor are sleeping bundles wrapped in blankets and greatcoats; and at the end, screened off by a waterproof sheet, is the linemen's room, piled with drums of cable, instruments, repair outfits, crooksticks, and all manner of stores. All over the walls are stuck files of messages, circuit-diagrams, 'flimsies,'[11] receipts, tables of delivery-services, duty rosters, and other details of office work.

Take the nearest instrument, which controls the four company lines: four spidery strands running out into the darkness to four little caves half-a-mile away at points in the Front line, where a man sits day and night with the receivers clamped over his ears, listening for the little sounds out of space. Over the operator's head hangs a switchboard of plugs and holes and lettered brass bars, by which he controls the whole system throughout the battalion. As he sits there he has his finger on the pulse of its whole life, and a stream of flimsies comes out continuously under his hand: reports, requests for ammunition, stores and bombs, returns, rolls, news, and all.

The other instruments are the longer-range circuits: to the watchful guns a mile in rear, to the Brigade Headquarters in their chateau, to the Division, the hospitals, the flank battalions, and the long trunk-calls to Army Headquarters and further.

Hanging on the wall is a curious little instrument, which is just a plain disc, and a most scandalous gossip.[12] It is simply a recorder – not a transmitter at all – and its business is to gather up all the news that is passing through and shout it out like a gramophone.

It wakes to life quite suddenly and gibbers and sings away contentedly, though nobody pays any attention to it, and gives away the most precious secrets. Two company commanders arguing over a bottle of whisky, No. 14 Platoon's complaint of short rations, an indignant battery commander on the track of his Forward Observing Officer, a Very High Personage being strafed by an Even Higher (this to the huge delight of the Signal Office) – there is nothing hid from it. Altogether a most human piece of mechanism.

If you are in at about seven o'clock in the evening, you will see all the lines grow silent one by one, and a certain hush of expectancy in the Office. Even 'Whispering Willie' on the wall feels it, and stops humming and buzzing away to himself. We are waiting for the day's casualty return: the tale of wastage that is flashed through taking priority over all other messages, every twenty-four hours; speeding on and on, gathered up and consolidated afresh at every office on the way, until it arrives in London in one long Roll of Honour and appears before you at breakfast next morning. But it was here in the Signal Office that we knew of it first.

The big switchboard wakes suddenly, gibbers a moment, and falls silent. The operator draws a pad of flimsies towards him with one hand, and settles down to write. As soon as the message is finished and acknowledged, another company takes up the tale and adds its own quota, and so on through the whole four; and each as it is finished is tossed over to the

Signal Clerk, who registers it, puts the office stamp and time of delivery on it, and passes it out for delivery to the Adjutant's dug-out. Five minutes after the last one has gone out, the runner comes back with the consolidated return and hands it to the operator at the Brigade instrument, who flashes it through to his own headquarters. Then the Signal Office wakes to life again, and soon every instrument is in full swing again and the whole dug-out is filled with their humming, buzzing, singing and clicking, and the rustle of paper, and the snores of the sleepers.

And a very weary Signal Officer glances through the day's files and registers, all docketed and done up in bundles, wakes his Sergeant, finishes this letter, kicks off his boots, and rolls himself in an invaluable Jaeger flea-bag for four hours' oblivion.

Nouex-les-Mines, 23 May 1916

We are out of the trenches for a few days, and all well and O.K. generally. I can't find anything to write about except my leave, which becomes due on June 6th. Not so long to wait now. If you come up to London, please bring me an old pair of grey bags and a comfy tweed coat. I promise not to wear them in Piccadilly.

Billy goes to-morrow, and Studholme on the 1st, and then (touch wood) myself. But lots of water may pass under the bridges before that.

I'm enclosing a few postcards that may interest you. The papers, now that you know where we are, will keep you better informed of our movements than I can. We go up again in a day or two, and I think I shall keep myself in the deepest dug-out I can find until June 6th comes along. Wouldn't it be maddening to be pipped just the day before one's leave came due?

Your parcel arrived yesterday. The postal authorities had carelessly packed a traction-engine or something on top of it; so the cake and the lighter pastries were 'nah poo,' as you might say. The things in tins were O.K., however.

By the way, before I forget, if you can send me a postal order or Treasury note for £1, it'll get me across London good and slick. Otherwise, you see, there will be a whole boatload of officers struggling to change their French money, and it may be hours before my turn comes, and I'll get the third or fourth train to Town instead of the first, or else I'll be standing half the day in the queue at Victoria Station.

I have no news for you, there never is in billets, and soon I'll be able to tell it you instead of writing it. I shall hit the middle of London, toss my mane into the air, paw the ground and champ, and throw up my head to the stars and howl like a lone wolf. Suspicious behaviour at 2 in the morning! (which will probably be the time I shall get into Victoria).

Philosophe West, 26 May 1916
Studholme has gone to hospital. I hope to arrive in London on or about June 1st.

Chapter 8

'We were all quite mad':
Raiding, June to August 1916

While Staniforth was home on leave, the battalion continued to be in trenches on a regular basis, both at Puits 14 Bis and and Hulluch. On 11 June, they moved to Mazingarbe for much-needed rest in billets before moving just a few miles to a new trench sector at Loos on 22 June. Up to this point, 47 Brigade had taken much punishment from German lines, facing heavy shell fire whenever they were at the front. But at Loos they had an opportunity to hit back against the Germans through a raid. On the night of 26/27 June, the 6/Connaughts and 7/Leinsters collaborated. Two units of the Connaughts provided smoke cover, while another two held craters and dug communication trenches back to British lines.[1] This involved laying wire around the edge, and constructing bombing posts to make them more difficult for the Germans to take back, and to ensure that they could be used as a base for further attacks on German lines. Considering that around two hundred men went out into the thick of the battle, the fatalities for the Connaughts, two in number, were light indeed, but they were heavier in the 7/Leinsters who carried out the actual raid.

The raid began at 12.15am on 27 June with two mines being exploded close to the German line.[2] At 12.18am, six parties of Leinsters entered German trenches, each party led by an officer and consisting of between twenty and twenty-five men. One piper was attached to each party, playing during the initial attack and subsequently acting as a stretcher bearer. Despite the mines and the noise of the pipes sowing confusion in German lines, parties one and two, led by 2nd Lieutenant T. Hickman and Lieutenant J. Johnstone, met with what the official notes of the raid describe as 'formidable opposition'. That came not from the trenches themselves, but from a machine gun at a strong point on slightly higher ground. The main fighting fell to parties three and four, led by Captain Lynch[3] and 2nd Lieutenant Reginald Hodgson. Lynch himself was wounded, and Hodgson was killed, but NCOs continued the attack.

The raiders threw bombs into dugouts with their effectiveness 'proved by the

110

shrieks and groans of the occupants.' Heavy casualties were inflicted on the Germans. Fighting was bitter with 'Desperate hand to hand' exchanges. It was noted that 'our raiders had to use their fists' when there was too little room for bayonets. A report in the brigade war diary stated that few prisoners were taken because, although some Germans surrendered when cornered, 'there were three gross acts of treachery'. This might mean that the Germans turned on their captors and were killed in the process, although Staniforth implies in his letter that six prisoners were killed as an act of revenge. There were fourteen dead (Hodgson and thirteen other ranks) in the 7/Leinsters, but for the information gained and the damage done (at least 140 Germans killed or wounded), it was seen by staff officers to have been a highly effective operation.[4] Meanwhile, it began to build a reputation for the battalion as skilled raiders.

Staniforth's next letter picks up with his return to France from leave in England.

Loos, 24 June 1916

[. . .] Here, things aren't as bad as they might be. I'm back signalling again, and living in a civilised cellar in the middle of the village instead of a front-line dug-out. I've a stretcher-bed to sleep on, and actually a table and chair.

The weather is beastly; a week of summer thunderstorms has turned the trenches into sticky rivers, and the masses of poppies and thistles and grasses which overhang them into dripping shower-baths. The Boche is also peevish, and we've had a good deal of trouble with broken wires. Still, I suppose even eighteen days must come to an end in time (they've stuck us on two extra days).

Loos, 29 June 1916

We have just done a bit of a raid on the Boche trenches here: quite a successful one. We blew a couple of big mines under his front line, and followed it up with an assault and some bomb-and-bayonet work. The artillery was magnificent. One of the 18-pdr batteries behind us fired 1200 rounds in an hour, and a couple of trench mortars (of the kind I mentioned to you at home) pushed across 220 shells in the first two-and-a-half minutes. This went on for a couple of hours, and it was fierce while it lasted. For the first three minutes after the mines we concentrated on his front line, with every gun of every calibre firing to capacity, and fairly beat hell out of him. Then the guns lifted and formed a 'box barrage:' that is, a curtain of fire on this principle:

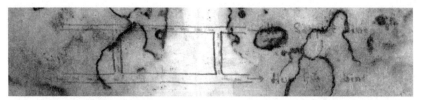

The label on the top line says 'hun support line' and the bottom one is 'hun front line'.

This cuts off the doomed bit of front line, you see: 'boxes it in,' and (in theory) allows nothing under it to get out, and no help to get in from outside. As soon as this curtain fell, we went 'over the bags' from our side and straight on. The orders were, 'Let no man stop to plunder, but . . .' you know the rest. It was only intended to last three-quarters of an hour, but the boys enjoyed themselves so much 'taking tea with Johnny Hun' that they stayed two hours.

I had laid several extra lines beforehand from Bn. Hq. down to the head-quarters of the O.C. Enterprise in our front line, and sited down there till the mines went off, to see that the concussion of 24,000 lbs of dynamite didn't wreck all the instruments before the start. (The mines were scarcely 100 yards away, remember.) When they exploded we were all lifted up and smashed against the walls of the dug-out like flies. I lay close during the three-minutes bombardment; the front line was like a volcano in eruption, spouting flame and rocks and earth and sandbags, with the heavies slog-ging away *crash, crash, crash*, and driving gusts of shrapnel that swept it clear of all life, as bare as the palm of the hand. The whole air was one long scream, with coveys of shells tearing over. The power and might of the whole spectacle, and the stupendous din (you could just hear the rolling thunder of the guns away back, mingled with the flames and crashes in front) was sublime. It was a glimpse of the British Empire really rising in its majesty – at least, that's how I felt. Then, when England had done her bit (they're English gunners behind us), the pipes lifted the Irish out of their trenches and sent them over the parapet with 'O'Donnell Aboo.'[6] I don't know how many times those wicked little war-pipes have played that old song up and down the glens of Munster, but they never did better work than when they played the Leinsters forward and set them racing straight in the teeth of the Prussian Guard. (It was they who were opposite, as we identified later from prisoners.)

At that point I left the front line and hurried back to the Signal Office, where I had to be. It was rather rotten turning one's back on it all right at the start and running like a hare to the rear, but it had to be done. For the

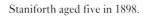
Staniforth aged five in 1898.

Here Staniforth is aged seventeen in 1910. He is pictured next to his sister Maisie, who is next to his mother, and his sister Mornie is seated on his father's knee.

One of the Leinster Regiment badges Staniforth acquired on transfer, worn on the cap and both lapels of the uniform.

Old Barracks, Fermoy.

Staniforth is pictured above the 'O' in 'Old Barracks'.

2nd Lieutenant J.H.M. Staniforth, photographed in Whitby in January 1915 while home on leave.

Kilworth Camp in early 1915.

Lieutenant J.H.M. Staniforth

The road to Guillemont viewed from Waterlot Farm, 11 September 1916. The Battle of Guillemont was fought from 3–5 September. In the words of the official history it was 'straight, desolate and swept by fire'. (Photo: © Imperial War Museum Q 1163)

German dead scattered in the wreck of a machine-gun post near Guillemont, September 1916. The photograph shows the destruction which occurred when the defence had no deep shelter. (Photo: © Imperial War Museum Q 4256)

The Battle of Ginchy, 9 September 1916. Carrying wounded across the battlefield under shell fire. (Photo: © Imperial War Museum Q 1304)

The Battle of Ginchy, 9 September 1916. Supporting troops move up in single file to support the attack. In the foreground a soldier ducks as an explosion occurs on the left. (Photo: © Imperial War Museum Q 1302)

The 16th (Irish) Division memorial at Guillemont.

1914 Do cum Ⱦóiɾe Dé aᵹus Onóɾa na hⱦiɾeann 1918

IN COMMEMORATION OF THE VICTORIES OF GUILLEMONT AND GINCHY SEPT. 3RD. AND 9TH. 1916. IN MEMORY OF THOSE WHO FELL THEREIN AND OF ALL IRISHMEN WHO GAVE THEIR LIVES IN THE GREAT WAR. R.I.P.

Captain J.H.M. Staniforth

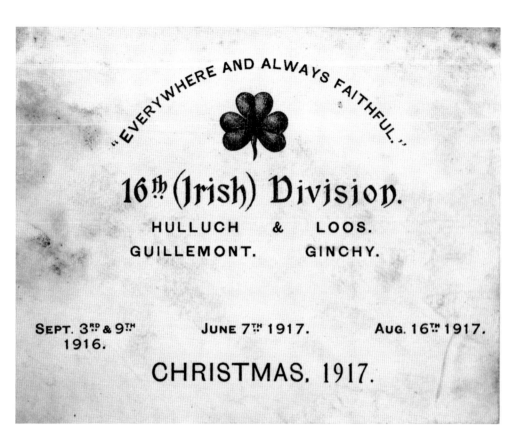

Front and inside of 16th (Irish) Division Christmas card, 1917.

Ulster – No Surrender. (Photo: © Imperial War Museum ART 15233)
A watercolour by Staniforth. It is undated and it is not clear precisely whom it depicts, although one can see elements of Staniforth's own features. Despite serving in the 16th Division (or perhaps because he did not hold the same views as many in the Division), his views on the Home Rule question were not made clear in his letters, except in his letter of 30 April 1917 when he said of anti-British sentiment in Limerick, 'just a glimpse of the iron hand would knock a vast deal of nonsense out of their heads'.

Biddie, left, in her Women's Royal Naval Service uniform, with her mother and brother Clive, known as 'Jim', who was in the Royal Flying Corps at the time.

Biddie.

Biddie and Max on their wedding day, 1 July 1922. Maisie Staniforth is pictured back left.

Max Staniforth *c*.1941-2. (Photo: © *Hampshire, The County Magazine*)

Staniforth in his study in 1982–3. His library shows broad reading tastes, including *The Hite Report* (which could be either the 1976 volume on female sexuality, or the 1981 volume on male sexuality) and a book about Wimbledon, in addition to a collection of leather-bound volumes. (Photo: © *Hampshire, The County Magazine*)

Staniforth's 1914–15 Star, Victory and British War Medals.

next hour and a half I sat in the office and was desperately busy with messages of all sorts flying backwards and forwards between the Brigade, Battalion Headquarters, and the front line. One circuit after another was smashed and pounded out of existence, and at last we were working on the very last wire – just one single strand linking us with the front line. Then at last, in the very middle of a conversation between the C.O. and the Major, there was a crash and the wire dropped as dead as a doornail. Couldn't get a thing out of it at all. The bitter part was that the communications had lasted as long and longer than I intended, for the whole enterprise should have been over by this. So I called for a volunteer to come out and see if we could fix things at all. My corporal said he was willing, so we found a spare coil of wire and some pliers and an instrument and went out. We fought our way down to the front line, kneeling down and tapping in where we found any protection. The Boche was putting over blizzards of shells, and some of them fell very adjacent. We were banged about by flying bricks and clods, and knocked about the trench by concussions, but not a blessed bit of a shell touched either of us except one that cut my boot and tore his breeches. At last we came to a place where a big crump had absolutely blown-in the trench, leaving a great mound which you had to hack your way through. We grubbed around in the mud and found the wire, and tested it, and found that the shell which had broken it had pulled in this great mass of earth on top of it. We bridged that gap all right by letting in a spare piece, but we hadn't gone far before we found another, and another, that would have taken hours to dig away before we could get down to the broken cable underneath. So we gave that up, and fought our way round to the flank company of the next battalion to see whether they had any better luck, but of course all their wires had been cut too. So then we came back to HQ.

The men were magnificent. One Sapper officer who had been looking after the mines said, 'I had no idea men could be as tough as you Leinsters.' They threw their bombs, and then they went in with the bayonet, and they went straight at the throats of the Prussians. One little fellow was found on the top of three dead Prussians, with his hands gripped round the throat of the tallest. The last that was seen of one sergeant was when he kicked one enormous Guardsman in the stomach, and laid out another with his bare hands, and then a rifle-grenade burst among the three of them. Another wee drummer came staggering back over no-man's-land under a torrent of shells and machine-gun fire with a helpless Sapper on his back. Oh, they were great. Of course they were all quite mad. Three lads were sent back to our trenches with six prisoners. On the way they stumbled across the body of one of our offi-cers [Hodgson] ... Those prisoners will never reach any internment camp now, I'm afraid.[7] As I said, we were all quite mad.

We are still holding the line; a little under strength, you will under-stand, and not quite the same battalion. There are some empty dug-outs, perhaps, and some fire-bays without sentries in them, and maybe a platoon or two commanded by a sergeant; but we are still holding the line, and we have not asked for reinforcements. And the Brigade and the Division and the Corps and even the august Army have wired congratu-lations, and within a few days we are to be inspected by various gentlemen with red tabs and medal ribbons and high commands when we come out to billets. For it was the first show the Irish have had, and we have done not so badly. Wherefore we are proud an' 'aughty, and the world is very good. [...]

Staniforth noted in his typescript:

The following was received a few days after the events recorded in this letter:

> Lieut. J. Staniforth, 7th Leinster Regt.
>   I have read with much pleasure the reports of your Regimental Commander and Brigade Commander regarding your gallant conduct and devotion to duty in the field on June 26th, 1916, and have ordered your name and deed to be entered in the record of the Irish Division.
>   (Sd) W. B. HICKIE
>   Major-General,
>   Commanding 16th Irish Division.

Unfortunately, the original has not survived.
Staniforth also enclosed with this letter a poem he had written.

What the Pipes Played. 27.6.16

Are you lonely over there, Johnny Hun?
Do you pine for change of air, Johnny Hun?
        'Nein, our trenches are cement,
        And our sausages unspent;
        We are very well content,'
                Grinned the Hun.

However that may be, Johnny Hun,
We are coming round to tea, Johnny Hun.
    ''Tis a cursed scanty brew;
    There is scarce enough for two,
    And we have no spoons for you,'
        Growled the Hun.

We will bring our spoons along, Johnny Hun.
They are Sheffield steel and strong, Johnny Hun.
    'The way is dark and far,
    And ye lack a guiding star;
    Ye are better as ye are,'
        Warned the Hun.

Never way was yet too dark, Johnny Hun,
For the Irish on a lark, Johnny Hun.
    'Ye will find the wire is deep,
    And the trenches plaguey steep;
    And what we have, we keep,'
        Snarled the Hun.

By God, then, show us how, Johnny Hun;
Here's the Irish coming now, Johnny Hun!
    'Quick, machine-guns! Fools, too late!
    They are racing for the gate
    Like Vater Rhein in spate!'
        Yelled the Hun.

Are we keeping you too long, Johnny Hun?
Do you like it hot and strong, Johnny Hun?
    'Gott! Their bayonets are red,
    And the trench is choked with dead!
    Break, oh break; let them ahead!'
        Screamed the Hun.

So you whimper like the rest, Johnny Hun,
With a bayonet at your breast, Johnny Hun?
    'Donner! None but Irish can
    Face you Irish – so we ran.
    Would you kill a wounded man?'
        Whined the Hun.

Get you back to fair Berlin, Johnny Hun,
And when they let you in, Johnny Hun,
    Tell them all about the spree –
    Tell them what Berlin shall see
    When the Irish come to tea,
        Johnny Hun.

J.H.M.S.

*July 1916 was one of the bloodiest months in the history of the British Army.
An anticipated 'great advance' was launched on 1 July in the Somme area,
partly in order to gain territory, but also to relieve pressure on the French. They
had been under heavy pressure at Verdun since February, in what would
become the longest and costliest battle of the war. The Battle of the Somme
began with an eight-day bombardment, followed by an infantry attack at
7.30am on 1 July. However, the bombardment had been largely ineffective and
British troops, rather than advancing rapidly, were soon unable to make any
progress in much of the line. Even in areas where targets were reached, such as
by the 36th (Ulster) Division at the Schwaben Redoubt, the lack of success
elsewhere meant that ground taken was soon given up again.*

*On 1 July, there were 58,000 British casualties, around one-third of them
killed, making it the worst day in the British Army's history in terms of casualties. However, the 7/Leinsters were not engaged in the Battle of the Somme
until its later stages and they lost only twelve men in July. Part of their time
was spent in billets at Nouex-les-Mines and Philosophe, and some in trenches
at Loos and Puits 14 Bis. Much of their work was routine labouring and that
continued into August, an even quieter month in which only four men were
lost.*

Puits 14 Bis, 23 July 1916
[. . .] The Brigadier has us all destroyed in the Signals with a terrible
code he has. This is a telegram I have just received. 'Please send IMPS
IDLE JIG at IVT GREECE but if HEAP GOBBIN HONE' – well, I
ask you. By the way, its predecessor on the file, not in code, is interesting
and instructive:- 'No. SCA 357 23/7/16. OC 7/Leins R. Please reply
reference to this office no. SCA 310 of 20th re gas-proof rations.'

There's no news. Billy and I, like Johnny Walker, are still going strong.
And everyone says the war will be over before October. I think that's all.
Oh yes, and I'm very lousy, and it's not a bit nice really. They have the
hide ate off me.

Loos, 10 August 1916

Times are not what they were with the push going on down south. When we come out of the trenches at the end of this tour, we shall have been in just thirteen days less than there are between Maisie's birthday and Mother's.[8] That's a bit different from our first tour, isn't it? I needn't tell you that this is not for publication. So the good old 16th Div. is still going strong.

Everybody is convinced that the war is on its last legs out here, and that's rather cheering. I'd like to spend next Christmas at home for a change. It'll be a great day when the 16th comes marching home – though 'not the Six Hundred,'[9] I'm afraid; continuous trench warfare is very 'attriting.' Leave, of course, is out of the question just at present.

I'm troubled horribly with the 'minor horrors of war' just now. Whether it's vermin really, or only 'prickly-heat,' I can't say; but I tear myself to pieces every night. I have searched all my clothes; and changed and changed and bathed and bathed, but I can't find anything, and it still goes on. I suppose it must be due to the weather (which is awful) and insanitary conditions of trench life. Anyway, it's damn irritating – literally.

[. . .] I've no news for you, I'm afraid. In fact, it doesn't seem as if there would ever be anything happening any more. It's all just heat, flies, and monotony. I'd give worlds for green fields and blue water, instead of stony white chalk, blinding in the sun-dazzle and scorching to touch. [. . .]

Loos, 20 August 1916

We're still digging along in the same old water-hole. (From July to August it's mostly hole; from August to July mostly water; hence the name.) I'm as spotty as ever, and afraid to go to bed and face what is in store for me every night. I am certainly as fully entitled to use the plural pronoun now as any royalty or tape-worm-fancier. The Doc doesn't think it's scabies, but isn't sure. He's going to give me sulphur ointment and a cresol bath when we come out.

Last night we took a gramophone and gave the Hun a concert. It was a great rag. We played it on the front parapet and up sap-heads quite close to him. As it was a glorious summer night, the music carried beautifully, even to the battalions on the right and left. We played from 1 to 3 in the morning. 'Let's All Go Out And Find Some Germans' left him cold; he didn't like 'We'll All Go Marching To Berlin,' and he hated the 'Marseillaise' and 'Rule Britannia.' However, he hated very badly, so it was all right.

By the way, we saw a woman and two children in the Hun support-trench the other day at daybreak. Curious.

Billy has just bought his engagement-ring and sent it home. We chose it with great care: a very slender diamond-and-platinum thing from Vickery's. It's an awful business, choosing rings; almost worse than hats; but I think Violet should be pleased with it. By the way, I've promised to marry my last billet-landlady (an irresistible stripling of 70) *aprés la guerre*, so you might begin to arrange about moving into the dower house, will you?

The Hun shot at us with a 110-ton gun the other day. Not a friendly act at all. Then he flattened the front line with 200lb Minnies. (They look like washing-tubs in the air: great big water-butts coming over, with a couple of hundredweight of T.N.T. inside.) When he had slammed it inside out, he played machine-guns up and down the ruins for half-an-hour. This being considered adequate preparation, nine stout heroes left their trench and advanced upon us. One of our snipers shot one, and the others left all and fled. ('All' was a nice little heap of hand-grenades, which we found in our wire and which made good souvenirs.) If it hadn't been for the labour of restoring the front trench, which was absolutely blown in from end to end, and for the loss of a man or two who were buried in a dug-out, it would have been quite ludicrous. [. . .]

Chapter 9

'Sitting in pyjamas in the sun': Hospital, August 1916

In Staniforth's letter of 10 August 1916 he had complained of the 'minor horrors of war' not knowing whether his itching was 'vermin' (he probably expected common lice) or 'prickly-heat', a rash caused by sweating more than one usually would so that sweat glands become blocked. The complaint turned out to be a rather nasty form of 'vermin', specifically scabies.[1] That involves very small mites, Sarcoptes scabei, *burrowing into the skin.*

Today, scabies is most often passed on through skin-to-skin or sexual contact, but it can also be passed on through sharing clothing, towels or bedding. During the First World War the close proximity of trench life often saw it passed between soldiers through the latter methods. When at the front, soldiers were often using beds which many others had slept in. Indeed, bedding might be in almost constant use on a rotation basis. Staniforth's letters about his treatment offer a detailed account of his treatment in isolation, but also show that a relatively minor illness could offer welcome respite from the front line.

Staniforth was seen at a field hospital on 22 August 1916, before being rapidly passed to 112 Field Ambulance and then on to a Casualty Clearing Station, from where he wrote on the same day.[2]

Casualty Clearing Station, 22 August 1916
They have taken me far, far away from the trenches and put me in a hospital for a change. It would be all very well if one were suffering from a less inglorious disease than scabies. As it is, I live in a nice little kraal of tents in the garden, surrounded by nice little pipe-clayed ropes and labelled 'Isolation Block – Out of Bounds.' This limits my exercise to a brisk stroll of fifteen paces to the right and a languid saunter of fifteen paces back again to the left. The rest of the Casualty Clearing Station takes its walks abroad all round and about my kraal, where I sit in solitary magnificence, and jerks its thumb and nudges and winks, and I gnash my teeth from behind the cords of pipeclay. I am bounded on the west by a gentleman called Diphtheria, on the east by another gentleman

called Enteric, and on the south by the Gas Family; and I'm bound to say that they're none of them very sociable companions.

Shortly after I arrived an orderly came to see me with an unpleasantly conspicuous board labelled 'SCABIES,' with which he proposed to decorate my tent. I told him that if he intended it to refer to the tent, I could think of heaps of nicer names than that myself – what did he think of something tasteful like 'Zepp View,' for instance? – or if he were really determined to be personal, that we had a regimental motto all ready to hand, 'Itch Den;'[3] or if it referred to me myself, my godfathers and godmothers had beaten him to it anyway, and I wasn't going to change at my time of life. 'Lieut. Scabies' doesn't appeal to me at all. However, he was soullessly determined and nailed it quite fiercely. So I hung a towel over it, and informed him with hauteur that I was travelling *incog.*

Anyhow it isn't for long, because I am off 'down the line' to-morrow to the base for a spell, to revel in the unhallowed delights of cresol baths and sulphur ointment. I'll let you know my address as soon as I have one.

I'm sorry in a way, because there were only the C.O., myself and one other officer who had never been sick in the nine months we have been in France. On the other hand I'm not sorry to be out of shell-fire for the first time for five months (except when I was with you, of course), and living in the lap of luxury, treated like a prince.

I'll write again when I'm settled somewhere. At present life is a procession of ambulances, motor lorries, and hospital trains.

Staniforth spent just one night at the Casualty Clearing Station before being moved overnight by train to No. 20 General Field Hospital at Camiers,[4] about ten miles south of Boulogne, arriving there on 24 August.

No. 20 General Hospital, Camiers, 28 August 1916[5]
Just a line to say I'm getting on splendidly. This life suits me down to the ground. I've had a whole week now doing nothing but sitting in pyjamas in the sun. Three hot baths a day; clean towel, pyjamas, and bedclothes every morning; books, papers, games, flowers, gramophones, and perfect weather. The final touch is provided by a contingent of about 250 from the Gunnery School here, who come and do two hours' gruelling physical jerks outside my tent every day!

Of course there are a few flies in the amber: one is the loneliness of a week in an isolation ward. I have even a reserved bathroom and latrine to myself. Another is anointing myself all over every day with powerful and smelly ointments. And the worst of all, of course, is the rash itself, which is maddening sometimes; particularly at night. I haven't had a solid night's sleep for a month now. But all these are small things compared with the absolute rest. The steamers in the harbour still make me duck when they blow off steam (it's exactly like a big shell coming), but I'm even growing out of that now. I expect when I get back and really do hear a shell I shall think, 'Oh, it's only another ship,' and forget to dodge.

The gas still annoys my lungs a bit, but the doctor says it hasn't done the least harm to my heart. I expect I shall only be here a few days more (two or three, perhaps), and then I shall take my place with the Base Details at Etaples, waiting for the first draft to go up-country. You see, when a man is invalided out of the regiment, even only temporarily, he is struck off its strength, and re-enters it through the usual channels as an ordinary reinforcement and begins fresh again. (Of course this doesn't affect seniority, or anything like that.) Worse than that, they have started a poisonous system of pooling all drafts at the Base and sending them to the unit that needs them most; so, although it's not often done with offi-cers, it's quite on the cards that I might find myself packed off to the West Rutlandshire Militia instead of the 7th (S) Bn. P.O.W. Leinster Regt., R.C.[6] I've lost several of my own signallers that way, who were incautious enough to go sick and get sent to a Base Hospital. Still, as I say, it's very seldom that that happens to an officer.

Riding down in the Hospital Train was a treat. A Hospital Train is just as much a military unit as a Field Ambulance or a battalion. It has its own permanent C.O. – usually a R.A.M.C. captain – and staff of sisters, order-lies, cooks, and so on, and its own quarters: 16 corridor coaches (15 wards and a staff coach), all painted khaki with the huge white panel and scarlet cross on the side of each. There are about thirty trains running in France, I believe; each up and down its own particular beat, starting right up at railhead and then calling at every C.C.S. along the line till it fetches up at its particular Base Hospital, where it stops the night and returns up-country next day. I came down on No. 20, which was a gift from the Great Eastern Rly. We had a mess-room on board for the officers' sitting cases. All the cots in the wards are, practically speaking, detachable shelves; so that a serious lying case, going straight home to Blighty, can be swung bodily out of the train and on board the Hospital Ship at the quay-side. A full convoy is about 450 patients.

We reached here about midnight of the 22nd, and were taken in ambu-lances to the Hospital, about a mile distant from the station. The place reminds one rather of Saltburn, and the hospital is formed of numbers of immense marquees on a plateau at the foot of a hill, overlooking the sea.

[Enclosure in] Letter to Billy, 25.8.1916

> Yestre'en in grots of clay I sheltered me,
>> Washed down my peaches (succulently tinny)
> With Black-and-White, and owned for *vis-à-vis*
>> The gentle Pruss and his attendant Minnie.
> In short, nor with prolixity to hymn it,
I was a fighting man, and found the life the bally limit.

> With Airy Archie and with Silent Sue
>> By day and night I was hail-fellow-well-met,
> Alert to dodge the nimble 4.2,
>> And slow to stir abroad sans shrapnel-helmet;
> And, strange to say, appreciating fully
Menus of petrol, paraffin, Maconochie, and bully.

> But now no sounds of strife assail my ear,
>> Saving perchance the far-off labouring-man's axe,
> The ululant perusal of *Le Rire*,
>> Or jodelling of convalescent Anzacs.
> All, all is silent as a peak in Darien,
All bully-less the wards within the realm of Sister Marion.

> Here rise pavilions of peace and plenty,
>> Where squads of P.U.O. and N.Y.D[7] doze
> Untroubled in their *dolce far niente*
>> By 'rum-jars' or by aerial torpedoes.
> One simply hauls a cushion and a rug out,
And straight forgets that such a thing existed as a dug-out.

> Wherefore, O William, wise wert thou to flee[8]
>> The mud, the map, the Minnie, and the mine,
> And come and share (*pace* the V.A.D.)
>> Th' auriferous Flake, the cheap and ligneous Bine,[9]
> And with a sheet (and very little more) on,
Forget with me there ever was a European war on.

No. 20 General Hospital, Camiers, 29 August 1916

[. . .] There's no news except that the fine weather has dissolved in cloudbursts, and all the marquees are flooded out and all the patients taking refuge in bed. (The M.O. is now being addressed as the Harbourmaster.) The R.A.M.C., *being* R.A.M.C., omitted to slacken any of the guy-ropes last night, and this morning the marquees are as drunkenly lop-sided as a company of the Leinsters after pay-day. If the wind gets any stronger there will be catastrophe. Feckless folk, these doctors.

I was telling you about the camp in my last letter when I was interrupted. It belonged at the beginning of the war to the Indian contingent, and all the marquees are the sort of thing one imagines for Indian rajahs. Immense vaulted pavilions, hung with Eastern tapestries and floored like a ball-room; and all lit with electric light, and covered ways from one ward to another. You would hardly know you were under canvas at all. And there are thick soft rugs on the floors, and a table and locker for each bed; and in fact it is quite wonderful after a dug-out.

The silver identity-disc you gave me dropped off last night, for the first time since December. The cord was rotted. *Absit omen.*[10] It must have been the unusual number of baths I've been having that finished it!

I haven't had any letters yet except one from Billy; but he says the regiment is on trek again (it *would* come out of the trenches the day after I left), and I suppose there's bound to be some delay and confusion.

Chapter 10

'One continuous ear-splitting roar':
The Somme, September 1916

Staniforth was discharged earlier than he had expected.[1] His next letter relating to the attacks at Ginchy and Guillemont offers vivid accounts of the key moment in the 16th Division's war, and an important successful phase of the Battle of the Somme. The 7/Leinsters had moved to the Somme, at Guillemont around five miles south-west of Theipval, in one of the more successful phases of the battle. 47 Brigade drew up for attack in the early hours of 3 September. The 7/Leinsters' A and C companies took their positions at 4am, with B and D companies behind them. At 8am, the Germans received the standard warning of an imminent attack: a heavy bombardment from British lines. However, some of the heavy trench mortars being used in the attack fell short. So in 'Rim Trench' the 6/Connaughts' C Company had to endure not only retaliatory fire from the Germans, but also 'friendly fire' from the British lines. By 12 noon, as the bombardment continued, their casualties numbered nearly two hundred. 2nd Lieutenant W.A. Lyon, an officer with the 7/Leinsters, later described the Connaughts' ordeal as 'a six hour plastering' and wondered how the men had carried on.[2]

However, the barrage also made a significant impact on German lines and, in advancing on the enemy, the Connaughts found 'Very little opposition . . . as the enemy surrendered at once' on the left of their advance. They were joined by the 7/Leinsters, who had not endured the problems of friendly fire, and both battalions found it comparatively easy to take their first objective. Resistance was tougher on the right of their advance, but they were still successful. Casualties might have been higher from a dug-in machine gun, which fired 'a hurricane of . . . bullets sounding like hosts of bees, whistling swooshing and shrieking past our heads with blood curdling intensity.' Yet many were saved because the gunner had fired a few feet too high.[3]

Two Victoria Crosses were awarded to members of 47 Brigade. One went to Private Thomas Hughes of the 6/Connaughts, a native of County Monaghan. He was wounded in the initial attack, but had his wounds dressed

124

before returning to the firing line. Having done so, he targeted a German machine gun which was causing great damage. Hughes ran out ahead of his company, shot the gunner and captured the gun. Although wounded in the process he brought back at least three prisoners. For these acts of 'most conspicuous bravery and determination' Hughes was awarded the battalion's only Victoria Cross of the war.[4] The Brigade's other VC was awarded to Lieutenant John Holland of the 7/Leinsters, once an Irish Volunteer, and from County Kildare. He led the battalion's bombers into Guillemont, not stopping even for British artillery fire. Starting out with twenty-six, the group was reduced to Holland and five others, but they brought back fifty German prisoners.[5]

Members of the 6/Connaughts joined an attack by other parts of the 16th Division on the final objective for the day, the 'Sunken Road'. Others dug in with the 7/Leinsters, whose war diary noted, 'The Battalion held on to its position with comparative ease, but great difficulty was experienced in the evacuation of wounded owing to scarcity of stretchers.'[6] Inevitably, Guillemont village, which they had taken, 'had been reduced to matchwood'.[7] In total over 2-4 September, the 7/Leinsters sustained 219 casualties among the other ranks, of whom thirty-eight men were killed. Ten officers were wounded, and one killed (Captain H.F. Downing). Another four men died of wounds in the three days after.

Vaux, 12 September 1916
This is the story of a week's adventures. I make no apology for telling it in full, because you will have read all about it in the papers before you get this; nor for seeming to talk about myself, because I can only give you my own point of view, as against Mr Philip Gibbs[8] and others.

I was discharged from hospital just after my last letter to you, and arrived in Etaples in time to take a draft up-country almost immediately. We spent 30 hours in the troop-train with no food but Army biscuits, being shunted on a siding for 13 hours at the back of Godspeed; during which time we made tea with the hot water from the engine's boiler, and drank it *sans* milk or sugar – whereby I scored, and the draft did not. All trains in France now move at a foot-pace, preceded by a merchant with a tin horn; at a big junction they have fugues and sonatas with harmony and counterpoint before they can let a train through. (The Second Tin Horn's part at Amiens, I remember, was peculiarly intricate and displeasing.) One of our fellows blew a few notes on one which he found lying about, and nearly caused a collision, because it appears he had inadvertently rendered a passage from the Third Tin Horn's part in the 5.15 Concerto, and the Fourth and Fifth Tin Horns took it up from different parts of the yard in the dark, and very nearly brought the 5.15 to grief.

When we arrived at Railhead we had a march of five or 6 miles to Divl. H.Q. It was an unforgettable sight. The road was simply one long line of transport convoys of every conceivable kind – supplies, ammunition, ambulances, guns, and everything space-space and lined with German captured stores of all sorts, from machine guns to Krupp howitzers every-where men were working like bees: sappers building the railway extension, with little engines puffing to and fro on flimsy construction lines, and carpenters putting up revetements, and new gun-emplace-ments being dark. The whole plane was a hive of industry. Later on we came to the men themselves. Imagine standing at Port Mulgrave and seeing the whole sweep of ground to Ellerby and the ridge there dotted with tents and picketed horses and troops wherever you could see. It was the Army of the Somme at rest. Beyond and over the ridge was the actual fighting which of course we could not see. When dusk fell, the camp-fires on the hillside were like the lights of the city. It really looked like a war on the grand scale, which Loos never did. At Loos one sat in a ditch all day, and had bacon and eggs for breakfast, and played the gramophone or wrote letters after lunch, and never knew one was at war at all. Here – but wait.

And the noise of the guns! It is simply one continuous ear-splitting roar from morning till night and night till morning. There are no words coined yet to describe it: the fury and frenzy of it are too appalling.

Well, with my usual luck I had walked out of hospital just in time for a battle. The order said quite simply, '—— Brigade' (you know which it is) 'will take Guillemont.' And by God, we did take it. Philip Gibbs and Beach Thomas[9] will tell you that it was the most important capture since the Push started, and that the fierceness of the fighting, which had seemed to reach the limit humanity could stand, was worse than ever before, and what it looks like to see flesh and blood walking into the thunderbolts hurled at them – but I was there, and I *know*.

You know the places; you have read about them all – Mametz Wood (a little spinney of bare poles such as you may see on the Staithes road), Delville Wood, High Wood, Trones Wood (all the same), Fricourt, Longueval, Mouquet Farm: the whole theatre is not as big as the Ellerby-Staithes area. The villages are heaps of brickdust now (men have walked down the main street of Guillemont at night now and fancied themselves still in the open – can you believe that?), but they are historic.

Exactly at noon we left our trenches and stepped into the open. I was with my Company (shortage of officers). What does it feel like to go 'Up and over?' I don't know. I concentrated my thoughts on keeping my pipe alight. It seemed to be the most important thing at the moment, somehow. Of course there was none of the 'wild, cheering rush' one imagines. We stopped outside the parapet to straighten the line, and then moved forward at an ordinary walk. I remember noticing that the air was just one loud noise – like moving in a kind of sound-box. And the machine-gun bullets snapped about your head rather like a swarm of angry hornets: all hissing and crackling; it was rather curious; I don't know quite how to describe it.

Afterwards we found some cigars in a German dug-out, which were very good.

They relieved us that night, and we went back about half-a-mile for 48 hours' rest. I think, as a matter of fact, that was worse than the other; because we had nothing to do but sit and be shelled. Of course there are no trenches that haven't been slammed flat anywhere, and what there are have only been hastily dug by battalions under fire. They aren't even continuous. It's funny now to think of the Loos trenches, stretching for miles, six and ten feet deep, with 40-foot wooden dug-outs. Here there are simply hen-scratches here and there in an area of absolute desolation, swept day and night by incredible tornadoes of shell-fire.

Following Guillemont, the battalion was in bivouacs at Carnoy, prior to being moved back to the front line on 8 September in advance of another attack, this time on Ginchy. Initially, the battalion was held in trenches in reserve and did not begin its attack until late afternoon on 9 September. Then, at 4.45pm, there was an intensive bombardment of the German lines for two minutes. Just like at Guillemont, some shells fell short. Fortunately, many were duds, and casualties were lighter than on 3 September. However, with duds also falling on German lines, the impact of the bombardment was not nearly as great as planned. When British troops moved forward at 4.47pm, they found German lines intact, very much as they had been when the battle began on 1 July. So in the first wave of the attack, the 6/Royal Irish Regiment and the 8/Munsters suffered heavy losses. The original plan had been for the 6/Connaughts plus one company of the 7/Leinsters and two from the 11th Battalion, The Hampshire Regiment, to follow behind the first attack, but with the Munsters so badly hit, their men had stopped advancing. A and B companies of the Connaughts realised what had happened and stayed in their trenches, but C and D companies plus the Leinsters and Hampshires did not. When there was a pause in the fighting, they judged that it was their turn to attack, but they could make no impact on the German lines. At 5.43pm a runner was sent back with a message for Divisional HQ saying, 'It appears that the trench opposite is full of Germans & that they were well prepared.' But elsewhere, 48 Brigade was more successful and by 7.30pm they had taken control of the village. The 7/Leinsters lost four officers and eleven men, with two more to die of wounds soon after. They had taken part in another successful advance, but it had been a bloody encounter, as Staniforth described.

Then they brought us up again to finish the job and take Ginchy. We moved up at night and dug ourselves in, in an advanced position ready for the morning. When dawn broke we were about five feet deep, and we crouched there all day. Of course we had no rations except bully beef and biscuits, and precious little of that; and needless to say nothing could get near us. At 4.45 it is 'Up and over' again; the same stepping out deliberately into that awful storm, the same slow walk forward (this time we had about six or seven hundred yards to go, instead of four or five), and men dropping like flies all round.

Then from 6 in the evening onwards we lay in odd shell-holes, and the Germans began the counter-bombardment. I saw the most sickening sights then; and the wounded had no way of getting back except over the open. It was then that I got knocked out. I had four machine-gun wounds before that, but they were only scratches (don't worry; I shan't even appear in the casualty list or get a gold stripe). But then a big shell burst right beside me, and a flying fragment caught me on the head and knocked me unconscious. When I came to, I was being carried back by some stretcherbearers. I was very shaken (that was probably lack of food and sleep more than anything, though), and had a big cut under the eye that closed it up completely, for all the world, like a prize-fighter. I told them to put me down, and after I had been very sick I felt better, and went back to the others. It was then that we heard the Germans were beginning their counter-attack, and we were told to hold our 'line' till the last man was dead. Then I really thought the Twilight of the Gods had come; it reminded me of the last act of 'The Darling of the Gods,' where the Samurai made their last stand, if you remember. There we were, just a battered handful; many of us wounded, crouching there in a few shell-holes in the middle of that fearful shell-swept desolation at midnight, some of us with revolvers, some with rifles we had snatched up, some with ammunition taken from the dead men; just waiting and watching the little ridge in front of us, lit up by the flashes of the guns, rockets, and flares. A shell-torn battle-field at midnight, with only gun-flashes for illumination and heaps of dead for landmarks, is a weird sight. I saw fifty men wiped out in ten seconds by a machine-gun at one point; they simply melted away and dropped before you could realise where they had gone. Of course we were cut off from all communication, so we could do nothing but wait and watch for the lines of running, tumbling German figures to top the ridge and come at us. We lay there till two in the morning; but I don't remember much because I got a bit light-headed then, and I only recall bathing in the sea and eating lobster salad; both of which were very far from the reality, I can tell you.

At two o'clock, however, shadowy figures loomed up out of the dark and materialised as our relief, and we gathered our handful together and began to pick our way out. That wasn't very much better than the other thing, because the whole place was a blizzard of shell-fire, it was pitch dark, and we were new to the place, and there were no landmarks; so we got pretty badly lost two or three times, and it wasn't the best place to get lost in. Also they had been gas-shelling Montauban pretty heavily, and the fumes were hanging about still.

However, to cut a long story short, we picked our way out somehow, and reached a spot a mile or two behind the lines, where we tumbled down and fell asleep by the roadside for two or three hours, and managed to get the men some hot soup and food.

Then we pushed on again to a bivouac for the night among the Army of the Somme resting behind. They didn't say anything, but they just came running up in hundreds from all over the camp and lined the road to watch us pass – quite silently. And we passed through them – just a handful.

Excepting headquarters, myself and one other were the only officers who came back of those that went over. All my old friends – all those who were with the battalion at Fermoy and Kilworth – gone. I am commanding the Company now, and giving myself orders in default of anyone else to give them to.

Of course, the general came round then and made us a speech: 'the famous 3rd of September and following days' . . . 'fresh battle honours for the colours' . . . 'heroes of Guillemont' . . . and all the rest. But that doesn't make up for empty chairs, shreds of companies, scraps of platoons.

Now we are away back, in a plague-spot of an agricultural hamlet at the back of Godspeed. There is a muddy trickle behind the billets. We look at it dully; it is the Somme, a river of blood and dammed with corpses.

So now you can read in the papers about the storming of Guillemont again, and read between the lines. I haven't told you half of what really happened because I can't, and you could never imagine it. Things like that can't be described. I have done little else but wonder in a dazed sort of way how it is that I am still alive. Somehow there are always a few who seem to come out of the most devilish bombardments. I'm still sick and shaky, and I have a proper Monday-morning black eye, but otherwise as right as the mail.

I haven't had any of your letters since leaving hospital, but that isn't surprising. I wonder if you could send along a magazine or two next time you are writing. Only if it's convenient, of course – if not, don't bother; only it's rather difficult to get anything to read out here.

My love to everyone, and I'm quite safe and content, really, so don't worry.

[P.S.] Billy has a real cushy one in the arm – just a scratch, and off to Blighty, lucky dog.

The only way to be here is to be philosophical. We have evolved a philosophy accordingly. What do you think of it? If you are a soldier, you are either (1) at home or (2) at the Front.

> If (1), you needn't worry.
> If (2), you are either (1) out of the danger zone or (2) in it.
> If (1), you needn't worry.
> If (2), you are either (1) not hit, or (2) hit.
> If (1), you needn't worry.
> If (2) you are either (1) trivial or (2) dangerous.
> If (1), you needn't worry.
> If (2), you either (1) live or (2) die.
> If you live, you needn't worry: and –
> If you die, *YOU CAN'T WORRY!!*

So why worry?

For the 16th Division as a whole, their operations on the Somme had not been as devastating as for those of the parts of British Army involved there in July. By September 1916, generals had begun to learn from their mistakes and that had a significant impact on both tactics and strategy. However, in sheer human terms, even if relatively low compared to earlier phases of the battle, the 16th

Division's losses were still striking. Between 1 and 10 September, the division lost 4,090 killed, wounded or missing from 10,410 other ranks, and 240 from 435 officers. At least 1,079 of those were later confirmed killed.[10] *It is no surprise then that in the story of the 16th Division, Guillemont and Ginchy loom larger than any other stage of the war, and so it is appropriate that the divisional memorial now stands in Guillemont.*

Chapter 11

'A nest of Sinn Feinery':
Limerick, March to April 1917

Following their involvement on the Somme, the 7/Leinsters were moved back from the front and a steady process of rebuilding the battalion began. They received new officers and men, often from non-Irish regiments, especially the Royal Sussex Regiment and the Bedfordshire Regiment. To some extent that transformed the character of the battalion, although the majority of its members had some Irish connection.

Throughout the winter of 1916-17 the battalion was holding lines in Belgium, usually around Kemmel near to Ypres. Most fighting ceased because the weather was so bad, with heavy snow and severe frosts. From the start of October to the end of January 1917, there were only twelve fatalities in the 7/Leinsters. Most losses came from shell-fire.

Staniforth was promoted to captain on 10 September, but none of his letters after 12 September 1916 and before 4 March 1917 have survived. These were in any case probably few in number, because he was granted leave from 24 October, supposedly until 2 November. However, while on leave he visited a dentist and was diagnosed with serious dental problems. A letter from his dentist noted that seven teeth had been removed and that more extractions were necessary. The area also needed to heal before dentures could be fitted and the dentist expected that this would take three months.[1] As a consequence, Staniforth was not judged fit even for home service until March, when he was transferred to the 4th Battalion, The Prince of Wales's Leinster Regiment (Royal Canadians), a reserve unit based in Limerick. Though still unfit for service overseas he was able to train new soldiers. He was to find attitudes to British soldiers in Ireland much altered in the wake of the Easter Rising and the steady change in public opinion which ensued.

New Barracks, Limerick, 4 March 1917
[. . .] This is a great place, if they'll let me stay here a bit. I think there are more old Seventh men than Fourth in it, and I've had nothing but cheerful grins and handshakes and 'Welcome back, sir' since I came.

Two of the old Fermoy officers are here as well, so I'm not alone in the Mess.

They've given me B Company to play around with, but as far as I can see nobody ever dreams of doing any work or attending any parades whatever, leaving it all to the N.C.O.'s. One subaltern hasn't been on a parade yet, and he arrived over six months ago . . . or so he says.

The C.O., Colonel Sir Anthony Weld, is a perfectly charming old fellow, and everyone adores him; he's been particularly nice to me since I arrived.

The quarters are quite good, and it's a change to have a room of your own, a decent bed, a bath, and a fire, after French billets. As for the town, it's better than I expected. There are some quite good shops, and one very nice little teashop, and a quite good club. Much the same stamp as Whitby, in fact.

The weather was quite good until yesterday, and then it broke up badly and has rained viciously ever since. A steaming barrack-square, grey sky, and puddles everywhere make up a most depressing outlook.

There's no immediate prospect of my going out to France, so don't worry. My teeth are settling down gradually; I don't think they're going to be so bad.

New Barracks, Limerick, 14 March 1917
I have been very fairly busy lately. At present I happen to be the only captain in the Mess – the others are all dug-out majors or unfledged subalterns – so I get dropped on for all the little jobs requiring a captain's services. Last Monday I was called for to sit on a court-martial on a recovered deserter; on Tuesday and Wednesday I was president of a couple of Courts of Enquiry on the illegal absence and kit-deficiencies of various soldiers; on Thursday we had to furnish a burial-party at the funeral of a Royal Irish captain, whose rank entitled him to a firing-party of 1 captain, 1 subaltern, and 100 rank-and-file; and on Friday the Limerick Assizes finished and we had to provide a guard of honour (1 captain, 1 subaltern, and 56 men) at the departure of His Majesty's judges.

The two last stunts were the worst, as there was 'business with sword', and I had to borrow a sword and freshen up my sword-drill. The guard of honour, in particular, was a nuisance; the band as we marched through the town attracted crowds of kids who ran in and out of the ranks; and then sitting motionless in the station square with a drawn sword for twenty minutes amongst a solid throng of sightseers, policemen, beggars, reporters and cinematographers, while the kiddies tried to commit suicide among the horses' hooves, was no catch at all. As one consolation, we earned praise from the *Limerick Leader, Chronicle and Times!*

The C.O. is a grand old man; a Carthusian,[2] too, by the way. Last Easter week, when the Sinn Fein trouble was on, there was a great panic here as elsewhere. The prominent Sinn Fein agitator here is the Roman Catholic dean, so on the night when a big meeting was to be held which was expected to end up with riots and shooting, the C.O. first of all slipped him an invitation to dine with the regiment in Mess, which he couldn't but accept (sound scheme, what!), and then, later on, went down town and addressed the meeting himself. Of course everybody in Limerick knows him and loves him, so he had a respectful hearing. 'Well, boys', said he, 'I hear you're determined to take up arms against the Government. Now, if you do that, they'll send for me, and I shall have to bring out my troops, and there'll be a lot of shooting, and a lot of women and children and harmless people will be killed or injured. Now, I don't want that, and you don't want that; so I'll tell you what I'll do. I'll march my men out to Ballycannon (about 4 miles outside the town), and you can march out too, and we'll fight it out fair and square by ourselves, nobody'll get hurt except those that are mixed up in it' . . . !

A most sporting proposition don't you think?

À propos, there's a lot of 'dark doings' over here even now, and the authorities are getting wind up about the forthcoming Patrick's Day and Easter Week. This town in particular is a nest of Sinn Feinery, and our men won't go through the riverside streets after dark unless there are two or three of them together. Officers who have been out in the country riding or motoring all day come back late at night with stories of lonely barns and stables by the roadside full of people talking and planning and that sort of thing; and the town is swarming with men of all ages sporting the Sinn Fein rosettes or buttons.

And I am acting Garrison Field Officer for the week (a major's job really, but they're all too lazy and hate responsibility), and as such responsible for the defences of a battalion of Leinsters, a battalion of Royal Scots, half a battalion of Durham Light Infantry, and a brigade of artillery, together with the whole structure and contents of the New Barracks, the Castle Barracks; and the Ordnance Barracks – and Patrick's Day is next Friday! Poor little me; it's almost as big a job as learning to play 'Dixie' on the piano, as I was trying to do when I was with you. By virtue of the powers vested in me, I may, if the whim takes me, blow the main street of Limerick into chicken-food with the guns and then send out 2500 men with fixed bayonets to mop up the ruins. Good luck – and *very* likely!

My sergeant-major was waxing eloquent the other day about the misdemeanours of one of the more notorious women in the garrison. 'An' there she is, sorr,' he wound up indignantly, after a long tirade against her vices and wickednesses, 'thumpin' her craw at th' altar o' God ivery Sunday along wid the best o' them.' It struck me as a particularly splendid expression.

I had a man by the name of McGrath whose mother died in Belfast the other day. So as a matter of course before giving him leave to go home for the funeral, I telegraphed the police in Belfast to verify the death, as it is a noticeable fact that during the furlough season the female mortality in the outlying districts of Ireland rises to remarkable heights. In this instance, however, the police wired back confirmation 'Mrs McGrath is dead.' Their telegram was delivered to the orderly room instead of to me; so the orderly room, with their usual brightness, turned up the battalion rolls, unearthed a certain James McGrath at present away on duty in the Curragh (no relation at all to my John McGrath), and without any investigation wired him, 'Your mother dead; proceed home on seven days leave.' Consequently they were a bit upset when James wired gratefully back from the Curragh that his mother was indeed dead – had in fact been so for some nine years – but still, if *they* didn't think this sudden interest in her decease was rather belated, why, who was he to object? – and departed cheerfully to spend a week in the bosom of his delighted family.

Just like an orderly room.

Two stories to finish up with. A newly arrived convict, taking exercise in the prison yard, was accosted by another. 'How long are you in for?' he was asked. 'Twelve years.' The other furtively produced a letter from his pocket. 'Post this for me when you get out,' he whispered; 'I'm in for life.'

Sandy was in the draper's, enquiring the correct depth of mourning for different relatives. He was told that black clothes were customary for the nearest and dearest, a black hat-band or arm-band for others of his family, while for more distant relations a black tie would suffice. Sandy pondered. Then, 'It's ma wife's mother,' he said, 'Gimme a shoe-lace.' [. . .]

New Barracks, Limerick, 23 April 1917
I've been away for the last week [. . .]. The Adj. asked me if I would like to go on a 10-days refresher course of signalling at Clonmel, just to see what innovations have come in since last year. So I went; but when I got there I found it was a recruits' course, beginning at the beginning and going on for 12 weeks! So after spending two days learning how to make

the letter A with a flag, I decided I was wasting my own time and everybody else's, and phoned back to the Adj. at Limerick to take me away, and got back here yesterday.

I found the following in a series of 'Regimental Nursery Rhymes,' and I've been straining the brain till it creaked trying to remember the original of which it's a parody, but it's still obstinately elusive. You'll probably recognize it at once, but I'm hanged if I can get it.

> 'I had an ancient charger, his name was Timbuctoo,
> I lent him to a subaltern (a silly thing to do),
> He thrashed him, and he kicked him, and he even made him trot,
> When, sad to say, poor Timbuctoo expired upon the spot.'

All is quiet on the Limerick front, and there's 'nothing to report.' The Boche has done a lot of 'retiring according to plan' lately, hasn't he? Only he doesn't say whose plan – his own, or ours.

New Barracks, Limerick, 30 April 1917
[. . .] I've no patience with these Governments; they're as weak as a gnat under a willow in a wet November. This city has a population of 32,000 and about a third of them are brawny young hooligans parading the streets shouting 'Hoch der Kaiser',[3] 'To hell wid King George!', 'Down wid the Army!', 'Up the Germans!' and other pleasant sentiments, and throwing half-bricks when they see a soldier by himself. And the women are worse. Of course they're irresponsible, but they don't realise how tolerantly they are being treated, and just a glimpse of the iron hand would knock a vast deal of nonsense out of their heads and make things a deal pleasanter for all of us.

New Barracks, Limerick, 13 May 1917
[. . .] I suppose you'll be pleased to hear this about myself. About a fortnight ago I had another Medical Board, and was passed fit for General Service. I didn't tell you at the time; no use. So I was expecting something in the way of overseas orders almost any time, as a good many of us are being sent out these times; there's rather a demand at the moment out there. However, I was surprised to find the other day that they are showing my name every week to the W.O. as 'Unavailable' still. You see, they are allowed a small number of officers as a kind of 'permanent staff' (C.O., Adjutant, Company Commanders, etc.), no matter whether they are fit or not: 'indispensables' granted exemption, in fact, who can't be

touched. So I'm figuring weekly as one of these, falsely represented as a Company Commander (as a fact, I'm not commanding a company at all at present). In its way it's a bit of a compliment, I suppose, as those jobs are usually kept warm for the old Regulars of the battalion, with much wire-pulling, and there isn't a great deal of love lost between the 4th (old Army) and 7th (Kitchener's) as a rule.

So unless anything untoward happens you can set your mind at rest; for the immediate future, as they seem to think I'm doing more useful work here than I should be in the trenches. How long it will be before some old frosty-face with a bigger 'pull' comes along, of course, I don't know. I feel rather a slacker in a funk-hole, but there you are.

I've just returned from eight days under canvas up in the hills with a couple of subalterns and 70 men, firing their musketry course. We had gorgeous weather till the last two days, and enjoyed ourselves enormously, though it was pretty heavy work from start to finish. When the week was over I was able to march the detachment back to barracks with a higher percentage of scores, more Marksmen, and more First Class Shots than any party which has fired from this battalion in the last two years – and more important, every man with a clean defaulter-sheet. So I'm rather proud of that. Of course we worked them pretty hard all the time when they weren't actually firing, and that kept them happy and out of mischief. And we had a rattling good lot of N.C.O.'s, which helped a great deal.

The enclosed is a sample of the sort of little incidents that beset the path of an unfortunate commander. Who am I to interfere between man and wife in these intimacies of conjugal life?

[Enclosure]
   Navan, Co Meath, 16 April 1917
   [To] Commanding Officer Leinster Regment
   Dear Sir I wish to let you know what is my husband's work. The last time he was home he threatened to take my life and the Baby I had to send for the priest the doctor told him he would warren the police he has caused me great illness since I was very bad on last Tuesday and there is no hope for the Baby the Nurse said it is head with the fright I had his conduct is very bad since he got with the Officer he is gone to the bad when he was in Dollymount last summer a girl there had a baby for him I ask of you for God sake to take him for the regment and not let him any more be a Officer Servant he has too good of a time I wish

he had been sent out to France 6 months ago and if so my poor Baby would be alive but God help me today my hart is broken between sickness and trouble all I am sorry for I did not get him arrested before he went back I did not wire for that I knew nothing about it I was so ill and afraid I do not want him back I never want to see him again I enclose you a stamped envelope would you be so kind to drop me a line let me know would it help to have a letter from the Priest for God sake take him from the Officer and let him be with the men again I hope you will forgive me for taking such liberty dont tell him or he will kill me

I remain yours faithfully Mrs Mary Byrne.

New Barracks, Limerick, 21 May 1917
[. . .] There's no news here. We continue to send out small drafts of 20 or 30 men every week (many of them old friends of the 7th, returning to France for the second or third time), but those of us who are left behind go on with the usual and uneventful round of duties. Occasionally a 7th man comes to us, but he has generally been three or four months in hospital or on sick leave since he was last in the trenches, and can give us no recent news of the old battalion.

Chapter 12

'Worse than the Somme!!':
'Passchendaele', June to August 1917

While Staniforth was in Limerick, the 7/Leinsters took part in the Battle of Messines in which the 16th Division was heavily involved. This was a prelude to the Third Battle of Ypres and has become iconic in Ireland's story of the war as the moment when the 16th (Irish) and 36th (Ulster) divisions fought along-side each other. Of course, by this stage of the war the Ulster/Irish identities of each had been watered down by drafts from English, Scottish and Welsh regiments. However, they still offered some a sign that perhaps pre-war disagreements and divisions could be overcome.

At Messines, 47 Brigade was in action from the first. On 7 June they witnessed enormous mines exploding under German lines as a prelude to the British attack. The 16th Division lined up to the left of the Ulster Division, with 47 Brigade on the right and 49 Brigade on the left, with 48 Brigade in reserve. In 47 Brigade, the first wave was provided by the 6/Royal Irish Regiment on the right and the 7/Leinsters on the left. Their target, as for the rest of the 16th Division, was the capture of Wytschaete village by taking a series of lines marked on the maps in colours.

The red line was captured by the 7/Leinsters in little over half an hour. The blue line was largely taken by 5am, although the battalion faced some stubborn machine-gun fire. By 7.30am, the Munsters, in front of the Connaughts, and moving through the Leinsters, had taken the green line, with the final black line secured thirty minutes later. The Leinsters took around sixty prisoners and killed between eighty and one hundred Germans, losing thirteen men them-selves. That was despite debris from the mine explosions which hung in the air and made some men 'visibly ill'. Meanwhile, the preliminary bombardment and mines had such an effect on the Germans that the resistance they offered 'was nowhere very formidable'.[1]

Staniforth returned to France on 23 June.

16th Infantry Base Deport, Étaples, 23 June 1917
Just a line to tell you of my safe arrival at the Base – that half-way-house between Blighty and the Line! I can't tell you how long I'll be here, of course: please the pigs, not long – it's a draughty, Spartan place of no comfort and crude makeshift and ancient leaky tents, suitable only to such a here-to-day-and-gone-to-morrow, floating population as ourselves. [. . .] I'm very tired and very dirty and very sick of travelling: I reckon I've done the thick end of 900 miles since I saw you – and that wasn't so long ago.

Anyway, here I am on my birthday night with two blankets, a dirty tent, two strangers for bedfellows, and no prospects! Cheerful, what? I'm writing to Col. Buckley to-night telling him I'm here: a big draft of officers went from here to the 2nd Bn. yesterday, so we ought to get to the 7th.[2]

On 24 June, Staniforth received orders to return to the 7/Leinsters the next day, taking a train of reinforcements from Étaples, acting as the O.C. Train. When he rejoined the battalion, he found it resting prior to beginning its preparations for the Third Battle of Ypres, better known as 'Passchendaele'.

Eringhem, 30 June 1917
The day after I wrote my last letter the oldest and dirtiest soldier in France crawled into my tent with a palsied salute and handed me a scrap of paper. I opened it and read 'You will proceed to-morrow to join the 7th Bn. Leinster Regt., and should report to the R.T.O., New Siding, Etaples at [time unclear] a.m.' So I told the veteran that his feet were beautiful on the mountains[3] and fell to packing my kit, with a light and carefree heart. Then I glanced casually at the paper again and observed a pencilled addition in one corner 'You are detailed as O.C. Train', and all beauty faded swiftly from the veteran's feet, because the command of a trainload of mixed reinforcements is a very poisonous job indeed. I called for a whiskey-and-soda and finished my packing thoughtfully.

Next morning I went down to the New Siding, which is a big shunting-yard built outside the station for military traffic, crawling with freight-cars of every kind and deafening with the whistles of a score of engines and the reeling bang of meeting trucks. Somewhere in the middle of pandemonium was a wooden rabbit-hutch of an office where the R.T.O. drove his unholy trade all day 'sending agreeable trains away: with one for thou and one for thee–and one for him–and one for he . . . .' and unfortunately, one for me also. So I went in, put my head through a sort of tickets-office-window, and shouted 'Shop!' until some one came. He seemed a bit irritable, and asked me rather shortly what I wanted. 'Somewhere', I replied poetically, 'somewhere a train is calling; calling for me. Lead me to it,' and I added corroborative details to convince him that I was really entitled to be issued with 'Trains, G.S., one; complete with engine.' and not a kleptomaniac collecting horseboxes to decorate my dugout with, or a connoisseur with a pretty taste in Louis XIV meat-vans and other knick-knacks.

Being at length persuaded of my bona-fides he told me my train was no. C163 leaving at 9.51, and carrying 120 officers and about 1500 men. He also shot a bunch of literature as thick as a chorus girl's ankle on me, dealing with the duties of an O.C. Train. Glancing rapidly through it, I decided that any O.C. who did his duty for 12 hours would require at least six months leave and would then probably be discharged into the Army Reserve, Class IV for the remainder of the war; so I used it to wrap my lunch in instead as a compromise; for which indeed it served admirably, and was unexpectedly grease-proof.

Then I went to look for my train. It was a dismal-looking and inter-minable string of the open French box-cars, all painted with the familiar 'HOMMES, 40: CHEVAUX EN LONG, 8', and studded at intervals with an ordinary second-class passenger coach for the officers. Around it struggled and jostled a Babel of men from every regiment in the Service, and a Pentecostal variety of tongues, from Billingsgate and Bideford to Blackburn and Belfast (not forgetting Brecknock and Bannockburn), rose to the sky. Lonely officers tossed here and there like corks: the multitude swirled about them, or broke against mountings of baggage and cliffs of grocery-boxes containing the 'repas de voyages' or travelling-rations for the troops.

Attached to the rear of the train was a palatial first-class coach, resem-bling the Americans' Private car and labelled 'Reserved for O.C. Train.' I should explain here that the charge of every troop-train in France is rested in two officers – the O.C. Train, who is responsible for the disci-pline of the troops on board, and the Train Conducting Officer, who represents the Railway Transport Service, and is concerned only with the correct running of the train and the picking up and sitting down of the various drafts at the proper stations. The T.C.O. is a non-combatant officer whose only job in life is travelling backwards and forwards on his trains (hence the Private-car, which is fitted up permanently with his own belongings), the O.C. Train is simply the senior competent officer of any given train-load. My own T.C.O. was a downy old bird who kept a very serviceable brand of whisky in his little pantry, and a quite efficient travelling chef for his servant.

I put my kit into the coach and returned to plunge into the maelstrom, from which I pulled out a reluctant subaltern by the ear, rather as a hawk swoops on a colony of small birds, and told him briefly that he was my adjutant for the rest of that journey. He started in to handout objections, but I told him anything he had to say could go into cold-storage till I had time to listen to it: and meanwhile he could hump his junk one-time into my carriage and wait there for orders. There I told off a couple of guards of one sergeant and ten men apiece and posted them in the first and last coaches, and drew a bundle of leaflets from the T.C.O. bearing instructions to draft-conducting-officers on matters of train-discipline, etc. These tracts I unloaded on my adjutant, and set him off along the way distributing them to the various officers – who also no doubt found them admirably adopted to wrap their various lunches in.

At last with a mournful howl from the engine (why is it that no engines on the continent have a healthy whistle?) and a chorus of troops from the shunters' tin horns, we jolted slowly out of the crowded yard – all the long, broken-backed length of us – and pulled out into our stride on a clear line at a steady ten miles an hour, and I settled down for that dreamiest of occupations, a long-distance journey in a French troop-train. The wild gallop of the untamed glacier is a breathtaking thing in comparison. At intervals the T.C.O. popped his head in. 'There are men riding on the roof of the 18th coach from here', he would say sternly, 'See to it at once, please.' 'Certainly, sir' I would reply in my briskest, do-it-now voice, and then, turning sternly to the adjutant in his corner, 'There are men riding on the roof of the 18th coach from here. See to it at once, please.' Or else it would be a door left swinging open, or jovial souls riding on the foot-board, or other harmless practices which are not right in the sight of the T.C.O. In the intervals I leaned back on the rich grey padding and dusty antimacassers peculiar to all French first-class compartments (remember them?) and dreamt while the train jolted along in the sun, and the tall grasses brush the footboards and the hayfields and harvests of France slid past all through the long June day.

In the evening, with much hesitation and heralded by fanfares of tin horns, we crawled into a big echoing barn of a station and grunted to a standstill. Doors flew open and erupted cramped and stiffened troops, who stretched themselves and stamped up and down the platform. Officers tumbled out, hastily buckling up straps and adjusting equipment, and presently the crowd sorted itself into compact little bricks of men each under their own commander. One by one after a final look-round and a washing up of packs and rifles, they moved off to [. . .] other trains elsewhere, some staying for the night before resuming their journey next day, and some to a march of ten or a dozen miles on the country roads to their units. The first lap was over; and I was left by an empty train, with nothing but the littered carriages to testify to these travellers who had been flung together for a brief space on their voyage towards the unknown. (That last sentence is worth 2d a line to any paper in the kingdom, don't you think. I'm proud of it.)

I spent the night at an officers' rest-house in the town, and resumed the journey at 7.30 the next morning. A short run of less than an hour brought me to a little wayside halt where all troops for the 16th Division detrained. The battalion, which was lying eight or nine miles across country, had sent the mess-cart for me – a light trap in which the mess captain goes to market; so I tumbled my kit into the back, climbed up beside the driver, and off we went.

That was a great drive. I'd had a good night's rest and a bath and break-fast, it was a glorious June morning and the roads were at their best, and I was going back to my own folk, – and I could have sung along as we bowled along.

And what a welcome [for a] relic of the old 1914 Fermoy days, [the] old stalwarts who first suckled the infant battalion, so to speak. I have become an Institution, and therefore Venerable. Metaphorically, I wear a covering of Moss and Ivy, and my weather-beaten stonework is crumbling with age. Now that the battalion has grown old in the pursuit of glory and made for itself a name that stands second to none in the Army to-day (of which more and anon) it still looks back over the past with gratitude to the men who grew up alongside of it in its kindergarten days. So there were smiles and welcomes and handshakes that warmed my heart: and the C.O. said nice things, and the men said nice things, and altogether I was very touched and my hat wouldn't fit my head at all. I dined with the C.O. that night, and with the Brigadier to-night: a sort of home-coming of the long-lost son!

Now for the situation at present. The division it seems did even more wonderfully at Wytschaete than we knew at home – did its own little bit faultlessly, and lent a helping hand to 2 other divisions as well. Its record is known now throughout the Army even to the Army and Corps commanders. Consequently it has been given a month's clear rest far out of the line.

Eringhem, 3 July 1917

Just a brief line to tell you where we are. I'm giving it to one of our fellows going on leave to post in England, so it will avoid the Censor.

At present we are lying in a village called ERINGHEM. It is about 17 miles NW by N of HAZEBROUCK. If your map doesn't mark it (it's only a tiny hamlet), follow the railway north from HAZEBROUCK to ARNEKE – about 10 miles – which is our station, where I detrained the other day. A good map might mark ZEGGERS-CAPPEL, the Divisional Headquarters; and that's only 4 kilometres away from us.

We are leaving here on the 15th, unless otherwise ordered, and shall go into training at a place called TILKES[4] [. . .] quite close to ST. OMER to be specially trained with a Scottish Division and the Guards as Assaulting Troops for a big push to take a place somewhere to northward. (Assaulting troops simply storm a position and are then taken out at once, leaving others to do the dirty work of 'mopping up', consolidating and resisting the counter-attack in these times, with such incredible artillery preparations, it's usually accounted the best job to have.) With luck there may not be a Boche left alive by the time the attack is launched. In the Wytschaete push, after 14 days preliminary intense bombardment, our fellows never met a Boche until the third line of trenches and only lost 11 lives in the battalion.

Eringhem, 5 July 1917

I went to-day with a party of other officers from the Brigade to a demon-stration of tanks[5] in action. A motor-bus picked us up at our headquarters at 8 in the morning: and a three-quarters-of-an-hour ride brought us to one of the many 'training areas' that have sprung up in France – a big stretch of waste ground given over for the construction of practice trenches, earthworks, barbed-wire entanglements, and field-fortifications of all sorts.

By the roadside where we halted stood four enormous bulks – squat, unwieldy and ironclad. Each was surrounded by a knot of mechanics, who tinkered at it with spanners and handfuls of oily waste. Just as we arrived one of them started her engines. There was a gentle purr which ran up rapidly to a shrill scream, hung a minute, and then dropped back to a deep throbbing note. Shuddering to the vibrations, her exhaust gently leaking pencils of blue vapour, she stood stick-still for a moment, and then with a sudden convulsive jerk plunged forward. Very slowly she lumbered forward nosing her way from side-to-side and recalling uncannily a giant slug with its sightless halting progress. She would feel away ponderously to the parapet of a trench, stop for a moment uncertainly with half her body hanging out over space, and then down went her nose, up went her tail in the air, and with a floundering crash she would pitch forward on her belly across the trench, and drag herself heavily clear on the other side. In the same slow and clumsy way she wallowed through barbed wire and shell holes and breast works, always wheezing for a moment doubtfully, and then, as if making up her mind, simply falling flat on her tummy all over the unfortunate obstacle.

Later on I went inside one. There is very little I can tell you of course: but the main impression was like the interior of a submarine – a narrow steel chamber, too low to stand upright in (a tank's external measurements over all are only about 25' x 8' x 7' and of course her internal dimensions are considerably smaller) and packed with machinery, levers, switches, and the shiny steel breech-blocks of the quick-firers. The walls are pierced with portholes (each closed by a revolving flat-shutter) and lined with rows and rows of shelves. The only bit of elbow room is in the semicircular bay or alcove in each side formed by the port and starboard sponsons.

She carries a crew, including the officer, equal to half Maisie's age [sixteen] next birthday – and how they all pack themselves away is more than I can tell you. Half are engineers and half gunners. Her tonnage is represented by the sum of Maisie's age and my own [forty in total] (enviously little, isn't it?), her maximum speed in m.p.h. by the number of months I was away from this battalion [eight[6]] (actually, over the rough ground of a battlefield, of course, such a speed could never be attained, nor one half of it) [. . .]

The pair of wheels at the rear of the tank were introduced in some early experimental models, but were then done away with. They were quite unnecessary and continually being shot away. (I told you I didn't remember seeing them, didn't I?). And the 'male' and 'female' varieties [. . .] are just those armed with guns – for the destruction of fortifications, concrete machine-gun emplacements, etc – and the lighter or 'female' type, which is somewhat fast and carries machine-guns only, for use against personnel not works.

Later I was allowed to drive one for a short spell & found the jolting & discomfort much less than it appears from outside. But the roar of the engines in that narrow space is deafening – add to it the explosions of the guns and the racket of machine guns all in a confined steel-wall space the size of a lavatory, and then imagine ten or twelve hours in a tank in a day!

Tatinghem, 22 July 1917

Your parcel arrived yesterday, with the breeches and washing. Most of it had to be consigned at once to storage, where I probably shan't see it again for some months: for the 35 pound limit is most rigidly enforced these days. When the division is always 'en état de partir'[7] at an hour or so's notice. I don't think this most salutary lesson in the elimination of unessentials will readily be forgotten in later years by some of us who may perhaps have been a bit inclined to [. . .] 'top-hamper'[8] before. An inventory of what I'm carrying around, other than on my back, might interest you: – a sleeping-bag, a spare tunic, one change of underclothes, a pair of boots, 4 pairs of socks, a towel, pyjamas, and three collars in my kit bag: a shirt, towel, washing and shaving gear, pyjamas and a pair of slippers in my pack – that's all! Not even a book (they are bought by the wayside, read, and passed on to hospitals and things) not a luxury of any sort. It isn't much to go around from month's end to month's end, is it? – less probably than you might take for a week-end! But when you are limited to just 3½ times the weight of that rifle of mine for your total possessions except what you can carry yourself, you have to cut down superfluities with a very unsparing hand – for a heavy larger sleeping-bag, a pair of field boots, and the cowhide kit-bag itself make a very big hole in 35lb, to start with!

Moreover they have a nasty way of stopping the battalion suddenly at mid-day on the road, weighing it, and ordering each piece over the regulation weight to be pitched then and there by the roadside. There is a story of one luckless subaltern who bent groping thus over his kit in a ring of stony-hearted quartermasters and transport officers, desperately seeking for something superfluous to throw overboard, while the battalion crowded round and grinned unsympathetically. Finally, after helplessly fishing in the depths for many minutes, he straightened up and tearfully produced a minute gold safety-pin, which he declared was the sole remaining thing he could possibly manage to do without!

We left our last quarters on the 16th, 'according to plan', and are now here, as I foretold. Moreover we do not much care how soon we get away, for 'intensive training', in which we are now indulging, is, in the language of Pte. Cassidy, 'the dizzy limit'. We have rehearsed the attack in gross and in detail, by companies, battalions, and brigades, the roots, backwards, and upside down, till we could do it in our sleep – from which indeed we have several times been routed out to do it.

An attack on a big scale nowadays is an interesting thing, which is worked out as mathematically and proceeds to its appointed conclusion as infallibly as a proposition of Euclid. It is preceded and prepared by an artillery bombardment of three weeks or so, beginning about mezzo-forte, and rising to fff immediately before Zero. (Zero is the precise moment at which the first wave of assaulting infantry leave their trenches, and on which all subsequent calculations of time are based.)

Suppose for a moment you wished to dislodge the Bosche from a line corresponding with the railway line at the Hinderwell station and drive him inland towards Ellerby. If you would divide your Brigade in two, first of all – the storm-troops, who take the first objective and then drop out of the game, and the 'pursuit-troops' who take up the chase and follow up the success to the second objective. Then you would prepare a beautiful little map, in all sorts of colours,

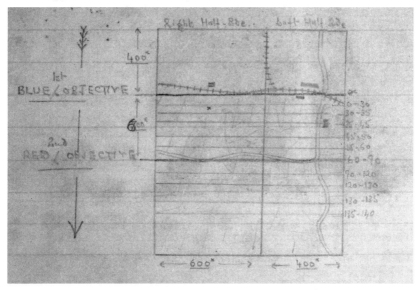

all barred and lined, with a table of figures running down one side, and a heavy vertical dividing line down the centre, something as I have indicated above, – and you hand these around in quantities till every officer knows all about them.

Look at the sketch for a moment. The Brigade attacks on a 1000yd frontage, into waves. Battalions 'A' and 'B' would form the first wave with the BLUE LINE (the enemy's front-line trenches) as their objective; battalion 'A', working on the left, would operate on a 400yd front, while 'B', having simpler, more open country to cross, might be given the remaining 600yds.

The battalions 'C' and 'D' would form the second wave, passing through 'A' and 'B' (who have halted at once on gaining their objective, and digging hard in the endeavour to consolidate the BLUE LINE), taking up the pursuit where the first wave left it off, and carrying it forward to the RED LINE.

(Of course, if you intend to have your success exploited to its utmost limits, you have additional BROWN LINES and GREEN LINES, with additional brigades to continue this 'hand-over-hand' or 'leap-frog' progression).

The row of figures at the side calls for explanation, as it is the key on which the whole infantry-work depends. It represents the 'Barrage Table' of the Artillery and is the Bradshaw, so to speak, which gives the time of 'arrival' and 'departure' at any point.

Lines are drawn across the map at short intervals – perhaps 100yds – and along each line the gunners let down a curtain of fire for a certain number of minutes before lifting forward to the next. Ordinarily quite a short time is enough for this curtain to rest, but on special features such as roads, banks, strong points, trenches, etc, it will hang for half-an-hour or more before going forward. This is the famous 'Creeping Barrage' theory, to protect advancing infantry, but you can see that if the infantry do not know thoroughly what the gunners are doing they will walk into their own curtain-fire if it hangs on one particular spot longer than usual, hence the absolute synchronising of all watches in all branches of the force before an attack, and hence also the Barrage Table, which shows on the map, in minutes, calculated from 'zero', exactly how the curtain moves.

So you see, on my imaginary sketch, the barrage lifts from the Bosche trench (the first). In which it has been bombarding for the past three weeks, precisely at 'Zero' (say 8 o'clock), as our own infantry go over their own parapet; and settles 100 yards ahead for a comfortable ½ hour (0–30) to allow them to start consolidating the trench. At 8.30 it moves off again with our *second* wave of infantry following in its wake, and creeps forward again until it reaches the RED LINE, which it deals with from Z+60 to Z+90, or 9.0-9.30, by which time the position should be ready for the infantry assault, which would come at 9.31, with the barrage then 100yds ahead.

(There is also a 'Swinging' Barrage, which moves forward from A to B for 5 minutes, and moves on to C, but come the survivors at B from their holes and dug-outs, mop their brows with relief, and set about repairing the damage, when – click! the barrage swings back from C to B again, and makes a second haul! That's rather a refined frightfulness.)

So you see there is no opportunity for commanders to show their strategy now by surprise flanking movements and things – the whole simply moves forward like a big machine, and one's only concern is to see that one is at one's right place at any given moment, according to the 'Bradshaw'.[9] Suppose, for instance, that I were the signalling officer of 'C' Battalion, the right Battalion of the second wave, where should I be at, say, 5 minutes to 9? – or Z+55. The barrage will be 100 yards behind the lateral road which is our 2nd objective (the RED LINE), at that moment. Now the Battalion works forward like this:

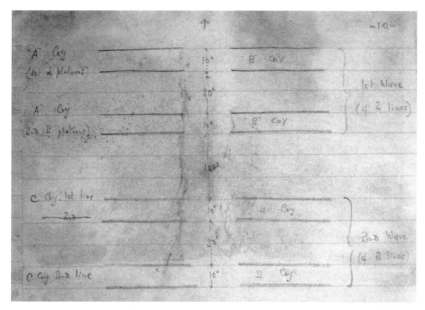

– in two waves 100yds apart, each of two lines 50yds apart. The signallers move 20yds in rear of the centre of the last wave, or 260yds from the first line. So at 5 to 9 I ought to be 460yds behind the RED LINE, or just 150yds past the lone house by the railway – and if I'm *not* there, there are plenty to know the reason why!

Well, as I say, we've rehearsed the thing till we're sick of it, at 4 in the morning and at 2 in the afternoon, and at 11 o'clock at night, with all the additional units to co-operate with us. The same slow-moving forward through standing crops and meadows under a blazing July sun, tanks lumbering on ahead, white signal-flags stuttering wildly all over the landscape, contact 'planes sweeping down with a sudden roar of engines, dropping a message on a white-lettered ground-sheet, and rising again, machine-gun-teams toiling forward in little knots with the guns, solitary 'runners' trudging back through the lines with messages for headquarters, drums thundering far in advance to represent the barrage, bandaged 'casualties' limping, hobbling, or borne by the stretcher-bearers through the tall corn, long lines of infantry breasting the slope in front, with the sunshine glinting on their bayonets, battalions of the first wave that have done their bit and reached their objective digging in desperate haste against a possible counter-attack, or pausing to wipe their faces and look after us as we pass through them and press forward – and the golden sunshine blazing down over all on hills and dales and woods and ripe yellow wheat-fields and little busy ants in khaki swarming across the landscape.

This is a dull and technical letter, I'm afraid, but there's nothing but hard work in the daily routine now, and no news.

[To his mother only]
Watou, 28 July 1917
Another birthday: – I hope and pray – and believe – it may be the last we shall be separated like this. Don't spoil it by worrying about me, for I'm quite safe and far away from the line; as safe as if I were writing this in your own sitting-room at Hinderwell instead of here. If I have any birthday message for you, let it be this: don't believe the pessimists that are painting such black and dismal pictures at home and in the papers. Out here there is a universal spirit, at the moment of writing this, of expectancy mingled with the firmest confidence that I have never known before. Our preparations are colossal, undreamed of before: dwarfing our previous offences to insignificance (as I have seen and heard for myself) and I do most confidently believe that perhaps even before this letter reaches you the last phase – I don't say the end, but the beginning of the final chapter – will have entered upon its course.

Passchendaele was regarded by Staniforth as being worse than the Somme, and he was not alone. Clear evidence of that view emerged in interviews with veterans of the Ulster Division, carried out by Billy Ervine. He recalled, 'During my many conversations with First World War veterans, almost all have expressed the opinion that Passchendaele was worse than the Somme'.[10] One such veteran, Jack Christie, went so far as to say that while he had some happy times on the Somme, 'Ypres was never like that. Ypres was hell from beginning to end.'[11] George McBride of the 15th Battalion, The Royal Irish Rifles remembered, 'It was awful, we were up to our knees in muck and water . . . . I was glad to see the back of it.'[12]

When the battle began on 31 July, 47 Brigade was in reserve behind the 15th Division. It was expected that they would advance once the 15th Division had gained ground. Yet after some initial progress, the 15th was driven back by the Germans and the heavy rain meant that a further attack was postponed and 47 Brigade was moved to the front in the Frezenberg sector.

3rd Battle of Ypres, 31 July 1917

It seems curious to be writing a letter a few hours after the start of the biggest battle of the war, doesn't it? But that's what I'm doing nevertheless.

At midnight last night we were roused in our bivouac, where we were snatching a few hours' sleep before going into action. It was a misty, overcast night, and black as ink, as the men stood to arms in absolute silence. There was nothing but a subdued rustle in the darkness as the companies fell into line; and now and again a shaft of white light from an officer's torch showed a glimpse of rows of faces under their steel helmets for a moment. We waited some time while extra ammunition, rations, etc, were issued round, and then with an occasional stamp and jingle from the pack-animals, or a whispered command somewhere out of the dark, we moved off. It was curious to think that all round us the night was filled with just such shuffling and rustling, and whispering as the unseen battalions and brigades and divisions massed all along the line – the background or minor to the dominant crash and thunder of the guns.

If I were a poet I could tell you how we marched up the Ypres Road that morning; the road so many feet have marched up to Ypres and – Beyond. It was just the hour before the dawning, and the east in front was already lightening. Ahead of us lay the crest of the ridge with the trees on the top silhouetted black against the gun-flashes every instant: and every step brought us nearer to that ridge, up the long straight road between the poplars, while each moment of dawn grew closer, and the knowledge of what was to happen in that dawn lay heavy on each man's soul, and the question whether he should see the day die that was being born. Then came a time when the men began to march with their watches in their hands, and lift their eyes to the skyline in front. One by one the guns fell silent, as if they too were waiting and expectant, and for a few moments there was a lull along the horizon.

Then, as the creeping hands touched the figure on the dial, there was a clap like thunder as the first mine went off, and instantly every gun leaped with a crash into action. Guns of England, guns of Belgium, guns of France, battery on battery, massed and concentrated to north and south as guns have never been massed before, sprouted flame and steel. Field-guns unnumbered chorused deliriously like a pack of hounds, gigantic howitzers coughed and shook and dribbled in their gun-pits while the crews sweated and raved over them, and the night reeled as thousands of tons of metal flew screaming through it. It was fierce and beautiful beyond imagination: it was the Apotheosis of the Gun. Minute by minute the pandemonium grew, rockets and flares hissed up, red and green and white, shells rushed and screamed and crashed, machine-guns drummed and thudded, aeroplanes swooped buzzing and circling, horns sounded, whistles blew, grenades burst – and somewhere in the storm-centre our wonderful infantry hoisted themselves out of the trench and walked deliberately into the heart of it!

Away back on the poplar fringed highway men said 'They're off!' in a kind of gasp, and then put away their watches and trudged forward again.

That was five or six hours ago. The tide of battle has rolled onward, and we're waiting now in a back-wash till our turn comes. I'm writing this in the front room of a chateau – such a room! From the walls – eighteen or twenty feet high: it is, or was, a salon of the most lofty – the paper hangs in strips and banners; the floor is mud, the doorway a mere jagged hole in the brickwork; the hall outside is a mountain of sandbags; splintered and crazy frames swing to and fro in the mined windows, and – last touch of all! – as I write a swallow flies thrice round the ceiling and disappears into her nest under the cornice, like a lonely ghost, there lingers one drawing-room chair, a pathetic frivolity of emerald plush and white enamel that has somehow escaped destruction, and looks among the mud and brick dust like an old chorus girl in a slum tenement.

If I raise my eyes, the Dead City is before me, with its empty, shattered streets, its roofless shells of buildings, and the jagged ruins of the Cloth Hall and the Asylum brooding gauntly over all. There is the road running down to the Menin Gate – that Gate has grown into a byword more sinister than even Traitors' Gate itself, among the regiments that have lived in its shadow – for it was the easterly gate, fronting the German trenches and not a rifle-shot away from them: and night by night it is a seething shambles of dead horses and struggling men as the ration parties and reliefs pass through it (there is no other way) and the German gunners pump shells as fast as they can load and re-lay their pieces. Other spots as significant are before me – 'Hellfire Corner', 'Hellblast Corner', and the like – can't you imagine how they got their names? Night after night at the same spot: the drivers lashing their horses to a gallop as they approach the clump of trees with the evil reputation – and then always, as they rounded the bend, the scream and swish of the salvo, and the kicking tangled heap of limbers, drivers, and teams in the roadway.

The landscape around is alive with the primrose twinkle of the guns –

batteries everywhere; in the hedgerows, in the cornfields, in every clump of trees and every ruined cottage – always a battery. There is an enormous how[itzer], scarcely a field from me as I write. Every five minutes – she is too ponderous for quicker delivery – there comes a soul-shaking crash of thunder, and the crazy walls of the chateau leap and rattle, and great lumps of plaster from the rotting ceiling fall upon the paper before me.

The highroad past the window is blocked continuously, as every roadway in the vicinity has been for a week. Now it is fresh troops pressing forward into the fight, and streams of fresh ammunition and supplies flowing forward, and guns and teams going up – with a steady ebb in the other direction of ambulances, walking wounded, and squads of dejected-looking Huns with their hilarious escorts. [. . .]

Ypres, 5 August 1917
This is the first time I've managed to get a line through to you. The battle still goes on – haven't had a *wash* since Tuesday (this is Sunday!) or a bite of hot food, and been soaked through all the time! The state of the ground between rain and shell-fire is absolutely indescribable. I'm writing this in an old Boche dug-out, the first roof we've had over our heads since we started, and there are 5 inches of water on the floor: we are all sitting with our legs in it, and have been since last night – everybody's legs are getting corrugated! It's a great show – wouldn't miss it for the world.

Toronto Camp, 6 a.m., 6 August 1917
O.K. Relieved last night – out for a spell in billets: writing to-night. Worse than the Somme!!

Toronto Camp, 7 August 1917
At last I can begin to tell you something of what we've been doing this last week. The only thing is that there's so much to tell it's difficult to know where to begin.

My last letter, I think was written in the old chateau the first day of the battle: so I'll try to pick up the thread from there.

A commanding officer may only take two of his four company commanders into a battle – the remainder being left out to form a nucleus in case of accidents – so in consideration of my recent arrival I was removed back to Battalion HQ, where I kept an eye on my old job of signals as the signalling officer happened to be away on leave. Throughout that first day messages kept coming in with news of the progress of the attack [. . .].

That night (the 31st) the rain began. At first we looked on it as only a summer shower, and no one dreamed of what it was going to cost us. That night also the Germans delivered their first counter-attack. I went up to the attic to watch it. Standing there amongst the brick dust, fallen plaster, and splintered beams, and peering out through a hole in the slates one could follow the whole battle going on in front. The sky all-round flickered with gun-fire like summer lightning, and streams of shells poured through the air from every battery near and far, converging on the storm-centre. It was like a gigantic firework display as each one flashed and burst and whizzed. Showers of golden rain went up, bombs and shells exploded with a red glare, while Very lights soared up in a long curve and hung shimmering with their peculiar almost saintly radiance, and a burning dump glowed luridly through the rolling banks of smoke. Alone up there on the ruined roof, with the night-wind on my face, I had a curiously exhilarated feeling as I watched it all, and knew that amongst all that hell-glare our own infantry were fighting like the splendid devils they are. The knowledge that at any moment we might be thrown in to reinforce the battle ourselves added a personal interest too.

That was Tuesday, the 31st. Wednesday brought in August in a blanket of mist and low-hung clouds and a silent steady pour of rain. By afternoon the country was a quagmire: freshly turned shell-holes became brimming ponds, hollows and ditches were lagoons and rivulets, and the hard ground turned first to heavy clay and later, with the constant passage of guns, troops, lorries, wagons, limbers and ambulances, to a soft slushy porridge with a substratum of gluey mire. Guns fired sullenly and blindly – there were no aeroplanes to observe for them – the infantry stood still in their shell-holes, and the columns splashed blasphemous lay along the roads, heads down and oilsheets pulled clock-wise over them, and took the spattering mud from every vehicle that passed. In the chateau the rain came in through the leaky ceilings, and blew across the floors from the hollow windows and doors: and we huddled in great-coats and mackintoshes and shivered in corners while we tried to avoid the drips from above.

At 4.30 came the order to move up. The battalion assembled in the soaked grounds, hooded in oilsheets and heavy with packs, rifles, bombs, and shovels, and trudged off by platoons at 50 yards interval down the road into Ypres.

I don't think there is anything which so nearly approaches my idea of Kipling's 'Cold Lairs' as this ruin of pride and pain. Perhaps the wreck of Pompeii may approximate to it – I cannot say. But as one passes through its deserted streets and squares, one's footsteps echo among the empty houses as its tragedies echo in one's heart. Jagged ruins, hollow walls, fallen beams and crumbling masonry – and a small population of British soldiers that goes deep down in cellars and creeps about after nightfall through the silent streets – that is all. And still the aimless shells fall into this city of the dead, flinging up the dust in houses where no man dwells and splintering the causeway in streets where no foot treads.

Through the city we marched, cross the ramparts by the eastern gate, and out into the country up the Menin road. That road is a chapter in the history of the war – perhaps the most famous road of all the British Army has known. Straight eastward into the German lines it runs – once an ordinary country road enough, where the lovers walked in the evenings outside the ramparts; now a way of horror and butchery, where every stone is stained with mud and suffering. Walk with me down it in [. . .] the dusk of a rainy evening; get the smells of death, corruption, shell-fumes, or lingering poison-gas that brood heavy over it into your nostrils: pick your way round that shell-hole – and that – and that – and a hundred more. A sudden flash and a roar at your ear – don't start: it's only one of our battalions beside the road: there are a score more within half a mile. A distant whistle that grows swiftly to a howl, flashes redly, and dissolves in a thunderous roar and a whizzing cloud of splinters, clods, and stones, leaving a burnt-out stench of brimstone in the air – the Bosche at his old games again. In the ditch to your right is a bloated, stinking carcass – a dead mule. A little further on, an overturned limber and two dead horses with their heads beaten in – remains of a battery transport caught at this spot the other night. At this corner, two sprawling heaps of clothes, with a stretcher and a third heap between them: the wounded who never reached [. . .] Blighty [. . .]. And so on, [. . .] miles of this nightmare of a world, the way is lined with the wreckage of war: men, horses, wagons, limbers, ambulances, guns and lorries – smashed, twisted, and overturned in the ditch: some hours old, some days, others weeks and months, till the biggest gun wheels rust and the rotting corpses fester and decay.

On we went and on, till we crossed our original frontline and were out of the battlefield proper. It was long since dark (it is difficult to move two miles in an hour amongst the congested traffic of battle-fighting) and the going was unspeakably exhausting. The shell-fire had reduced the ground to plough-land, besides destroying all natural drainage, and the men, burdened with the extra kit and two days' extra rations and ammunition, laboured and floundered their way forward, past field-batteries brought up to advanced positions now firing furiously in the open, past derelict tanks bogged to the flanks in the mire and abandoned earlier in the advance, past smashed and flattened trenches and crumpled entanglements, past dead already half-sunk in the mud with the rain falling on their faces – past all the backwash of two days' fighting.

That night we spent in an underground [. . .] gallery in an old German trench. It was like the workings of a coal mine: fifty feet underground, shored up with pit-props, with the moisture dripping from the ceiling and forming inky pools that glistened in the candle-light – a dark, noisome cavern where we dozed uneasily for a few hours till daybreak, and then pushed on again.

At this point I must digress for a moment to explain something of the tactical scheme insofar as it immediately concerned ourselves. Our particular Army Corps[13] attacked on a frontage extending from the Ypres-Roulers railway on the right to 500 yards beyond WIELTJE on the left – in all about 2700 yards. On the right was the 15th Division – Highlanders whom we knew since the old days of 1915-16, when they laid beside us at Loos – on the left was the 55th. Behind the 15th came ourselves in support: behind the 55th came the remaining division of the Corps.

Each of the three brigades of the two attacking divisions had its own objective. The two first brigades (one from each div) went side-by-side to the BLUE LINE – about 700yds past the German front-line trenches. The next three brigades carried on the good work as far as the BLACK LINE: another 1200yds deeper, with its centre on the famous strongpoint POMMERN CASTLE. Finally, the remaining brigades were to push on to the GREEN LINE, 1300yds further, or about 1000yds short of the village of GRAVENSTAFEL. At this point they were to stop and be relieved, while we either passed on through there and took up the pursuit, or, if the resistance was too strong, consolidated and held the ground gained against counter-attacks.

That was the plan. In point of actual fact, although a Highland battalion did at one time penetrate as far as the GREEN LINE, they were unable to remain upon it and had to fall back as far as the BLACK LINE, which their second brigade had meantime placed in a state of defence. The Corps on our right, across the railway, had also been unable to get further than the BLACK LINE, which made it difficult for us to maintain an isolated forward position on the GREEN LINE.

This was the position when the whistles blew in the cold grey dawn of Thursday, and we climbed up out of our mine-gallery and started forward once more.

In charge of about 30 men of the Battalion HQ staff, I had no orders except to find and takeover the battle headquarters of the Gordons, who were at the moment in close support just behind the Camerons, who in turn were hanging on to the BLACK LINE.

There was a dressing-station close beside us, where I enquired of wounded Gordons where the headquarters were and got a rough direction. Round about the entrance to the dressing-station (which was only a dug-out scooped out under the railway embankment) the wounded lay sick on stretchers in the slush, just as they had been brought out of the fighting. As I passed I was just in time to see an officer of the Argyll and Sutherlands, who was lying groaning in the rain waiting for his turn, grope blindly for his revolver and blow his brains out. Poor devil, he was shot through the stomach, and I suppose the agony was too much for him.

So I collected my 30 men, and in straggling Indian file we struck out across the battlefield. The rain was still coming down, and the heavily laden men sank to the base rock at every step. They were nothing but stumbling figures of mud: every now and again they would slip and fall full-length in the sludge, rifle and all, so time after time we had to stop and pull one man or another out, who had sunk to the thighs and was helpless. And all the time the German shells whizzed and tore into the ground, burying themselves in the swamp and throwing up fountains of mud and water over us. My signalling sergeant, whom I had known and trained since he enlisted in my platoon at Fermoy before Christmas 1914, was blown to pieces as he struggled to release himself from the mud: the corporal had both his legs mangled and lay in a foot of slime till he died: another shell buried two men beside me and tore a gash in the palm of my hand. The country was barren of any landmark: just a shell-torn sweep hidden in mist and rain and rising gently to a crest-line in front of us. So at last I stopped the men, put them in any cover they could find in shell-craters and ditches, and went out with an orderly to reconnoitre a bit.

As we topped the sky-line I saw the remains of a trench-system, smashed and flattened and water-logged past all usefulness, but still a trench. At the same time we were aware of a change from the scream and crash of shells: there was a vicious 'phwit – thump' into the clay beside us that could only be small-arm-ammunition fired from fairly short range. So I judged we must be in sight of the Bosche snipers now. This was confirmed when the bullets followed us as we scrambled along, varied by occasional bursts of machine-gun fire spattering into the mud around. As it took us five minutes to advance 50 yards, heaving one leg after another out of the mire, and stopping to extricate each other when we sank unusually deep, it was a quarter of an hour.

Presently we came to the ruins of a house, just a few piles of bricks five or six feet high. Underneath was a cellar, where we found an officer (a second lieutenant) and a couple of men. This was the commanding officer of the Camerons and his headquarters staff! (The battalion was about 30 strong, I believe.) From him I learned we had come too far – the German front 'line' was only about 600yds ahead, in fact – and the Gordons' HQ was some way back. So back we floundered again to the men in their shell-pits, picked up our burdens, and started to retrace our steps across the slough.

To cut a long story short, we ultimately found what was left of the Gordons in a concrete pill-box in Wilde Wood. (The 'wood' was repre-sented by a score of splintered match-sticks.) They were delighted to see us, of course: they had been there since Tuesday mostly with no food or fire or water, under a blizzard of shell-fire and drenching rain.

So they cleared out and we took over the pill-box. There are numbers of them about, built by the Hun where the ground is too wet to allow of deep dug-outs, and are small circular redoubts of enormously thick concrete reinforced with steel rails, with a blind side towards our lines and a low hole to creep in and out at the back.

This was the only shelter in the neighbourhood, and standing so conspicuously was certain to be a target for shell-fire: so we disposed the rest of the battalion, when they arrived, in craters and old trench-works at some distance from it and crawled into it ourselves – the C.O., adju-tant, doctor, padre, intelligence officer, sergeant-major, two or three runners, a couple of orderlies, and myself: total, a dozen! (The interior of the pill box was 8 feet across!) Those of us who could, sat down on the floor; the remainder stood or crouched against the walls. This was about noon on Thursday, and we remained there until 9.30p.m. on Friday. We had a drop or two of stale water in our bottles, and the bully beef and biscuit of our iron rations, and a bottle of whisky, so fortunately we weren't so badly off for rations, as there was of course no earthly chance of getting fresh supplies to us. The shelling was absolutely incessant the whole time we were there, as the Bosche, having only just evacuated it himself, knew its position to a hair's-breadth. To give you some idea of the shooting he made, we had three men killed actually in the trench-mouth through which we crawled in (the brains of one were blown all over my steel helmet) and to put a shell into a doorway less than 3 feet square at something over 2000yd range is pretty good shooting. Again, of four shells of a single salvo, three were direct hits which put out the candle we had lit with their concussion. And this never stopped for two minutes together during the whole 30 hours we were there. We even had to use an old tin for a W.C. for to go outside the shelter would have been madness. Fortunately the accuracy of his shooting was the salvation of the rest of our fellows, for outside a radius of 200 yds the shelling was only normal.

Most of the time we dozed uneasily as we stood or sat. Now and again someone would wake, and asked drowsily 'Is it still raining?' or 'Are they still shelling?' and the answer was always 'Yes.'

So the hours wore on and on, till on Friday evening it was time to move up the last stage and relieve the Highlanders in the very front line. The original plan was for the Munsters and ourselves to relieve side by side the frontage held by the Camerons and Seaforths. The Munsters however sent in a position petition to the G-O-C, pointing out the exhausted condition of their men, and requesting that fresh troops should be put in the line instead, as we had done our bit already. They wanted us to join in the petition, but we thought we might as well make a good job of it once we had begun, so we said we'd take over their little front as well and hold the double length by ourselves, and they could go back into support. [. . .]

So once more, shortly after dark, I ducked my head and ran the gauntlet of the shells round the mouth of the pill-box, and was lucky enough to get through safely as far as the trench where my 30 men – now sadly reduced – had been crouching since the previous noon. Two more had been killed, six wounded, two shell-shocked, and one died of exposure: but the remainder, though stuck over their knees in the morass, were cheery as larks. They heaved themselves out of the mire – or rather heaved each other out – and off we started again. These walks over the battlefield are emphatically not to be recommended. It is pitch dark and raining steadily: each step is a labour; one troops into shell-holes and falls into water-logged trenches, stumbles over remnants of rusty barbed-wire entanglements and rips one's clothing to pieces, loses one's direction in the dark and mist, and walks a mile out of the way, tramples on dead (and sometimes wounded too), and as a final thrill is heavily and blindly shelled all the time. Battlefields, like Skegness, are *so* bracing!

All these delights and more befell us: but the last straw was when some division somewhere decided now was the hour and now the minute for a counter-attack. We saw the Bosche S.O.S. rockets soar up into the sky, and the next thing we knew was that the blind shelling changed abruptly and settled down to a steady barrage, with each gun firing top speed: and the line of the barrage stretched right across the open ground we were endeavouring to cross! It was the counter-attack I had watched from the chateau attic repeated, with the difference – that instead of being a spectator at a comfortable distance in the rear, I was out in the open with a handful of men at close quarters!

The only thing to do was to stop and lie down in what we could find, and wait till things blew over a bit. So down we plumped into pools and rivulets and anything that looked like hollows in the ground, and took the earth to our bosoms while the Hun barrage crashed and flashed and thundered around our ears. I could feel myself sinking deeper into the glue as the minutes passed, and I rejoiced at the knowledge: the less I was exposed, the better I was pleased! It was chilly, though, when one was really in the grip of the mud. We lay there for about an hour, and then the situation seemed to have cleared up a bit and the shelling dropped back to normal. Luckily the enemy were firing mostly H.E. shells which didn't burst till they struck the ground, with the result that half the force of the explosion was lost in the soft slime. It was only the high-bursting shrapnel overhead that made us uncomfortable. A red flash and a bang twenty or thirty feet over your head, and the air is full of the whine and whizz of bullets and steel slivers, that drive past your ears like the crack of a whip and in an instant are buried five or six inches deep in the ground about you – that's much worse than the really big groups, that bury their snouts in the mud and kick up a geyser of birth and gravel and black smoke, but don't do much harm unless they really land on top of you.

To resume, we reached our destination at between one and two in the morning. This was the FREZENBURG REDOUBT, which you've probably read of in the Press afterwards. It was the German brigade-headquarters, and consisted of an underground concrete fortress on the highest point in the neighbourhood, just beside the cross-roads that marks the site of FREZENBURG VILLAGE – now more utterly destroyed even than Guillemont and Ginchy. Inside were five compartments; living-rooms, sleeping-rooms, servants and orderlies' quarters, etc. In all it had about the accommodation of a large-sized flat.

The old Bosche brigadier had skipped so hurriedly that he left behind him on the table his staff-map, with all gun-positions and strong points carefully marked on it (which the Seaforths had gleefully dispatched to the rear the day before), besides a quantity of strange Bosche delicacies – cold bottled coffee, tinned sausage, and the like, which we carefully threw out.

There was a drawback, however. The continual rain had flooded the low-level rooms (there was a step down into them from the trench outside) and seven or eight inches of black, greasy water swirled and eddied to and fro on the floor, on which bottles, cigarette-tins, papers, scraps of equipment, and all manner of litter floated depressingly. Even the chairs were awash, and bobbed buoyantly unless one sat down upon them.

However, it was a good headquarters as battle-headquarters go, and we tumbled cheerfully into it. (And, to anticipate the narrative a little, I might say here that I took off my clay-caked putties and soaking socks at once, and from then until we marched out 48 hours later I lived in bare legs with unlaced boots on my feet, whether sitting in the redoubt with my feet in the water or scrambling knee-deep in the sticky clay of the trench outside: and I was *the only one* of the officers and men in that redoubt who was not crippled with frost-bite and trench-feet when we came out.)

We relieved the remnants of the Camerons and Seaforths – gaunt, ragged scarecrows who have been hanging on since the first day, in the teeth of repeated counter-attacks, incessant shell-fire, and indescribable weather conditions, and at last found ourselves face-to-face with the Bosche again. The advance being held up, there was nothing to do but hang on to a scattered line of outposts and piquets until the weather cleared up and made the second phase possible.

The German outposts were about 600yds in front of the Redoubt, with our own line along a ledge opposite them. No one knew the exact position of either line: it's changed almost hourly, with little scraps between patrols and advanced posts: so neither side dared shell the extreme front. About the only thing the Hun *did* know definitely was the redoubt itself, and he let himself go 'all out' at that. If the shelling of the 'pill-box' in Wilde Wood had been bad, this was worse. On the other hand, the spirits of our men were twice as good, now that they were definitely faced with the enemy instead of being hammered helplessly in the back areas. I got a telephone line run out to our outposts, and then returned to the redoubt, where I spent most of the next two days.

At the time, of course, things were eventful enough, but looking back now I don't find anything outstanding to put on record. The most of us simply sat with our legs in the water and waited, and occasionally gnawed bully beef and biscuit. I needn't say luxuries like plates, knives, or cups were unknown. We managed to bury some of the dead – both Scottish and German – who lay thick around, and to collect some of the wounded, many of whom had been lying out since the first day.

Once the Hun counter-attacked heavily on our immediate right, just across the railway; and we all seized our rifles and revolvers and 'stood to arms' expectantly in the trench outside; but nothing materialised on our front. In the main it was a history of cold, wet, hunger, exposure, and shell-fire more intense than any I have seen.

On Sunday night came the welcome news that we were to be relieved, and a battalion of Dublins turned up to take over. In small parties, as each section was relieved, we turned our faces homeward, scrambled out of the trench, and set off down the track. But we were not by any means out of the wood yet. All the way down the track the Bosche was shelling furiously, and we had our proportion of casualties. And it was the same up the Menin road, as always. The rain had stopped and a full moon was shining through the mist. I wish I had been a painter: there are two pictures I could have immortalised 'Dawn on the Menin Road' and 'Ypres by Moonlight'. In the one, the grim half-guessed shapes of broken guns and corpses in the shadows by the roadside, the shafts of moonlight falling on wrecked and ruined buildings and making the shell-holes pools of darkness in the roadway, or revealing broken men that struggled home by ones and twos from the battle, the mud deadening their footsteps till they passed like wraiths in the mist – in the other, the vast and lovely wreck of the Cloth Hall rising in the moon-blanched square, an occasional pigmy figure at the corner of a silent deserted street – a traffic control post on night-duty among the ruins – or a twinkling light on a pile of bricks and mortar, indicating a subterranean life in the cellars: and from every quarter of the empty, lonely city echoed the bursting of shells and the clang of falling masonry.

So we came through Ypres and [. . .] the fields outside the city as the grey dawn was breaking, we came out to a train standing on the line with steam up. Wearily we piled into the carriages anywhere and anyhow, and with the echoes of the shells we had left still in our ears and the morning mists soaking up from the fields around us, we dropped off into oblivion.

That is the end of the story. We woke to rest and peace, the first hot food for eight days, the first wash or shave, and the first dry clothes – but these things are too sacred to write of!

Our casualties totted over 300, and many sick – mainly trench-feet, from being water-logged for a week, and wrinkled like crocodile-skin. We could not have put 50 effectives on parade out of the battalion.

I don't know why I'm alive (we lost three out of four company commanders) but I'm getting used to my luck nowadays!

This is the last sheet of the pad – it's just lasted out nicely. I'm giving it to be posted in London – I wish I could take it myself!

Meanwhile I'm as well as ever and still 'in the pink', as Tommy says.

The rain persisted at Frezenburg. The battalion was next in action at Langemarck. The 16th Division's attack there was initiated at 4.45am on 16

August by 48 and 49 brigades, with 47 relieving them in trenches in the
evening. By this time, Staniforth had been given command of a company of
reinforcements, so he was not at the front at Langemarck.

Eringhem area, 14 August 1917
A dreadful thing has befallen: bend your ears while I whisper it. I have
got a job!! No more for me the dug-out and the Maconochie:[14] instead,
the hut, the bed, the furnished quarters, and a superior smile. Far away
from the shells I apply my peaceful trade [. . .]. Behold me at last in the
ranks of the full-fledged 'embusqués'[15] behind the firing-line. I consort
with quill-drivers in the gate, and sit in the seats of the ink-slingers. How
it has happened I cannot pretend to know: I possess none of the qualifications for the usual 'cushy' job – the complete ignorance of front-line
warfare, the lofty contempt for the mere fighting infantry man, the uncle
at the War Office – I lack them all. Yet is the thing accomplished:
nothing remains but to wait for the end of the war and in the fullness of
time to draw my Military Cross.

   This must be startling news to you after my last – and still fairly recent
– letter, which I suppose must have had rather a stink of blood and gun-
powder. It was no less startling to me. Yesterday while I was sitting with
the others waiting for orders to go up and resume the boost in the dear
old salient, a telegram was handed to me. 'You will proceed at once to
M——,'[16] it ran, 'and take over command of the 47th Bde. Coy, 16th
D.D.B. from Capt. V.J. FARRELL who is to rejoin his unit immediately.' And two hours later I was on my way, in a wholly delightful little
narrow-gauge train, the very twin of the Cavan and Leitrim Light
Railways, that meandered in a fascinatingly intimate manner through the
meadows and cornfields in the sunshine, while the distant rumble of guns
on the horizon grew fainter and fainter, and the salt breezes swept in more
strongly from the invisible sea.

   Life is made up of contrasts, they say. And if I had wished to point the
contrast between this week and last I could have chosen no more effective
means than this little country train. The leisurely progress, the primitive
track – a simple pair of unballasted rails that wander at will, now along
the dusty highway, now winding through a field of standing corn – the
rustle of the tall grasses against the low footboards. The fields of
haymakers and romping children and country-folk, all make for an inti-
macy with the peace and restfulness of the countryside which is altogether
missed in your up-to-the-minute express. A normal English train would
probably have whirled me from the beginning to end of my journey in

something under an hour, leaving behind a confused impression of speed, discomfort, and clatter: in my 'petit tram-way', the hours succeeded one another through the long summer afternoon, & the shadows lengthened into the golden sunset mist of evening; and still we meandered pleasantly along by brook and field, deep in the heart of the country.

But I'm digressing – though this pastoral strain tempts me to dwell on it, by contrast with recent less restful scenes. (Hasn't the full-fed turgidity of it got into my sentences beautifully!) You will be anxious to hear about my new job.

There have recently been formed what are called Divisional Depot Battalions – or more shortly, D.D.B's – which are in essence, small advanced replicas of the Infantry Base Depots which I described in an earlier letter. All reinforcement drafts – including men from hospitals, C.C.S's, etc, in France – collect here before proceeding to join their units in the firing-line. We keep them in our hands here, complete their training if still unfinished, fit out deficiencies in equipment, and are ready when called on by the battalion in the line to dispatch them with the least possible delay, fully equipped and ready to take their places in the trenches at once.

This 'battalion' has three 'companies', corresponding to the three brigades of the division. No. 1 Coy. takes all men of the 47th Bde, No. 2 the 48th, and No. 3 the 49th. Similarly each company has its four 'platoons', representing the 4 battalions of its parent brigade: thus in any company we have a Leinster platoon, a Munster, a Royal Irish, and a Connaught Rangers, in one of which every man on the 47th Brigade who is posted to us finds his place. The battalion, in fact, is a copy of the 16th Division in miniature, with companies for brigades and platoons for regiments. Your dutiful servant is the 'company commander' of the 47th Bde. Coy, and controls all reinforcements sent up to any of the regiments in that Brigade. [. . .]

This news will, I am sure, take a big load of worry off your mind. For that I am glad: otherwise, it's rather rotten to be doing office-work in the rear when the old battalion is adding fresh laurels to its crown every day. However, somebody has to do it, and I suppose in its way it's useful work.

I can't tell you in this letter where we are, except that I can see the sea once more, about eleven miles to the northward, and that we're very close to where I first found the Leinsters six weeks ago.

I got your parcel, by the way, – except the honey, which had broken. In its place was a ticket from the Overseas Parcels Committee, or some such organisation, who take all damaged parcels, remove them, re-pack the parcel neatly and strongly, & forward it to its destination with a printed explanatory slip enclosed. Rather a good form of unostentatious war-work, isn't it? – and very badly needed in the case of many soldiers' parcels, I'm afraid. [. . .]

Eringhem area, 15 August 1917
[. . .] This would be quite an agreeable spot if it weren't for the weather. At home it's only a conversational cliché: but in an outdoor life over here it's a consideration of the first importance. And it's been vile ever since I arrived. A depressing, 'nagging' kind of downpour that spreads itself every now and then into a vicious strain of really torrential rain and then relapses to a dull drizzle again. The camp is a filthy quag, and the tents are shivery, comfortless places to sit in – mostly leaky. I'd give a lot to see a fire, or even a brazier; but that's been out of court since I left England, of course. The papers come out with pictures of girls in bathing-dresses with sunshades, so I suppose you're luckier than we are. However, it would be a sad day if we had nothing to grouse at; & it's all in the seven.

I've no news for you: the weather is holding up the Push, of course: I suppose it's our own fault for kicking up such a deuce of a shindy of gunfire, but that doesn't help matters much.

47 Brigade was relieved at the front over 17 and 18 August, leaving the Third Battle of Ypres for good. In the first half of August, there were thirty-three dead in the 7/Leinsters. The battalion had endured its worst conditions of the war. 47 Brigade as a whole had lost heavily at Ypres: total casualties were nearly a thousand from 26 July to 19 August, including 117 killed.[17]

Chapter 13

'The milk and whiskey are blocks of ice': Cambrai and Paperwork, August 1917 to January 1918

Following Passchendaele, the 7/Leinsters were sent to France, to the Bapaume area. Staniforth's time at the Divisional Base Depot was short and by the end of August he had rejoined the battalion.

Achiet-le-Grand, 25 August 1917
Only one small piece of news. The division, reduced and exhausted by recent fighting, has been moved out of the battle-zone to another of portion of the line for the winter – and where do you think we are? Within gun-range of where we were exactly a year ago, and throughout the memorable first week of September! I thought when we left it then that I never wanted to see it again: now it seems like a haven of rest after the Salient. Breezy, sunny stretches of rolling uplands: scarcely a shot from morning to night – a really 'cushy' spot.

Don't be surprised at the address. When the division moved, the reinforcement depot was broken up and everyone returned to their units, till we settle down in a new area, when it will be re-formed and established somewhere in the new Corps headquarters again. Meanwhile I'm living at our Battalion Headquarters – doing nothing!

Throughout his life, Staniforth enjoyed writing poetry and rhymes, often humorous. He sent one short piece to his parents on 29 August:

Metrical Meteorology
It rains upon Mouchy-le-Preux;
It rains upon Bullecourt, too:
　　　And Infantry Hill
　　　Is a positive swill, -
What is a poor devil to do?
'Somme' weather.

166

In early October, Staniforth enjoyed a short leave home. On 16 October, about 100 men from the 7/Leinsters (not including Staniforth) raided German lines, losing one man killed. They obtained useful information about a German position known as 'Tunnel Trench', part of the Hindenburg Line. Such intelligence-gathering was part of the preparations for the attack at Cambrai.

The raid also prompted another of Staniforth's ditties, which he sent to his parents on 23 October. The rhyme was presented to an American general (the USA had entered the war against Germany on 6 April 1917), visiting the battalion, who attended a dinner put on for him and the officers of the battalion's raiding parties:

The Raiders
Here's wishing them all promotion and STARS,
Here's wishing them Military Crosses and BARS,
And here's to our ally, Old Glory, to-night,
Where the STARS and the BARS in splendour unite!

At Cambrai, the target for 47 Brigade was Tunnel Trench, which extended about thirty feet underground, with ferro-concrete pill boxes at the top.[1] The attack began at 6.20am on 20 November with a four-minute barrage of the German lines followed by a successful attack by the 6/Connaughts, who were relieved on the evening of 22 November by the 7/Leinsters. The next day, the Leinsters gained some ground which had briefly been held by the Connaughts in the days before. They found many of the Connaughts' dead in that area. The 6/Connaughts' war diary notes, 'One of our dead was actually found locked in grips with a dead German.'[2] By the time of the battle, Staniforth was acting as the battalion's Adjutant and so was focused on administrative tasks.

Cambrai area, 10 November 1917
You asked for some account of an average day, so I made rough notes on a piece of paper to-day as various things happened, and here they are.

First of all to set the scene: Battalion Headquarters is a colony of sand-bagged dug-outs in a disused railway cutting, which happens to run parallel to the frontline and about 1200 yards behind it. They are mostly of the same pattern: a semi-circular steel arch or culvert driven in under the bank, and the end boarded up, with a door.

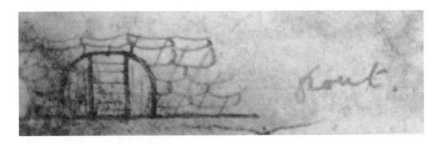

Average measurements about 5' x 8' x 7' – not too bad at all. I used to have these: one where I sleep, shared by the second-in-command, and the Orderly Room itself, where I live most of the day. Both are furnished the same way with tables and seats made by the battalion pioneers. My own dug-out has a couple of 'sapper' beds: i.e. four log posts, and wire-netting stretched between them for a mattress. The office has a long table down one side for me, and two small tables at the other for my two underlings, the Intelligence officer and the Asst. Adj. At one end is the door, at the opposite end (the 'face' of the cutting) is a rough brick fireplace. I have a row of pigeon-holes in front of me made of boxes, and over the fireplace in the centre hangs a letter rack I had made for me by the pioneers for outgoing correspondence to the 4 companies, Headquarter officers, Transport officer or Quartermaster (who are 3 miles behind, at the 'base'), Intelligence officer, Brigade, Circulars (i.e. memos to be passed round companies, noted, and returned), overseas post, correspondence with Records,

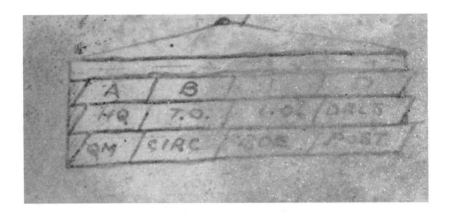

At my elbow is the inevitable telephone, behind me an enormous communal waste-paper-basket for the three of us (it's a tinned-meat packing-case really) and that's all the furniture.

Paymaster, War Office, etc, and D.R.L.S. – Despatch Rider Letter Service – to other units in the area, e.g. hospitals, the battalions, batteries, etc.

My servant woke me at seven this morning. I was sleeping half dressed, of course, so it didn't take long to wash and shave and dress. Then I strolled round to the mess and found porridge, coffee, toast, and bacon-and-eggs, and ate till I felt strong enough to face the daily round.

Then I lit a pipe, went round to the office, and attacked the morning's work. It was Saturday morning, and rather a lot of weekly returns were due – including the bane of all Adjutants, the B213, the weekly fighting strength return, which is a 'combing out' of every man borne on our books and needs a clearer head than double-entry book-keeping to make the columns balance (see specimens enclosed).

The returns from the companies which form the basis of this were ahead on my table, so I tackled them at once. I had been working for about ten minutes, when a signaller brought me a pink telegraph form: – 'Please detail one good visual signaller to report by noon for attachment to Bde. Signal Section, and one day's ration and two blankets to be brought.' I turned it over to the Asst. Adj. to arrange with the signal officer, and went on with the B213. Another five minutes went by: another pink telegram. 'Please send escort at once to DUNKIRK for 10685 Pte —— A.P.M.' a reference to the battalion which showed Pte —— as a deserter six weeks ago: evidently he has been caught. Also turned over to the A.Adj. to arrange with the culprit's company commander.

Somebody appeared in the doorway. I looked up and found the Brigade Bombing Officer, come to see about some new red and green flares that were very susceptible to damp and must be stored in a dry place. I went out with him to look for a good place to store them: found one, & promised to inspect them daily and keep them warm and dry. I notice the S.A.A. store was in a very bad position and very poorly protected: send for the R.S.M. and gave orders for it to be moved elsewhere. 100,000 rounds of ammunition are not things to have next to your dug-out unless they're fairly well sandbagged.

Went back to the office and worked uninterrupted for 5 minutes. Then enter a runner from A Coy in the front line with a note: they have no candles & no whiskey – can we do anything for them? Damn them heartily, but give the runner 2 of my precious store of candles (can't spare any more) & send him to the Mess President to see if we can afford to let them have a bottle of whiskey. It's rotten to run short in the line.

Glance at the watch hanging on the wall, and stopped work on the B213 for a quarter of an hour to arrange the working-parties for the evening with the sergeant-major. We have to find 170 all told: so many to X for carrying ammunitions, so many to Y for repairing and improving a trench, so many to Z for construction-work under R.E. supervision, etc. Companies in the line can't be touched: they have enough work of their own: consult strength of remaining two coys in reserve: 86 & 75: total 161: eke it out with H.Q. personnel, & divide up the various parties between the 2 coys. Fill in printed slips through each coy giving number of men required & details of place, time, tools, etc & turned over to A.A. for signature.

Another minute or two and a runner appears in the doorway '7am-twenty post, sir. Just starting'. (I have organised a runners'-post, leaving stated times, calling at each Coy H.Q. in order, and returning to head-quarters, to deliver and collect routine correspondence – the whole thing running up to time like a Bradshaw, worked out to margins of 3 minutes (it saves much trouble and runners, & the companies like it, as they know just when to expect a messenger).

I have nothing more for him – the clerks clear the letter-rack 20 minutes before each post, so as to have everything addressed & registered by the time the runner is due to leave – and off he goes. I go back to the 213.

At 10.30 the messenger from the Brigade arrives with the morning's post in a satchel. The A/A opens the letters, deals with a certain amount himself, and turns the remainder over to me. It is a fairly small post this morning – most of it requiring only to be endorsed 'Passed to you please' and forwarding to the proper quarter – and another hour sees my table clear again and the letter-rack dripping with outgoing matter.

I have hardly finished when the C.O. breezes in from his daily trip round the front line, with a string of notes as long as a late breakfast. B Company's trench is falling in, and they must have assistance to repair it: C Company's permanent 'house-maid' party [. . .] aren't doing their job & small blame to them they are 3 men and a lance-corporal, and the communication-trench they are supposed to keep in order is over 1600 yards along): the telephone-wires in PELICAN AVENUE have been pulled down in the night & must be pinned up again: and a hundred & one little things like that. I make copious notes, & promised to see to all of them, & he departs.

Another glance at the watch: 11.45, & the daily casualty wire must reach Bde. by noon. The companies haven't sent in their returns to me yet, strafe them. Reach for message-book and write urgent telegram for all coys 'Casualties not yet received, all expedite'. Ring bell & signaller appears from the bowels of the earth next door, and takes the message. Re-light pipe and wait for replies. In ten minutes they are all in: 'NIL',

'NIL', 'NIL', 'NIL', splendid. Despatch wire to Bde. and go back to 213 for the n-th time.

Pious hope. This is the busiest time of the day: everyone comes round the trench, everyone enquires first of all for the adjutant. Have visits in rapid succession from officers of the M.G.C., Trench Mortars, 18-pdrs, 7.5 howitzers, Bde. Intelligence Officer, Bde. Major, a very small subaltern who says he is the 12" How[itzer]s, and lastly a Sapper & staff officer (I deduce it is a quiet day in the front line). They all want something: the M.G.C. officers want to shoot, & inquire if there is any thing the infantry want strafing, the Bde. I.O. is thirsting for information about new Bosche trenches & suspected minenwerfer & things, the sappers want working and carrying parties, the Bde. Major wants the C.O. [. . .] and I say 'No', and they all say 'I'll just take one of these cigarettes, if I may?', & I say 'Do', and they all say reluctantly, 'Well, I must be getting along now', and I smile between my teeth at them and get back to the 213, and then a mess waiter pops his head in at the door and says suddenly 'Lunch is served, sir'.

I finish entering up the extra Orderly Room clerk on the B213 (we aren't allowed one really, so he has to be shown week by week as an 'additional Butcher', which we are allowed. He doesn't like it being a very gentlemanly clerk, but it's good for him. The 213 is full of little gadgets like that, in reconciling what we really have with what we are allowed to have. For instance, the H.Q. Mess Cook appears [. . .] as a 'tailor under instruction' and the mess-waiter can only be squeezed in as an 'assistant company sanitary man') [. . .]

So much of the remaining thirteen pages has been damaged that it is not possible to reproduce lengthy sections which are meaningful. However, enough can be read to be clear that among the tasks on which Staniforth worked were approving leave, arranging a Court of Enquiry to discover whether a soldier's wound had been self-inflicted, and touring battalion trenches to assess the needs of the men. His conclusion has, however, survived intact.

I don't know whether this has bored you profoundly, or interested you at all. Anyway it's just, as I said at the beginning, a record of one day's work, actually jotted down from hour to hour. Reading it over, I'm inclined to think it reads as rather more strenuous than it really is – most things can be dealt with more quickly than they can be described. Another day, of course, the set of problems might be completely different. Usually, there is a lot more telephoning than on this day –

sometimes the damned thing seems to ring all day. Also, I've omitted a lot of stuff that falls to the A[cting]/Adjutant to deal with.

On the whole I'd be inclined to describe an Adjutant's day as a succession of petty obstacles to overcome. There's very little that hangs over – most things crop up, are dealt with, and forgotten. Mainly, it's a hurry to keep up with scheduled time – doing nothing as it comes up is absolutely essential, or it never gets done – but in the main it's very interesting.

Cambrai area, 29 November 1917
[. . .] things are considerably quieter now. You saw in the papers, as you said, that we had our own little part to play in the push – but it was quite a subsidiary part, though interesting. [. . .]

I received your parcel all right. It turned up, as yours seem to have a happy knack of doing, just when it was most wanted, when we were away up the line and rations very disconnected. It had been re-packed [. . .] & a note inserted saying that the bananas (bad) had been destroyed. Everything else was O.K. 'A special word of praise is due' to the black currant & bacon pasties which aroused great enthusiasm. [. . .]

Tincourt, 7 December 1917
The Western front has been considerably disturbed of late, and we have done a good deal of short-notice trekking. One day about a week ago I went and had a hot bath & went to bed early. That same night we were pulled out for a false alarm. It was freezing cold, and I collected a really A1 dose of flu. The next day we started on the move, and I had no chance of knocking off. That night we bivouaced in some derelict tents on a bitter hill-top – there was a North-east wind and beaucoup snow, and I felt like a poisoned pup – blinding headache, shudders chasing each other up and down my spine, gorgeous temperature and a pronounced aversion from bully beef and biscuits – which was all we had!

We spent three or four days wandering round the wilderness, sleeping sometimes in tents, sometimes in trenches, and most of the time I crept about like a sick kitten. The weather was beastly: snow and hard frost every night, and as cold as the pit. Rations slipped a cog, too: one loaf amongst 13 for 24 hours doesn't go far. That's the worst of these offensives!

However, it passed off in course of time, and I managed to escape being sent down. Now I'm pretty well O.K. again except for the aftermath, which is eating (or rather drinking) up hankies at a prodigious rate.

I rode over to our last year's battlefields yesterday, and wished I hadn't. The country is extraordinarily like the moors at home: leagues of barren heath, with a few roads, many tracks, and infrequent little villages. Riding through this at the dusk of a December day was very eerie. Each one of them was a famous battle: – Le Transloy, Lesboeufs, Ginchy, Guillemont, Morval and so on: exactly like Ugthorpe, Mickleby, Scaling and the rest – little pleasant places far away from railways and high roads. Now they are gruesome places: level heaps of brickdust, with the grass beginning to grow over the bricks & the heather in the streets, and silent wooden crosses everywhere. Not a living soul anywhere – simply abandoned to the wilderness and going back to it again. As [. . .] I rode down the main street of Lesboeufs two rats ran across the road and a bat flew out of some ruins. Just rats, and bats, and regiments of lonely crosses. It was worse than Ypres, I think, because there there were at least soldiers of our own: here there was nothing but our two selves.

But on the open moors between the villages it was just the same. It was a 7-mile ride, and there were crosses, crosses, all the way: dotted about in the brown heather wherever you looked. The whole country is a giant cemetery. Also the year-old debris of battle that is still uncleared: broken wheels, rusted rifles, rotten bandoliers, rags of uniforms and so on. I found our old assembly trenches at Ginchy, and the graves of some of our fellows who died there, and went over the whole battlefield again. I looked into one shell-hole, full of water and frozen over, and on the bottom, staring up through the ice, lay a corpse that had escaped the burial parties somehow. Why it wasn't a skeleton I don't know: but it wasn't. Altogether, I rather wished I hadn't come.

All the Irish battalions have been moved out of Ireland & replaced by English troops, to prevent Sinn Fein contagion. There is a reserve battalion at Redcar containing many officers who were out with their service battalions in this brigade at Loos & the Somme: and probably many personal friends of mine. Also I heard that our 3rd was at York, but I believe it isn't true.

There's no news at present: it's abominably cold, as I said before, and I wish to the Lord we could move into a civilised area again. I haven't seen the civilians since we were in Flanders, and one gets very tired of soldiers & war *all* the time. I'd like to go into a French town again, and have a decent dinner & see some shops & people instead of these blasted deserted ruins. I suppose it's Christmas unrest, that's all [. . .]

If you're sending out for Christmas, I'd like one of the mufflers I left behind. Nothing keeps out the cold these nights, but one might as well try. (There are 7 H.Q. officers sitting in this canvas hut as I'm writing: four are trying to play cards & cursing each other for mis-deals because their hands are so cold: one is warming his fingers over the candle: the other two are stamping up & down to get the snow off their feet. Everyone has greatcoats, gloves, mufflers, leather jerkins, British warms,[3] Balaclavas, & all manner of swathed round them!) Also if you love me send something to eat that was made in a civilised kitchen at home, and not in an army cannery! [. . .]

By mid-December, Staniforth was acting temporarily as battalion Quartermaster in addition to Adjutant. His next letter described some of the problems of supplying provisions to soldiers.

Ste Emilie, 18 December 1917
Christmas week in such a Christmas! Seasonable is no word for it. Some of the roads are level with the cams (six and eight-feet drifts) and the frosts are some of the hardest I remember. When you wake in the morning everything – sponges, brushes, socks etc – is as hard as a board: the milk and whiskey are blocks of ice and have to be thawed into liquids again, and the ground is iron-bound for 6 inches under the surface. A pick axe will just splinter it.

This is my last day as Quartermaster. To-morrow I shall be relieved. It isn't a job I'm in love with, but at times it has a certain fascination: taking rations up to the line, for instance, is an incident which would always give material for a good picture or poem. The routine goes something like this.

The regiment's base (Quartermaster's stores, horse-lines etc) are in a village usually about 5 miles behind the trenches, and conveniently near to the railroad. A battalion in the trenches is fed in the following manner. Base Supplies sends up trains full of food every day – as it might be from London: assuming the battalion were holding trenches at Port Mulgrave Harbour. Each division has a divisional 'Railhead' – i.e. its nearest point on the railway. In this case Hinderwell would be our railhead, Staithes & Kettleness the railheads of the divisions on our flanks. Accordingly the daily train from London would dump all its stores for our division at Hinderwell (great distress of Messrs Moody and Lewis). The Divisional Train (i.e. A.S.C. Train, of waggons & lorries) meet it there, and take the stuff to the various Brigade Refilling Points. Ours might be, say, at the Ship Inn. It is then the duty of the regimental QM and Transport Officer (who would be living, perhaps, at the Long Row) to send their transports to the refilling point, take over the rations in bulk from the A.S.C., bring it back to the Quartermaster's Stores at the Row, where it is divided up into 5 portions for the 4 coys and HQ, and then take it on to the ration-dump – usually near Bn. HQ or as near the line as it is safe for vehicles to approach. The coys in the line then send up ration-parties to meet the transport at the dump (say the top of the Harbour steps) and each party receives its company's rations for the following 24 hours and returns with them to the front line.

Our refilling point here is fortunately only about 500 yards from the transport lines, so we have no distance to go to meet the A.S.C. Train. More often it is 2 or 3 miles.

I take the limbers down there every morning about 11, and load up with bread, meat, biscuits, bully, tea, sugar, oatmeal, rice, dried fruits, vegetables, tinned milk, pickles, jam, cheese, butter, candles, rum, etc, for the ensuing 24 hours, and bring them back to the QM stores, where the cases are opened and the contents broken up according to the strength of the companies.

The remaining articles of supply – i.e. not food, but things like clothing, whale-oil, paraffin, fuel, letters etc, I have drawn earlier in the morning from the Ordnance Depot (not the A.S.C.), together with the material required for work in the trenches, such as timber, sheet-iron, sandbags, gabions[4] for revetting (which comes from the R.E. Store) and ammunition, bombs, flares, detonators, and similar fireworks (from the Divl. Ammunition Dump). So that my morning is very like a round of shopping at various places, from which I return very much laden indeed, in that I require 8 double limbers (pair-horse), a spring cart, 2 G.S wagons, and occasionally the loan of a 3-ton motor-lorry to take back my purchases!

The road to the trenches is 5 miles long, mostly uphill, and takes an hour and a half to cover. Of course we can't arrive in daylight: which means we can't start till half past three (in the summer we frequently can't start till nine at night, and have been known, at Loos, to get back from the daily trip at 5 or 6 A.M. every morning!)

At a quarter-past three I push my nose out of the office, where I've been snowed under with indents and waybills[5] for the last hour, and find the daylight fading already, a bitter north-east wind blowing, and a light snow-blizzard in progress. Splendid night for a ten-mile ride – at a walk all the way! (all horse-drawn vehicles proceed at a walk in this country, except under fire). I yell for my servant, who produces top-boots[6] (size 12½ – I must show them to you some time), three pairs of socks to go inside them, leather jerkin, Cardigan, greatcoat, and woolly gloves, and assists me into them. Swaddled and bloated, I waddle out to where my groom stands with two horses, stamping & blowing on his hands (the groom, not the horses), and climb ponderously into the saddle, the groom following my example. The wagons are already lined up in the road waiting to start, with the 4 quartermaster-sergeants walking in the rear. There is a pause while we make sure that certain small things are on board alright (soda water for the HQ mess, case of whiskey for C Coy, cigarettes for the Adj., & so on) then I ride up to the head of the column – 'Walk March' – and the whole convoy rumbles off up the road.

We have three ruined villages to pass through, X-, Y-, and Z-, and one rather nasty bit of road where some of our batteries are, which naturally comes in for more than its share of shelling – otherwise the road is quiet enough.

Darkness is coming on very quickly, as the hedges slip by in the twilight, with the open snow-fields stretching on each side. Far ahead over the horizon the first Very light soars up and hangs glimmering over the front line trenches. The old mare ambles sleepily along the long line of carts and waggons lumber creakingly behind, and I suck a pipe, stick my hands in my pockets, and think drowsily of many things. The sergeant, just the red glow of a pipe visible under the curve of his steel helmet. I often wonder what he thinks of.

We pass through Y-, and I space out the vehicles to intervals of 60 yards, just in case. With the cursed Germans you never know: and it's better to lose one cart than two or three.

Windy Corner has evidently had its daily dose earlier in the day. The road is plentifully starred with new shell-holes, one of the guns lolls drunkenly in its emplacement beside the road, and we pass a smashed limber & a couple of dead horses in the ditch. The old mare catches the smell of blood & and shies violently. However, all is quiet now: the hate has exhausted itself.

A kilometre beyond Z- there is a crucifix by the roadside, among three or four bleak-looking trees. Here we leave the road & strike across the fields for six hundred yards to the ration-dump. We are within 1000yds of the trenches now, and machine-gun bullets begin to harm around, while every now and then the Very lights reveal each stick and stone in a ghastly white glare, throwing up lines of struggling men & horses against the snow for a moment.

The dump is at Bn. Hdqrs, and the ration-party, hearing the creak of wheels & the jolting of the limbers afar off, are assembled ready to meet us. Each party crowds round its own limber in the darkness, while I leave them to squabble about rations, candles & things, climb stiffly out of the saddle, throw the reins to the groom, and waddle ponderously down the trench. After the long ride in the winter nights, the trench looks very homely – glimpses of light and the glow of braziers from dug-outs, little timbered villas lettered on the doors 'C.O.', 'Adjutant', 'HQ Mess', 'R.S.M.', and so on, with lights showing through their oiled-silk windows, all making a pleasant homely contrast to the snow & darkness outside.

I go on to a door marked 'Orderly Room', push it open, & find the Adjutant working inside. We spend a quarter of an hour discussing waybills & shop generally, swop gossip from the front line and back areas, & then go round to the mess for a cup of tea and a cigarette.

Then I gather my papers & receipts, make notes on various commissions for the morrow, have a farewell drink for good-night and good-luck, & push off.

Out of the dump it is snowing bitterly & you can see nothing ten yards ahead of you. The limbers are waiting, & the groom holds my mare, head & tail down against the glass. It is not a night to waste time, so I scramble up as quickly as possible & we start back.

Till we get back to the road it is a tricky business, for the fields are pitted with shell-holes, & it is pitch dark. I ride on a few yards ahead & let Polly have her head – she can avoid holes more instinctively than I can. At last we strike the road – one limber nearly upsets, stumbling down the cam into the roadway: a drop of 3 feet, & probably unnegotiable by any vehicle on earth except an Army limber – & turn homewards full into the teeth of the storm.

As we approach Z-, two big 5.9's[7] whistle overhead and burst in the village. Query: will the hate be over by the time we pass through it? Apparently not: as we get nearer & nearer, it quickens & gets more intense. We have struck a bad moment: one of the brief bursts of fire which he indulges in for two or three hours. The shells are all falling at the cross-roads in the village, and the interval between them is not long enough to get the whole of the transport through. We shall have to hurry through – which I hate doing: it's bad for the horses & for the limbers. However, can't be helped. So I hold them 100yds from the cross-roads, & give orders to wait for the next shell, & then make a dash for it. I drop back to the rear of the column, & we wait. Next minute there is a scream & bang, & a cloud of brickdust. [. . .] 'Walk-march! – Trot – Canter! – GALLOP!' and the whole train goes off with a roar of wheels & thunder of moves, the drivers' whips rising & falling & the light limbers bounding

& bucking 3 feet in the air. Poor Polly gets wildly excited, & it is all I can do to hold her. However, we get through all right, & are a hundred & fifty yards past the cross-roads before the next one bursts behind us. We pull up smoking & panting, & a still rather fidgety & excited horse (horses hate the reek of sulphur and brimstone that hangs round a spot that is being shelled) & proceed at a more dignified pace then. The rest of the journey is uneventful except when one limber bolts on a steep hill, & I nearly get an awful toss galloping beside it in the dark on the slippery roads before we can pull up the team. At last we get back to the lines.[8]

Tincourt, 11 January 1918
Have I or haven't I thanked you for your Christmas parcels? If I haven't, it wasn't because they didn't reach me safely or weren't appreciated, but because the adjutant has been away on leave since Christmas day, and I've been very busy, with no persistent and only one clerk. But thank you very very much for them, and specially for the silver bracelet, which I'm very proud of. But when I come home there are one or two more entries to be engraved on it.

[. . .] We had a very Merry Christmas, though not a very happy one (a distinction with a difference). It was just before we went into the line fortunately, so we could give the men a comfortable Christmas dinner in billets. We bought a big cake for them and five barrels of beer in addition to their rations so they didn't do so badly.

Chapter 14

'The Division has ceased to exist': Disbandment and the German Spring Offensive, February to April 1918

Cambrai was to be the 16th Division's last major encounter with the enemy before it was reorganized. At the end of January 1918, five battalions in the 16th Division were wound up, including the 7/Leinsters. Two battalions joined the division, the 2/Munsters and the 2/Leinsters. This allowed the division to be reconfigured, like the rest of the army, into brigades of three battalions each. The 6/Connaughts remained in 47 Brigade, joined by the 2/Leinsters and 1/Munsters.

A small number of 7/Leinsters went to the 11/Hampshires and 200 formed the 19th Entrenching Battalion. Staniforth refused the role of senior captain in the latter, and eventually went into another infantry battalion, the 2/Leinsters. That had taken the bulk of the 7/Leinsters (fifteen officers and 330 men), although Staniforth did not join them properly until early May. He first spent two months at 'L' Infantry Base Depot at Rouen, was home on leave from 7 to 24 February, and then had a recurrence of earlier dental problems as he so vividly describes.

Grand Hotel, Calais, 22 February 1918
Two nights in billets: 4 on a camp on a hillside, 2 at the Officer's Club P——; 1 in Amiens, 1 in Boulogne, now here, and to-morrow to the Base Camp 6 miles outside the town. The regiment broken up, and three of us (HQ staff) sent down to the Base to wind up the show. Shall be here for some time and after that God only knows what. Have been travelling around France for the last week without any kit. This is a rotten hole: why on earth Mary[1] had it written on her heart I can't think.

Rouen, 28 February 1918
I'm feeling very much like the sole survivor of a wreck. The old Battalion was simply disbanded – not amalgamated at all: a big proportion of offi-

cers and men was absorbed into the regular Bn., the remainder went to form – of all things – a new Entrenching Battalion. (I was offered the post of senior captain in this – but not for this kid, thank you.) Three of us – the Adjt., 2nd in Cmd,[2] and myself, then repaired to this place, with the Orderly Room Staff and many boxes of papers to wind up the battalion. They have given us a hut among the sand hills overlooking the sea, and we sit and answer correspondence all morning, and then do a cinema and dinner in town. It's a lazy life, pleasant just for the moment but will be very wearisome soon, I see. After that I don't know what will happen to us. [. . .]

French rationing is very strict. Afternoon tea in the town consists of tea (no milk, but a dollop of *honey* for sugar) and little apples. No bread or butter. A poor blow-out for a growing boy.

Rouen, 10 March 1918

[. . .] I have no news from the Leinsters. To-morrow I'm taking a draft up the line for some division and returning. Shall probably be away three days and two nights. I'm still not posted to my unit – in fact as I am only on the books of the 7th Leinsters, and they have ceased to exist, I'm beginning to wonder whether I am in the Army at all! I suppose if I hopped aboard one of the leave-boats which I see weighing anchor every day the point would be settled fast enough, though. [. . .]

Rouen, 17 March 1918

I have just come down from a trip up country with a draft. [. . .].

'The Irish on the Somme'[3] is a silly book. He tries to keep up with the old stage-Irish, 'Donnybrook' tradition. Where would we be if we were really fire-eating mountebanks like that? But as far as historical facts and records go, the book's sound enough.

[. . .] I was thinking this morning that as most of the work is done now, it might not be a bad idea to get someone to look up my teeth before I was sent up the line again. It looks so bad to go to the M.O. after you have received your orders! So I went round to the Medical Hut and got a chit to the Dental Surgeon in the Base Hospital here, 'Please examine and advise Capt. J. Staniforth, etc'. I wandered off to the Hospital, was passed through seventeen officers and twenty orderly rooms, answered the same questions each time, and watched the same answers being faithfully tran-scribed on enormous buff forms (the first question was invariably 'Are you under orders for the Front again yet?' – it was lucky I could say 'no') and at last found myself in the consulting-room flat. There was quite a decent chap there who put a few questions to me, and after I told him all about Bridges' work last year and so on, put me in a chair and said 'Let me look.' I sat back comfortably, opened my mouth, rolled up my eyes and relapsed into contemplation of my own scalp the way one does almost at once. I felt a prick in my palate and a big injection of something or other (the man was babbling pleasantly about Patrick's Day or some such nonsense all the time).

Next moment something like a claw hammer wandered into my mouth, and there was a sound like the crushing of a lump of sugar, and a gory eye-tooth rattled into the basin before me. While I was still too speechless with indignation to protest, and before I detached my eyes from the top of my head back to reality again, four more followed the first, and my opening attempts at outraged profanity were drowned in a rush of blood. By the time I had spat it all out he had fixed up my next appointment and was bowing me out!! The whole thing hadn't taken five minutes!

The net result was five extractions (mostly stumps) and I am to be here for 4 weeks from to-day until the treatment is complete. I shall be transferred from 'L' to 'K' I.B.D. to bring me nearer the hospital I expect. I am to have an upper plate on each side, leaving only my three front teeth, which are to be filled for the present – though he says in time they will have to come out too, and three more added to the plate.

He is an awfully good chap, and didn't hurt me a bit. I believe he was rather a big dentist before the war (HELYARD, W.A., is his name), and it seems that Calais is one of the first-class centres of B.E.F. dental work, where you can get as good work done and as good plates made as anywhere in England – not rough-and-ready Army work at all – so I might just as well get it fixed here and now as wait for Bridges. Particularly as H.M. Government will foot the bill. What do you think?

There is no other news, except that I have been posted to the 2nd Leinsters, which relieves my mind a lot. I was afraid I might get to some other but I'm afraid they won't see me for a while yet

[. . .] We had nothing to celebrate Patrick's Day, really. We got out some shamrock dished it out to the men on parade in the morning, and they had a bit of a sing-song in the evening.

[. . .] We once lived in a cosy front-line trench for weeks and weeks we got to know every inch of it stop one day Fritz suddenly blew 4 mines under it. It took us two days to get used to it again – owning craters all at once instead of the familiar fire-bays, and so on.

. . . That's what my mouth feels like.

For those former members of the 7/Leinsters who had gone directly to the 2/Leinsters, life had been quiet since Cambrai. However, based at Villers-Faucon, they bore the brunt of the German Spring Offensive which began in the early hours of 21 March. The battalion war diary recorded how all officers in the area of fighting except one were casualties by 11.30am. Over the next three days, casualties throughout the ranks were so heavy that the battalion was reorganised with remnants of Connaughts. When the battalion was withdrawn from fighting at midnight on 23/24 March it was down to only 175 men, but went back into action the next afternoon until 29 March. From 21 to 29 March approximately[4] sixty-nine members of the battalion were killed. When this took place, Staniforth was still at Rouen. He did manage to get into action by volunteering to take a draft of soldiers to the front. However, he was clearly traumatized by his absence from his own battalion, as his first letter home about the German offensive suggests.

Rouen, 31 March 1918[5]

Just got back from the line, taking up a draft. The Division has ceased to exist. Wiped off the map. You know where they were; they took the Boche attack full smack, the first day they were in the trenches. They died fighting, while I was hanging round a Base Depot. I'll tell you about it later. I don't want to just now.

Calais, 6 April 1918

I've had a small experience of the push, which may interest you – God knows it was nothing to what I ought to have had if I'd been with my regiment: I'll never forget that as long as I live.

On the 23rd, as soon as we knew the big thing had started at last, I went to the Staff and said I wanted to take a draft up the line. (I'm marked 'unfit' till they have finished my teeth, so it would have been useless asking to be sent up to the Leinsters for duty, and a draft was the next best thing.) I arranged to take a small draft up to a certain divisional-report-battalion behind Arras the next morning (Sunday 24th).

At 3.30 on Sunday morning we paraded and marched down to the station to entrain. There were a number of officers waiting with drafts, totalling about a dozen subalterns and 1200 men. I happened to be the senior present. At about 6 the train started. We had an uneventful journey, except for a man who travelled on the roof of his carriage till we came to a sudden bridge and was killed. And a Boche plane which bombed the train with good-will but no success for a few miles, during the morning: but of course terribly slow. The congestion on the lines was very bad, with troops and guns and horses going up, and wounded coming down. (At one place we passed nine full hospital-trains standing buffer to buffer on a blocked line, followed by long trains of cattle-trucks carrying other stretcher-cases.) This congestion had a direct bearing on our route. If you look at the railway map of France you can see that the line runs CALAIS-BOULOGNE-ETAPLES-NOYELLES-ABBEVILLE thence by the AMIENS line as far as LONGPRÉ junction: thence eastward to DOULLENS, and so direct to ARRAS. Instead, we ran through LONGPRÉ straight on to AMIENS, and turned N.E. towards ALBERT and ACHIET. I suppose the idea was to work round through ALBERT and then northwards to ARRAS again, via ACHIET. Anyway, the halts began to get longer and longer, and the news at each one more ominous. The situation was changing every hour, and no one quite knew how much ground had been overrun by the Boche. At HEILLY (the same country-station where we detrained in 1916 for GUILLEMONT & GINCHY) we found a wild-eyed R.T.O. who hadn't been to bed for three nights, and had handled traffic under almost continual bombing since Thursday. (He had arranged to get married in London that very day.) He could get no news from any station ahead beyond MERICOURT – the next – and nothing from ALBERT at all: wires down evidently. From wounded and stragglers it seemed that the Hun must be just the other side of ALBERT. Considering that up to then we had not even heard of the fall of PERONNE, this was news with a vengeance. It was like when setting out from Hinderwell to meet the Boche in Sheffield, and being told at Malton that he was already in York. Anyway, there was no prospect of our train being able to get through to ARRAS by ALBERT. The R.T.O. said he could not push it further than the next station (MERICOURT); & we should have to detrain there and try to make our way north across country, to our own divisions. So I did a bit of thinking, and I said 'Damn their divisions', and I sent for the officers. I told them as much as I knew of the situation, and told them I proposed to take command of the train, run it through to ALBERT, where the fighting was, and turn the mixed reinforcements into a fighting force, roughly equivalent to a battalion, which it seemed to me would be of more use on the spot than various small drafts could be to their respective divisions, if and when we ever reached them. So we climbed aboard again and I told the driver (luckily he was an English R.O.D. man[6]) to run straight on through MERICOURT into ALBERT. By this time it was about eight o'clock and getting dark. The men had had no rations since we started in the morning, except what little they carried in their haversacks. Fortunately, however, they all had their 120 rounds of ammunition.

The noise of gun-fire and aeroplane bombing grew louder as we neared ALBERT, and the sky was aflame with flashes and searchlights. When we pulled into the station it was evident the battle was very near. I got out, ordered the officers to detrain their troops as quickly as possible and stand by, while I went off to find the R.T.O. He was in his office, dismantling and destroying it, and burning papers and things. In an excess of zeal he had already destroyed the telephone – which accounted for me being unable to get through from HEILLY. The Telegraph however was luckily still intact – though there was no operator, so it wasn't much use to him. He told me he had received orders from Army HQ to evacuate the station by midnight, with all rolling-stock. There was only one loco-motive in the yards – ours made two – and any God's quantity of stock, so he wasn't happy. So I called up MERICOURT (there's some use in being an ex-Signal officer), told them to send along as many locos as they could spare one-time, and if possible to notify the Army of my misap-propriation of 1200 reinforcements – not that anybody was likely to be worrying about them – and marched them out of the station, which wasn't a healthy spot, and reported to the senior officer in the town, who was taking over all stragglers and organising the defences. From him I got 100 men and one subaltern (I haven't the slightest idea what regiment they belonged to) and went out through the town eastwards. We picketed the road and sent out patrols to have a look-see. There was a continuous trickle of stragglers coming back, but like all stragglers they were very vague. There were reports of Hun cavalry patrols about 5 miles down the road, which dwindled to 3 subsequently, but no evidence of them. There was a good deal of shelling.

We waited there until about midnight, and then I received a message that we were to withdraw to CORBIE. So we never actually got in touch with the Hun at all. We marched back through the town, which was in a filthy state. It was crowded with troops and vehicles, all pressing west-ward under a brilliant moon (how I cursed that moon) and the Hun had sent over squadrons of 15 and 20 planes which were shovelling out bombs as fast as they could release them. The whole town was reeling and crashing round our ears, and half of it was in flames. The big Expeditionary Force Canteen was blazing, and all the stores had been flung out hastily into the streets. The passing troops looted what they could as they went by. I saw a case of champagne broken open and running down the gutter, and men staggering away with cases of Bass on their shoulders, bags of fruit, tinned meat, biscuits, vegetables, etc. Lorries were lurching past, top-heavy with all sorts of kit: one gave a jolt and half-a-dozen officers' valises fell off into the street. Nobody gave them a thought. There were a few distracted civilians, who screamed at each splitting crash as the bombs fell among her strengths. At last we got out of the town on the westward road. It wasn't much better there. It was a high-road, white and bright as day under the moon, and treble-ranked with vehicles, all moving forward like carriages in a theatre-queue, 10 yards at a time, as far as you could see – lorries, by the score, limbers, guns, ambulances, staff-cars, motor-bicycles: everything on wheels. Every now and again the Boche planes came low and emptied a drum of machine-gun ammunition at the column. I took my men a few hundred yards away from the road into the fields (not fields really, but moorland) where we were fairly safe, dropping and lying flat if the planes came too close. Now and again we would pass a big siege-battery position, the guns all harnessed up to their teams, and the drivers sitting on their horses waiting for the word to move off. The scraps of paper littered about in the mud, and the debris of long occupation, and the whole battery sitting mutely on their horses at one o'clock in the morning, instead of sleeping as they had slept for months past, was rather moving. (It's not often you know, that for miles and miles all round you there is not a single person sleeping, everyone up and busy in the small hours of the morning. Even in a battle there are some asleep somewhere. There, everybody was on the move.)

Ultimately we fetched up at CORBIE, where the Army was re-organising. My original draft had of course been handed over to ALBERT (some of them were in action by this) so I dumped my 100 men and their subaltern at the first Major, and wished them luck, and began to think of making my way to my original destination and reporting the disposal of the men and handing over their papers. Evidently I couldn't be any use here.

It was then about 3 in the morning – perhaps a bit later. I pulled out a map and decided to make to DOULLENS, where with luck I might get a train to MONTICOURT where I wanted to be about 7 kilos east. DOULLENS was about 45 kilos away.

I was very hungry by this, so I found a house in CORBIE where I got three new eggs – it was all they had –and the end of a loaf. I broke the eggs and swallowed them, put the loaf in my pocket, and struck off across country. I hadn't gone far when I met another fellow going the same way, so we went on together. We tried several lorries, but they were all packed with gear or fugitives. Presently we came on one standing abandoned in the ditch (it sounds unusual, but you see a lot of queer sights in the retreat of an army). It wouldn't have been any use to me, but the other fellow was a motor-sharp, so he popped in while I cranked up and we soon had the old bus moving off along the road quite professionally. We picked our way from my map (they were country roads, and abominable) and we hadn't gone three miles before we came on an abandoned car – a little four-seater runabout this time. So we affected a transfer and carried on. Shortly after daybreak we ran into a little hamlet like Etherby, and decided to break the journey, and have a bit of sleep, and finish the odd 10 or 11 kilos after-wards. We knocked at the biggest house we could find, got no answer, pushed open the door, and went in. The place was empty, but had evidently been abandoned a few hours ago when the old woman heard of the retreat, for the kitchen fire was still warm. So we ran the car into a yard, hoped it wouldn't be seen by another strolling couple, and went into bed – in the best bedroom. I was pretty fagged by then (I'd gone to bed at 11 on Saturday night, got up at 2 am on Sunday morning, and this was 5 o'clock Monday morning) and didn't wake till, as they say, 'the sun was high in the heavens'. I looked at my watch and found it was 10 o'clock. So we got up and rummaged round for breakfast. We found eggs, bread, butter, and coffee. So we didn't do so badly. We left a five-franc note hidden away where the old woman would find it if she came back and passing soldiers wouldn't. After then, washed, shaved, and fed, returned to 'our' car and went on to DOULLENS. Here we parted, as the other fellow (I never found out his name) wasn't going my way. We left the car in the middle of the town quite openly, where it may be this minute for anything I know. I went down to the station and found a supply-train running out to MONTICOURT at 1.30. I went back into town, hung round a bit, saw the Guards being rushed through on motor buses to relieve the pressure ARRAS way, had a bit of lunch at the cafe in the square, came back to the station, and found the train was cancelled (wasn't it you who remarked that there is no stability about Army arrangements?). However, there was the ubiquitous lorry going in quantities down the road, so I easily got a lift over the 7 kilos and dropped off at MONTI-COURT about half-past-two. I found my D.D.B., handed over my papers and explained why I was 80 men deficient. I stayed to tea in their mess, told them what I knew of the situation down south, heard the news in return – from the BULLECOURT-CROISELLES front, which ground I said I knew as well as they did – including a fight round my own old billet at ERVILLERS: and left them with mutual expressions of goodwill and a farewell whiskey-and-soda at about 6 o'clock. I jumped on a French lorry driven by a poilu[7] for the return road to DOULLENS. Rather a funny incident occurred there, it was chilly driving in the lorry, and I saw him taking his hands off the controls several times and blowing on them to warm them. I had a pair of woolly-gloves on, and an extra pair of leather ones in my pockets. So I pulled off the woollies, and handed them to the driver, & wore the leather ones myself. He grinned amiably at me, slipped the gloves unconsciously in the pocket, and went on driving! I didn't feel capable of explaining that they had been intended as a loan, not a gift, so I had to let it go at that. They were a jolly good pair of gloves too. However, it all helps to cement the Entente – what?

I got off with thanks at DOULLENS, and made inquiries at the station. No, there was nothing going to ABBEVILLE that night except a light engine. However, a light engine was as good as a whole train to me, so at eight o'clock I climbed into the cab of a monstrous Chemin-de-fer-du-Nord, all pipes and gadgets, greeted the 'mécanicien' and 'chauffeur' cheerfully and pulled out into the night. With reasonable luck we should have made ABBEVILLE before 10: as a matter of fact it was exactly 5 A.M. when we got there – which will give you some idea of railway conditions at the moment! (To do them justice, I believe there was a breakdown somewhere) [. . .]. I must have looked rather a sweep when I got down. They were a very amiable pair, but the fireman's idea of stoking was to throw down half a hundred weight of briquettes on the footplate and turn a hose on them till the whole cab ran with inky water and steaming coal-dust. He explained volubly that 'Les charbon brûlent beaucoup mieux tous [. . .] comme ça: y'a plus de chaleur, voyez-vous, 'ce-pas?'[8] He was also considerate enough to build up a little rampart of a dozen briquettes for me to sit on, similar to one occupied by himself and his mate. Lucky I had my third-best, or first-worst, uniform on. However I picked up a rough idea of how to drive a French loco, which may come in useful sometime.

At Abbeville I dossed down for the rest of the night (it was there I first heard rumours of a long-range gun shelling Paris, and wondered what sort of people could be found to start, and believe fairy-stories like that) and the next morning I picked up a slow local to ETAPLES, where I caught [end of letter missing].

Calais, 18 April 1918
[. . .] Entraining is a hobby peculiar to Bases, and therefore not without its humorous side. (I have personally entrained 15,000 troops since this

push began, so 'experts credo'.) You must understand that one of the fine old crusted traditions which have made the British Bases what they are to-today is that no job of work can be done by the man who is paid to do it. He must have assistants detailed to 'help' him: assistants who if possible know nothing whatever of the work, who come down in rotation daily, and very rarely come twice (this last to prevent all danger of their acquiring elementary knowledge of the job). The idea is mainly to find employment for the hordes of reinforcement-officers who passed through the bases on their way up to the line.

Now at every station in France used by the B.E.F. there is an established Railway Transport Officer. He is one of the lowest forms of Staff life, wearing blue tabs, instead of red, and acts as a stationmaster for us. (There was once an R.T.O. who put some troops on the [rest of paragraph badly damaged].)

Anyway, in the old days, before organisation became the miracle it is to-day, the Base Depots arranged a draft of 100 men, put a subaltern in charge, and sloshed it off to the station, and all was well. The subaltern enquired of the R.T.O. how to get to the 156th Div, and the R.T.O. said 'North-bound train, no. 17 line, departs 10.50'. The subaltern collected his following, put them on the South-bound train, no. 8 line, departing 12.30, and so reached his Division without loss of time. It was all very simple.

Too simple, in fact. The sub. had no other job but to get his men into the train; the R.T.O. no job but to indicate the right train. Every draft had its subaltern to look after it, too. This, as you can see at once, would never do. So, as a tentative experiment, a Blanket Officer was introduced: and drafts were forbidden to entrain until they had previously drawn a blanket per man from him. This worked well for a time: because there are usually ten to fifteen drafts on a train, and they all had to wait their turn to file past the Blanket Officer. Additional advantages were (1.) the Bl.O. was detailed fresh daily from one or other of the depots, and invariably arrived down in a state of the blissful ignorance of his duties. (2.) Army blankets are issued in bales of 10, and the breaking up the bales to equip drafts exactly created a pleasing diversion. (3) There were no platforms on most French stations; consequently, the huge dump of 1000 or so blankets had to be piled up in the [. . .] way, and it was always possible to arrange for the arrival of a train on that particular line of rails, necessitating the complete suspension of all business while the pile was hastily torn down and erected elsewhere out of harm's way.

Finding this operation was not a gigantic success, the Circumlocution

Department went into committee again and announced their next 'turn', the Entraining Officer. This was enormously popular, as all three R.T.O's could now live simultaneously and continuously in the canteen, while the Entraining Officer broke into the office, searched through the papers till he discovered something about trains (usually slipped into the current 'Vie Parisienne'[9]) imparted the contents to the expectant draft-conductors, whom he then led off to the nearest train, and, after writing cabalistically in chalk all over the carriages, ushered them 'by fifties and fifties' into it. This being done, it only remained for the R.T.O. to unleash the panting engine driver, and all was well. (The creation, however of an Unleashing Officer is momentarily expected.)

The night before last I was awakened at about 12.30 a.m. by an orderly with a chit. I lit a candle and read 'You are detailed to superintend the entraining of troops at 9.30 a.m. to-morrow. You will report here on completion of duty.' (This lest, becoming absorbed in the work, I might inadvertently entrain myself with blanket complete – and proceed to join some unsuspecting division at the front.)

Accordingly, I rose somewhat earlier than yesterday, and took a train to the station [. . .]. I saw a score of draft-conducting officers surging round the R.T.O's office, waving buff forms, and about 1 million men grouped picturesquely in the background. Having some slight experience of the job (a fact doubtless overlooked by the orderly-room when selecting me) I entered stealthily by the back way, and found the R.T.O's clerk reading a paper by the fire. He consented grudgingly to furnish me with some details of the train-surface for the day. I then collected a pencil & paper, and commanded the portals to be flung wide. A small and spectacled 2nd-Lieutenant, very breathless and crumpled was instantly shot like a pea from a pea-shooter. He picked himself up, saluted most flatteringly, and intimated that he had 46 Argylls, 23 Gordons, 17 Black Watch, and 20 Seaforths, (producing documentary evidence of it all) and what was I going to do about it. I despatched him to the Blanket Officer . . .

Others followed – all 2nd Lieuts. and all originally inexperienced. A sample conversation will represent them all:-

2nd LT (reciting his little piece) '35 Lincolns, 18 Staffs, 22 Bedfords, 14 Northants'

MYSELF 'All Umpty-first Division, your train goes at 9.45 on the 2nd line from here. Have [you any] rations?'

2nd LT 'No, ought I to?'

MYSELF (patiently). 'You must [. . .] take on the train [. . .] the

Detail Issue Stores [. . .]. 20 men will do it for them, and don't forget to get a signed slip from the issuing N.C.O. Have you got your blankets?'

2nd LT 'No. Where can I get them? How many do I want?'

MYSELF (wearily). 'Find the Blanket Officer, draw 110 blankets from him, and issue one to each man. Have you had your breakfast?'

2nd LT 'Not yet, no.' (Explains at length why not: early start, things to be done at last moment, etc.)

MYSELF 'Better get something at the canteen here, they'll give you X and sausages and coffee – it'll be a long time before you get anything else. When you've drawn your rations & blankets, I'll have your trucks chalked for you. When you have your men safely in, come to me for your movement-order.' (Army equivalent of railway-ticket.)

2nd LT (with visions of a good morning's work in front of him). 'What time did you say the train was due to start?'

MYSELF '9.45; so I should try to get the majority of your men in by about 10.30 if I were you.'

(Exit a rather muddled and mystified subaltern to endeavour to draw rations, issue blankets, feed himself, and entrain his men (in a carriage marked 'Chinese Labour only') simultaneously. In which praiseworthy attempt he is fortunately foiled by a watchful Military Policeman.)

After disposing of the last officer, I collated the totals on their buff slips. There were 1188 men to go. At 36 to a truck this means 33 trucks, with two men over. They can ride on the roof, or the footboard, or something. I take a lump of chalk and go out to the nearest train. There are 100 men for the xth Div. so I mark the first 2 trucks 'x' and the 3rd '28 X, 8 Y' and so on, till an R.T.O. materialises from nowhere, watches me in silence for a while, and then informs me kindly that this train is a 'returned empty' and doesn't go anywhere. In return, I inform him of some hitherto unsuspected details of his ancestry, and begin again on another train about 2 lines away. Then Wilfrid and Herbert lend a hand.

Wilfrid and Herbert are respectively, the chef and sous-chef de gare. They control the French part of the traffic (including the guard and engine-driver of our own troop-train) and may be known by their partiality for dirty blue jeans and tin horns. Also by their unanimous and complete ignorance of the English tongue. (As the highly complicated operation of despatching seven or eight thousand troops daily is entirely dependent on their slightest whim this point has the straw backs.) They now proceed to do the first of their never-failing turns.

I have said that there are no platforms on our station. There are, however, 19 sets of parallel lines. The train I am concerned with is standing at No. 4. It is obvious then that the long suffering soldiery must carry all their rations, in bulk (and 3 days rations for 1200 men is some bulk), all their blankets, all their equipment, and finally themselves across the first 3 lines. This they are now in process of doing – sixty score men struggling at random all over the yard.

This is the cue for Wilfrid and Herbert, and they come out of their office, armed with flags and tin horns. Wilfrid begins: he advances among the soldiery and makes a noise like an offensive. 'En voiture! (toot-toot) En voitu-u-ure, tout le monde!! (toot-toot) Le train part tout suite! Depêchez, depêchez – En voiture [. . .] là – vite, vite, vite!'[10] – and so on. (Tin horn obligats, and gesticulation.)

The sight of Wilfrid doing his song and dance naturally causes a panic among the troops. Laggard D.C.O's hurriedly seize their parcels, the canteen vomits a throng of revellers, fatigue parties, staggering under crates of biscuits and cheese, hasten their tottering steps and the whole multitude surges across the lines.

Meanwhile Herbert has produced from nowhere an exceedingly fine specimen of the French goods-train, measuring about half-a-mile from tip to tip. Seating himself upon the front buffers of the engine, without jubilant fanfare on his tin horn, he brings this into action at the psychological moment – on No. 2 line!

The multitude is cleft in two. On one side are about 500 men, who have got safely across, and Wilfrid now making noises of extreme panic creating the impression that our train is about to depart [. . .] in three seconds.

On the other are 700 frenzied men [. . .]. Between is Herbert, idly rolling his immense train past at the rate of about half-a-kilometre per hour – the wheels just perceptibly moving. Tableau!

Wilfrid gibbers at Herbert. Herbert, as he is carried past, jabbers gleefully from his perch on the engine at Wilfred. The two masses of soldiery uplift their voices to each other across the barrier. The engine-driver emits a Satanic screech from his whistle. And the train continues to drag its slow length along.

15 minutes elapse. The rear of the train comes reluctantly into view. Burdens are picked up again, and we prepare to resume the crossing. The train stops dead . . .

We endeavour to carry on, by clambering through the carriages and hoisting the luggage after us. For about two minutes this arduous labour precedes unchecked. Then there is another mocking screech from the far distance (the engine is long since out of sight), a banging and jolting of couplings, and the train is in motion again – backwards! And we have to sit down again and watch the whole infernal string pass us for the second time . . .

The second turn is something of an anticlimax after this. It merely consists in seeing the last man in the train, forbidding anyone to get out as the train is now about to start at last, and then going instantaneously away and leaving the train to stew in its own juice for anything from ten to 40 minutes.

The 2/Lieut. is no longer mystified as to why he was told to have his men in by 10.30 when the train was due out at 9.45.

And that's my work at present: it's easy to be frivolous about it . . . [. . . .]

Chapter 15

'Keeping on keeping on':
The 2nd Leinsters, May 1918

The Spring Offensive had stalled in early April and though German forces made further ground in the Lys offensive from 9 April they sustained heavy casualties and their advance had halted by the end of April. The 2/Leinsters' month was spent behind the lines until 27 April when they were back at the front at Vieux-Berquin close to Hazebrouck. By this time they had been joined by a draft of most of the officers and 281 men of the 6/Connaughts, whose battalion was effectively wound up on 13 April. Meanwhile, the 2/Leinsters were transferred to 88 Brigade in the 29th Division on 23 April. Enough of a badly damaged letter of 30 April has survived to tell us that Staniforth was on his way to the 2/Leinsters by then, but little else. Joining the battalion on 2 May, Staniforth acted as Adjutant in his first stint with them, until 10 May when his predecessor, Captain A.H. Whitehead, resumed duties having returned from hospital.

Vieux-Berquin, 2 May 1918, 8.30pm
Left Corps Reinforcement Camp 12.30 this morning, and marched with a draft about 11 miles to here to report to our new battalion. Very dusty and hot. Very pleasant to be in this part of the country again, after the devastated areas of the Somme. It is like marching through your country at Hinderwell: green fields with cattle in them, hedges full of birds, rutty little country lanes that twist up and down between high banks, and villages with little shops in them. The men picked cowslips and stuck them in their caps.

We are encamped in a field full of daisies, at the top of a little hill over-looking a village. The battalion transport is in the village, and we shall rejoin it to-morrow morning. Eastward the war is very close; flash and crash follow each other incessantly. It seems so curious to have this war in peaceful countryside, without any of the familiar accessories of approaches to the trenches, shelled areas behind the lines and so on. I wonder if they felt like that in 1914. It seems somehow like giving a performance of a familiar opera in suddenly strange surroundings, with none of the usual scenery or props.

I'm writing this at the door of my tent, and now it's too dark to see the words any more. Goodnight.

Friday, May 3rd. One of the things – two of them, rather – that sometimes fill me with envy of the people with jobs at the Base are, firstly, the sense of permanence which enables one to say, 'I shall be here this day month.' and to make arrangements accordingly; and secondly, the sense of freedom implicit in having no men to consider. I fancy every infantry officer gives way to these two grouses occasionally. Never since I came to France have I known definitely that the lapse of four weeks would find me still in the same place – and not often the lapse of one. And there are times when all my life seems to have been spent in dragging bodies of men blindly round the country in search of somebody or something. Bless them – but they take years off one's life.

On coming into camp yesterday we were informed that guides and wagons (for the men's kits and rations) would be sent separately for each unit in the morning. Sure enough, they turned up about 10.30 – for every regiment represented in the draft except the P.B.L.'s.[1] Nobody knew anything about us, and nobody wanted to know. So after waiting about in an empty camp till noon I walked down into the village, dug up the Area Commandant, and found out from him where the 2nd Battalion of the Leinsters was. He showed me one billet on his map marked 'L.R.'[2] about a mile and a half away. So I walked back to the camp, detached one man to guard the rations and told him I would send a limber back from the battalion for him, and took the others along with me. Arrived at the billet about one o'clock. It certainly was occupied by our regiment, so that was O.K. But only by a handful of them, known as 'surplus personnel' and left out of the trenches with a couple of officers. The battalion transport lines were about three kilometres further on. It was a very hot and chokingly dusty day, so I decided against taking the men any further (there might be no accommodation for them at the transport lines, and then they would only have to come back here again), but billeted them pro tem. in an adjacent barn and cadged some dinner for them. Then I took one man with me and went on to the transport lines. Got there about 3. Found the orderly room (this battalion maintains its administrative headquarters *out* of the trenches), but no officers. Apparently they were all away at a court-martial: the C.O., the Q.M., the Transport Officer and all. So I found the transport sergeant and told him to get a limber at once, and send it back in charge of my one guide to collect the derelict rations and take them on to the men who were waiting for them. Then I sat down to wait for the Colonel's return and report myself.

I waited for four hours, and felt very miserable. You know how I hate making new friends and starting afresh anywhere; and sitting alone in a tiny bare room watching the shadows lengthen while I waited to take the plunge into a new life wasn't just the cheeriest way of starting. More like being kept waiting a very long time in a dentist's parlour.

However, the C.O. came in at last, and shook hands, and we sat down to dinner. He is 39, very soldierly-looking, brisk and energetic, and occasionally nervously unreasonable. Some people dislike him, but I can't say I did. He is also an Old Carthusian (1892 vintage). Name, H.W. Weldon; the brother of old Sir Anthony, who commanded the 4th until his death last year. He told me he wanted me to take over command of C Coy, whose skipper was killed last Saturday. He asked me various questions as to service, experience, etc., and on the whole was quite a good sort, if a bit curt. I don't know yet what he will be like to serve under. Shortly after 9 o'clock I left, and started to walk back to the 'surplus' camp, to pass the night there and go up to the line to-morrow.

For your information (but don't put it on your letters) we are in the 29th Division, 88th Brigade, and our Brigadier is the famous Freyberg, V.C.,[3] so we are in good hands.

Turned in about 10.30, very tired. Goodnight.

Saturday, May 4th. Lay in bed till 9 this morning, and got up very refreshed. Had a cold bath in the sun outside the tent, and put on a complete change, which always raises the morale. Packed what I wanted for the line, and despatched the rest over to the Q.M. stores for deposit. [. . .]

Vieux-Berquin, 4 May 1918, 1am

We set off from 'surplus personnel' camp at 7 this evening (no, yesterday evening), and after a long walk not wholly devoid of incident made port about half-an-hour after midnight. The artillery activity round all these areas is incessant night and day. The night was close and muggy, and we all had heavy kits, but we skipped along the last two kilos like two-year-olds. No stragglers, believe me. The world-weary ones who long for a new sensation should try escorting 70 men they don't know along a road they don't know to a destination they don't know on a dark night under shell-fire. And just to show you how perverse my guardian angel is, the whole of my Company-to-be happens to be out on a working-party tonight, officers and all, and won't be in till daylight (three hours yet).

The new company commander, arriving jaded at midnight to his new command with threescore men, finds only the duty signaller to welcome him. What a picture.

Meanwhile – query, where are the men's billets? Are there any rations for them? May they show lights here at night? What do they do in case of alarm? Should there be guards posted? If so, where and what strength? Which are the dangerous spots? Where are the latrines? Are we under enemy observation or not? Where is the O.C.'s billet? . . . And Echo answers, 'Search me.'

This war is getting beyond a joke.

1.10 a.m. The signaller has just informed me chattily that three men were knocked out at the corner of the road this afternoon. Cheery bird.

We have been stripped of the good old Leinster maple-leaves[4] at last. I enclose them herewith, not without a pang. Take care of them; we carried them over many a bloody field, not altogether dishonourably. Instead, we now sport on either arm a loud scarlet triangle, recalling the familiar sign that decorates a pint of Bass all over the civilised world – but a trifle flatter than the original, as is only appropriate in these days of Government swipes. Inset is a drawing, made at great expense by our special artist and guaranteed accurate in every detail.

I heard a new term for the shrapnel helmet to-day from that cynical humourist Thomas Atkins.[5] He now speaks of it sardonically as his 'battle bowler;' or, in the manner of the vocabulary of the Ordnance Stores, as 'Bowlers, battle, one.'

We are now living in a house. Possibly this does not strike you as extra-ordinary. But when I add that the house is in all respects exactly as it was left by the retreating inhabitants a week or two ago, you will see how unusual it is – for us. The grandfather clock in the kitchen corner is still ticking and chiming; the brasses on the chimneypiece have not lost the lustre of the last polishing; we have not yet eaten all the food stored in the larder. All is ours – to loot if we wish. Curious.

1.30 a.m. To add to the cheerfulness of my first-night welcome, the d[amne]d battalion in front of us is now going over on a 'trench raid' (minus the trenches), just to stir up Brer Hun.[6] Our artillery (and there are as many guns here as there were at Ypres; guns in every lane, ditch, field, copse, and farmyard; including two 6-gun batteries within 100 yards of me as I write) is making night hellish with a top-speed barrage; the windows of this room leap and rattle, and I can hardly hear myself think.

Seems odd to be sitting here talking to you in a perfectly civilised room

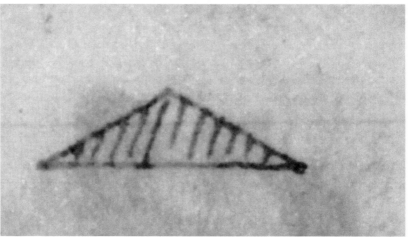

Staniforth's forest green maple leaves and his sketch of the scarlet triangle which replaced them.

while all hell is raging outside and many a Boche is (I hope) meeting his fate scarcely a thousand yards away even as I write these words.

1.40 Boche retaliation now commencing. Our quiet little village street distinctly noisy at the moment. Wonder if we got many prisoners.

When this racket dies down – as it will soon, when the raiders have returned and the situation eases off – I'll knock off this and try to doze a little till the company returns. Signaller tells me you're not supposed to sleep at night here, only in the daytime. All very fine, but he's had his day's sleep and we haven't. Still, I don't feel a bit strong even after a sixteen-kilometre walk in full kit and much mental wear and tear. Overstrain, probably.

1.45 Situation still apparently tense. Guns hammering away like mad things. Hope it is a good killing. Query: shouldn't I look fine if the Boche followed up our returning raiders and did a little show in his turn! Am, figuratively as well as literally, absolutely in the dark; don't know where I am, or where my company is, or where anything or anybody is. Must instruct all hands to light enormous camp-fires, broadcast, and make a noise like an Army Corps in bivouac, I think.

1.49 Gunning slackening a shade. Good egg. I think I'll knock off these incoherent jottings and have forty winks. I suppose you're both sleeping peacefully. I can see every inch of your room in my mind's eye, down to the latest bunch of seven pennies on the bedside table. Heigh-ho, what a world it is. Sleep sound.

Sunday, May 5th (as indeed the foregoing ought also to have been dated, since it was after midnight last night), *2.30 p.m.* Company returned at 3.30 last night, and I met my subalterns and we had some supper. After that it was time for morning stand-to, and we went and stood in a gloomy farce of a trench 1 ft. deep at the bottom of the back garden until 5.15. Then we came in again and had breakfast, and I lay down from 6.30 till 8. Washed and shaved then, and bucked into the company-business with Holden,[7] from whom I take over.

Raining then, but has cleared up and come out warm and sunny now. Brings out the trees and flowers nicely – also the gunners and aviators. This place has rather a reputation for gas-shells, but so far we haven't had any. In fact the old Hun has been fairly quietish this morning, except for some 4.9's crumping into Merris now and again. [. . .]

Vieux-Berquin, 6 May 1918, 4.30pm
Still keeping on keeping on. Had a bit of an alarm about 3 o' clock last night, when enemy shelling set the next-door cottage on fire, but all ended well.

Heavy thunderstorms yesterday evening made trenches in ploughland *'no bon.'* Picked up half a ton of sticky clods on boots at every step. If you dig one foot below the surface here, you strike water at once, and the deluges which fell yesterday have added to the supply.

Cottage opposite this on the other side of the street is occupied by the R.A.M.C. as relay aid-post. It has a high thatched gable-roof. RAM Corps came out this morning and found that one of Fritz's shells last night had passed clean through the roof from front to back, leaving a neat round hole in the straw thatch. Being non-combatants, decided this was good enough notice to quit, and are moving on elsewhere to-day. But curious how shell didn't detonate on its way through the gable. Perhaps it was a dud anyway, and didn't detonate at all.

Haven't seen a paper since I was at the Corps Reinforcement Camp, and then it was two days old. Wonder if anything is happening in the real world.

1 a.m. Just returned from working-party with whole company, beginning 8.30 p.m. The profession of arms is noble and splendid. We filed up in the dark to an irrigation drain behind the front line, and splashed about in it like mudlarks for four hours to an accompaniment of star-shells, stray bullets, profanity, and a beautiful effluvium from the disturbed drain itself. We left it finally, two feet wider and a lot smellier, and came home to change our wet boots. Doubtless it cements the Entente for us to repair the sewers of the French for nothing. But if we are told to occupy it as a fire-trench tomorrow (of which I have the strongest suspicions), the Entente will come unstuck again.

Home again in the rain, to a fire, tea, and bread-and-butter. Compensations, after all. There will be time for a couple of hours sleep before stand-to.

4.15 a.m. Stand-to, and a dull morning spitting with rain. The Hun has set a farm on fire about a mile away; it looks a cheerful, warm blaze as we stand and shiver in the sodden daybreak. Stood-down at the earliest decent moment, and back to breakfast.

5.15p.m. Nothing of interest all day. Sun came out this morning, and the day has been hot and steaming with muggy mists. All this country is terribly waterlogged. Got your letter dated May 1st, re-directed from Calais. That ought to be the last of yours addressed to 'L' I.B.D., as you must have heard by now that I am at the war again.

Am very hot on salving foodstuffs now. Almost every cottage in this village has its attic or outhouse with a store of peas, potatoes, wheat, bran, flour and so on. And there are lots of swede-stacks in the fields. We collect it all and send it back to Salvage in the ration-limbers every night.

I'm sorry for Clayton[8] – but at least he's out of it. That's a lot to be thankful for, you know. Of course one wouldn't do anything deliberately to get sent home, but I couldn't help being glad if one were decently out of it for good. After the war I shall take a house for 99 years and sleep in the same bed in the same room every night and change all my clothes three times a day and never never go out digging o' nights.

We have three subalterns in the company now, all boys with one pip and all good boys. Holden is the senior, and was running the show till I came, since the last skipper was killed. Good stuff, but washes with his shirt on – you know. Father probably a top-class tradesman, or perhaps in an office somewhere. Next comes Mallins[9], our stylist, a regular Line commission, good family and education and all that, not yet 21, and rather prides himself on the elegance of his repartee. Not up to handling men yet, but high ideals, I fancy, in a quiet way; and not so blasé or affected as he'd like us to think. Lastly Chapman,[10] son of a printer in Eastcheap, a dear, honest soul, as willing as possible and as open as the day. One ambition: to go to Cambridge after the war. Don't know why Cambridge; should think he once knew a man who'd been to Cambridge, and it stands for his ideals – as Cheltenham used to do for you. It's difficult to tell him it wouldn't benefit either the University or himself, because he's old enough to have acquired the Eastcheap manner ineradicably, and he only wants the business education which of course Cambridge will never give him. Leeds or Birmingham is his mark, not a place where he'll go up thirsting for facts and knowledge and be given an elegant stone.

Salved 7.5.1918

	Beans	Bran	Flour	Oats	Potatoes	Wheat	Coals
Sacks	3½	5	4	20	13½	3	4

and one sack of Sulphate of Ammonia fertiliser
Not bad for C Company's day's work

Vieux Berquin, 8 May 1918, 5.45pm
Very little news to-day. We went out on the usual working-party last night. Our guns put down a barrage on a short section of the Boche front at about 10 o'clock, and we felt rather nervous that he might retaliate (we were working out in the open, only a few hundred yards behind the front line) but he didn't. One of his shells set a farm on fire which lit up the neighbourhood – including ourselves – rather too brilliantly for comfort. We got in early last night, and were all back in quarters by midnight. One fellow fell in a stream in the dark coming back. He sent his clothes to the cooks to dry and appeared in a weird rig belonging to the French people who had left his billets, crowning the effect with a scarred old top-hat. I had to laugh at him.

Tried to snatch a few hours' sleep before morning stand-to, but was awakened at 3 by a violent increase in the artillery fire. Reached for my tin hat and went out into the streets. All guns were firing top speed, and a lot of stuff coming back from Fritz's side. Was very puzzled as to whether we ought to turn out and man battle-positions or not. However, I listened hard and although the bombardment showed no signs of decrease I couldn't detect the small-arms fire which would certainly have been heard if there was an imminent attack, so I took a chance and let the men sleep on. Stayed up for about an hour and then things eased off a bit and I went back and turned out all hands for stand-to.

Bde. Gas Officer came round in the forenoon. (*NB.* 'morning' and 'forenoon' quite different: former from 4 to 8 a.m., when nobody is about except front-line folk; latter from 8 to lunch-time, when the rest of the world may also be seen). We had a jolly morning inspecting the Company's respirators together.

After lunch we went over to call on Jack Farrell, commanding B Coy in the next hamlet. They have a much better farm than ours. Borrowed as many radishes from his kitchen-garden as I could carry, and a bunch of pansies for our mess. Walked home over the fields to tea. You wouldn't know there was a war on, except for the guns. The land lay and basked in the sun – wide level stretches of crops and pasture, dotted with farms in thin little clumps of trees: rather like the view over to Hinderwell from Borrowby. The war hasn't had time to damage the landscape perceptibly yet.

Vieux-Berquin, 10 May 1918

Another quiet day, and nothing to report. Usual working party last night; arrived back shortly after midnight. A Boche plane was around dropping 5-lb bombs all over the shop; funny little cusses they are.

I was looking through some of the abandoned houses here, and came on one that roused my worst passions: an office-furniture store evidently. Fumed oak roll-top desks, cabinets of drawers and indexes, a beautiful little printing-press in the basement, evidently quite new, all shining steel levers and rollers, with complete founts of type mostly still unused. We found a few sheets of what had evidently been experiments with his new toy. The temptation to loot is a fearful thing. Try to imagine wandering about in Selfridge's, at liberty to take away anything you could carry, without anyone to ask for payment or even question you about it. It's the same thing here in a smaller way. I sympathise with the Crown Prince as never before. I simply had to pick up a few small things which screamed to be used in the Company office: an indexed spring-file for documents, and a wicker basket-tray for letters, and a small letter-rack. The three would probably have set me back half a Bradbury[12] at home.

The men are living like fighting-cocks. Potatoes, flour and turnips are there for the picking up, more than they could eat; and if they hunger, they slay a pig or a hen from the deserted homes; if they are cold, they go to the cellars for coals. Open warfare has its advantages.

The Hun put the wind up us last night by setting a near-by cottage on fire (there's always a house burning somewhere; they're mostly thatched, and he's for ever throwing his phosphorus incendiary shells about) and then flinging over 7,000 gas-shells to follow. No casualties, of course; but it does keep us humble.

I must stop, and censor some letters. They are funny; I wish you could read some of the unburdenings of Private Gavin, an honest soul who invariably concludes his laborious epistles to the wife of his bosom with 'God protect you from your lovin Husbin.' [. . .]

Vieux-Berquin, 11 May 1918
Have run altogether out of writing-paper [. . .] I went to the school-house to-day in the hope of finding some blank paper or exercise-books. It was rather pathetic; left just as they had abandoned it, except for one shell which had crashed through the roof and made a mess of some desks and a blackboard. I could have believed myself in Hubby's schoolroom at home: same rows of forms, same coloured charts on the walls of anatomy, botany, etc., even the same jam-pots on the window-sill with frog-spawn or seedlings maturing in them. Just one difference: two or three of the kiddies had left their wee gas-helmets still hanging on their pegs. The Hun must be very proud of himself . . .

I can't resist sending you one of the compositions I picked up; it rather catches me about the heart. Poor wee Hélène Verhie; I think of her solemnly going to the cemetery to see 'our dear deads,' or with all the world (*'surtout moi aussi'*[13]) to Mass to hear the curate preach of them. *'C'est bien sur,'* she philosophises sadly, *'qu'on ne les verra jamais plus.'*[14] And she, like everyone else, has someone *'mort sur le champ de bataille.'*[15] Poor mite; in spite of her profound wisdom she can still write *'j'ai pensez;'*[16] her grammar isn't up to her philosophy. I hope Hélène wasn't there when the shell came through the roof.

I glanced through the school ma'am's report-book. I couldn't love her, I'm afraid. Listen to this: – *'Duhamel, Emilie. 8 ans. Très mauvaise carac-tère. Fort peu intelligente.'*[17] One sympathises with eight-year-old Emilie in spite of her load of crime. And again:- *'Dubenthal, Meurice. 9 ans. Excellent petit garcon. Pas une absence pendant l'année entière.'*[18] He must have been an awful little stinker, don't you think? – the sort of kid that waits to walk home hand-in-hand with teacher, or brings her a bunch of flowers at morning school. [. . .]

I could go on all night picturing these vanished schoolchildren. There is a scribble chalked on the wall, scarcely four feet from the ground, *'Paul aime Melanie.'*[19] And another hand (I hope not Melanie's) has added contemptuously, *'Paul est un sot.'*[20] I wonder if he saw it, and crept shyly away — or went out and socked the writer in the eye.

Grand Hasard, 18 May 1918

We came out of the line on the 14th, and have been having a grand time here for the last four days. It's a hut-camp, about seven thousand yards behind the line, with baths in it. You can turn out at 6.30 on a glorious May morning (we've had top-hole weather) and walk straight into a shower-bath, hot or cold, and start the day as fresh as a daisy. Every other day we have had to find big working parties up to the line (A and B Companies to-day, C and D to-morrow, and so on), but on the odd days in between one can get the whole company out on parade to play with and that's almost an unknown thing out here, as anyone can tell you.

I'm getting to know the company quite well now. We won the prize for the cleanest field-kitchen yesterday, and had less rifles for overhaul at the armourer's inspection to-day than any other company, so we're not doing too badly. (Also we had more cases of defaulters at the C.O.'s orderly-room, but we don't mention that!)

It was great to come out of the line on Tuesday. One appreciates it much more with a company than at Bn. HQ. Already I'm beginning to look on Bn. HQ. as people with soft jobs, far behind the line!

We had a long walk out, very dark and across heavy country; it was two o'clock in the morning before we got here, and three before we had the men bedded down and fed. That was the first time I had had my clothes off since we came to the Reinforcement Camp I told you about, best part of a fortnight ago. So you can imagine what it's like to sleep eight hours a night in clean pyjamas, even if it's only for four days.

We knocked up some sports this afternoon, and beat the [4th] Worcesters soundly. Of course the Leinsters were always a fine sporting regiment. They held the Army tug-of-war championship for years before the war, both in India and at home. I made sixty francs out of Worcester officers, whose esprit de corps did them more credit than their judgement.

The post has been rotten; nothing for the last two days.

Billy is getting married on the 1st of June — did I tell you?

There's a Hun overhead now. There always is, these fine nights.

Vieux-Berquin , 20 May 1918, 6pm
– or rather, In the Wood. I feel like a combination of Robin Hood and
the Rosalind of 'As You Like It.' We are in a forest: a big forest full of
glades and clearings and rides and rabbits and pheasants and deer. The
contrast is very striking: the rustle of leaves all round, cuckoos, jays and
nightingales everywhere, and then the whistling flight of shells through
the trees – a new kind of bird that the 'forest primeval' has never known
before.

Come and see our 'Company Headquarters.' One of the biggest trees,
a huge gnarled oak with spreading roots, was chosen, and a shallow semi-
circular pit about eighteen inches deep and twelve feet across was dug
behind it. This was then roofed with sheets of corrugated galvanised iron
sloping up to the trunk of the tree, comme ça:–[21]

Its extreme height, where it reaches the tree-trunk, is four feet six; but
at the 'doorway' we are reduced to two feet of headroom. It is necessary,
when desirous of entering, to lie flat on the stomach, insert the head and
shoulders into the doorway, and then drag in the remainder by means of
abdominal wrigglings copied from the worm. Once within, turn smartly
over on to the back, and it will be found entirely possible to sit upright
(after previously removing the steel helmet). When the entire strength of
the mess (5 officers) is mustered, sardines are estranged and solitary creatures by comparison. Once inside, we replace the branches and greenery
over the door-hole (very necessary camouflage), light a candle, and sing:

'Under the greenwood tree,
Sing heigh-ho,the holly,
This life is most jolly.'

In passing, I may say that conducting office-work and correspondence horizontally in a rabbit-hole is a new sensation for the world-weary.

Among the disadvantages of the simple greenwood life, an easy first is the mosquito. The wood is a maze of paths and swamps, the sun is incredibly hot these days, no wind penetrates the leafy aisles, and so the mosquito comes into his own. From fingers to shoulders, and from forehead to chest, we are a mass of burning, stinging red lumps. Nothing will keep the little demons away.

Now come and visit our outposts. (Did I mention the company is on outpost duty?) You must wait for nightfall for this; a move in daylight anywhere would be fatal. Five minutes pushing through the dense undergrowth from company headquarters brings us to the fringe of the forest, and to fields and hedges. Creep along a hedge – the Boche is not so far away now. At the corner of the hedge you are suddenly challenged in a low voice, and a bayonet appears from nowhere at your chest. Look closely, and you will see the sentry; more closely, and you will see the rest of the post, crouching in a small slot of trench, silent as the grave, staring watchfully out.

Cross the field, move along the hedge, another low challenge, another group of still, vigilant men around a machine-gun, peering out through the hedge. Beyond them, out in the moonlit ground-mist, you can faintly discern moving figures: a working party, strengthening the barbed wire. Suddenly from that dark clump of trees two hundred yards away in the distance comes flash-flash-flash, and a burst of machine-gun bullets whistles past you. The wiring party drop flat . . . the sentry sinks to his knees behind the hedge . . . a moment's breathless pause . . . then, up again and carry on.

So it goes on, all through the night; everywhere the groups of silent men, straining their eyes into the night; everywhere the dark shapes of machine-guns, poking their muzzles out through hedges, around bushes, out of ditches with the still, watchful crews around them.

At dawn everyone drops silently into his little trench, pulls the branches over his head, and curls up to sleep motionless through the day. We get our dinner at 9.30 at night, and our breakfast at 3 in the morning; beyond that, nothing. Outpost duty is perhaps the most exhausting part of warfare.

All night long there is the menacing hum of enemy aeroplanes, high up among the stars; not a match, cigarette, or electric torch must be seen. Every now and then there is a quick gust of shells; sometimes tiny pip-squeaks, sometimes big crashing heavies, sometimes gas, that tear through the wood, splintering the trees and plunging into the under-growth. And all night long the nightingales sing full-throated among the leaves overhead, the bull-frogs croak in the pond, distant pheasants drum and whirr, and the moon silvers the glades and glistens on the dewy bushes. What a life.

Water is rather a trouble. One bottleful per man in the twenty-four hours for drinking, cooking and washing doesn't go far in this fierce heat. This afternoon we left a canvas bucket half-full in the shade outside the door of our palace (it was the remains of our ration), and a damned splinter from a Boche crump[22] made it a casualty about half-an-hour ago (just after I started this letter). Fortunately we spotted it leaking in time.

There's no chance of leave just now, of course; but they're sending me away on a machine-gun course to Le Touquet on the 4th. Proper embusqué I'm getting: two months in Calais, then a short month with the battalion, and then off again to Le Touquet for three weeks!

Must stop now. Damn these mosquitoes; I'm half-crazy with them.

Vieux-Berquin, 22 May 1918, 11.30am

Yesterday wasn't one of the Hundred Best Days. I told you that these posts can only be visited by night, and everything has to be covered up in the daytime. One of the posts is outside the wood, separated from it by a ditch full of stagnant water, about six feet wide and four feet deep. At night this is bridged by a duck-board, to allow communication with the post; but before daylight the plank is taken up and hidden in the bushes, so cutting off the post for the day.

I had been talking to the officer in charge of the post, last thing before leaving him for the day. I must have stayed too long, for it was almost daylight when I started back, and found the bridge up for the day and myself cut off from my own HQ in the wood. However, there was a young sapling lying across the ditch, and so I tried to balance myself and do a 'Blondin'[23] across it – with the inevitable result that I slipped in the middle and went souse into the water up to the waist. I waded across, and scrambled out dripping on the other side.

Well, in the line of course one only has the clothes one stands up in; no change of garments. So when I got back to our palace under the tree I could do nothing but take off everything, borrow a couple of overcoats, and lie down till the sun dried my things later on. Lying on the ground with no clothes on at four o'clock in the morning brings its own reward; I dozed for a couple of hours, and woke feeling like a poisoned pup. Rheumatism in every joint, abdominal muscles aching so that every breath or cough hurt, and as light-headed and tottery as a hospital patient getting up for the first time after six weeks in bed. Twopence would have bought me twice over.

When the sun got warm I crawled into a patch of it and lay there like a sick kitten all day. Couldn't eat anything; had to get Mallins to write my reports for me. Lord, I *did* feel cheap!

In the afternoon a chit arrived from battalion headquarters saying that the unit on our flank was making a raid at 11.30 that night. This meant re-arranging my patrols, cancelling a wiring-party, and arranging to withdraw the more exposed posts temporarily. So as soon as it grew dusk I got into my clothes again – quite dry now, except the boots which were as hard as purgatory – leaned heavily upon the arm of my faithful runner, and tottered feebly off like an old man of eighty.

After we had seen the first post and were going on to the second, the Hun took a notion to hate the track we were on, and for five minutes he kept us dodging and jumping in a manner becoming neither my age nor my habits. However, it was probably the best cure for my debility, though perhaps a trifle heroic. One minute I was crawling along in a paralysed sort of way; the next I was leppin' like a two-year-old. It shows how many of one's ailments are imaginary.

We got the posts withdrawn, and bundled them into a trench behind a hedge. Then the raid began, and down came Fritz's barrage hot and strong, right on the top of us. A trench raid isn't exactly the Battle of Ypres, of course, but a barrage is a barrage all the world over, and this one was a daisy. They came swishing into us like clockwork: pipsqueaks, heavies, gas, phosphorus – all the fun of the fair. I made myself as much like a decimal point as possible, and hoped the Boche would find out as soon as possible that it wasn't we who were doing him any harm, and transfer his attentions elsewhere.

In about two minutes I heard what I had been expecting: the old familiar cry of 'Stretcher-bearers!' I pushed along the trench and found a couple of men groaning on the ground; one with a splinter in his hip, the other with nineteen or twenty tiny scratches all over him. (The first case was a tough little scoundrel called O'Connell, who had been up before me for a drunk while we were resting the other day; I was chatting to him while we patched him up and happened to ask him if this was his first wound. He was hugely indignant; it was his fourth! I apologized profoundly.)

That was a bad beginning: two casualties in as many minutes. But after that the luck turned, and although it was fifteen minutes before Fritz slackened at all, and another fifteen before he finally eased off and took to machine-gunning instead (which was quite harmless to us in the trench), we never had another.

When things were quiet again we came out of our hidey-hole, re-occupied our posts, and got busy wiring again. The whole wood was rotten with gas and the brimstone stench of H.E., and there were many 'dark strangers' (new shell-holes) everywhere. We wired till three in the morning when it began to get light, and then came back to my rat-hole under the tree and turned in till seven o'clock. Woke as fit as a fiddle, and ate a breakfast as big as a house. Did a few physical jerks to get the stiffness out, and when I've finished this letter shall sleep again for a bit if the mosquitoes will allow. Hands and arms are like a smallpox patient's, pitted with little old red scars and scabs and hard red new lumps. However, we shall be out of this again in a day or two now.

I don't suppose you could get hold of some lemonade powder or crystals or something like that for me, could you? The demand for lime-juice and lemonade this hot weather is too big for the supply, and we front-line people who only get to the canteen at rare intervals never have a chance; it's all bought up by the 'harmless soldiers' in the back billets. If you could, I should be very grateful.

Morbecque, 24 May 1918
Out again for a spell, and very glad, although it's a filthy wet day. The fine weather has broken at last, and we're in canvas bivouacs.

I'm writing this in bed, so forgive scribble. I got a bellyful of gas yesterday. Fritz drenched the forest with it, and it was everywhere. I made an awful idiot of myself, too. When the regiment came up to relieve us I was lying in our dug-out coughing and choking, and could only croak at them in a palsied sort of whisper. Then I started to show them round our posts, hobbling round on my orderly's shoulder. 'This' (cough, cough) 'is No. 6' (pant, pant, pant) 'post' – that sort of thing, like an asthmatic old man of eighty. However, that was all right; gassed folk are common enough nowadays, and no one thought anything of it. But then one of their officers asked me some commonplace question about something, and all at once my face screwed up like a baby's, my lip quivered, and I dissolved in floods of tears! Before I knew what I was doing, I found myself sobbing great helpless sobs like a child, and the tears running off my chin end.

Inside I was calling myself every kind of dam[n] fool God ever breathed life into, but I couldn't stop. After that I had to be led gently home like a baby.

I sent the company out as soon as they had been relieved, and the sergeant-major and my orderly said they would stay and help me out. I don't know how they did it; all I remember is hobbling along, choking and strangling, between them; sitting down to rest every five minutes; and weeping idiotically if anyone spoke to me. The path out leads past several heavy batteries of ours, and I remember crying piteously and imploring them not to go round that way, and hiding my face and cowering when the bangs came. Oh, it was a very degrading exhibition.

We made camp at about four this morning, and I went straight to bed, reported sick as soon as I woke (about 10.30), and here I've been all day. I'm as fit as a fiddle now, after a decent sleep, but I'm taking a day's laze.

There's no news. We're making great preparations for Der Tag[24] tomorrow. Perhaps we'll be in the thick of it when you get this. And perhaps not.

Chapter 16

'A "blighty one" at last!'
Gassed, May to June 1918

On 30 May 1918, the Staniforths received a telegram from the War Office:

Regret inform you that Capt. J.H.M. Staniforth Leinster Regt reported twentyninth May admitted Fifth Red Cross Hospital Wimereux suffering from the effects of gas severe.

The sight of a telegram being delivered would have shocked them, but once they had opened it, the above would have been better news than they might have feared.

Staniforth had been admitted because of the 'bellyful of gas' he'd written about on 23 May. He seemed to have coped with the initial effects enough to stay with the battalion but, as his next letter records, his health took a turn for the worse and by the next time he could write he was in a Casualty Clearing

Station at Watten, about five miles north of St. Omer, before being transferred to a hospital in London. His letters home, initially from no. 64 Casualty Clearing Station at Watten, offer a detailed account of the symptoms and treatment of victims of gas.

Watten, 26 May 1918
- and no one more surprised at the address than myself. My last letter to you was on Friday, when I was taking a 24-hour 'easy' after coming out of the line. On Saturday morning the M.O. looked into my tent again and asked how I was. I didn't think there was anything wrong with me that a day's rest wouldn't put right, and said so. However, he insisted on taking my temperature, and the merc[ury] climbed up to 103, so that tore it. Tried to get up, and found I couldn't; and the next thing I knew I was on my back on a stretcher (never been there before; it's a queer sensation), and in a Red Cross ambulance. Then I was hawked round the country from Field Ambulance to Divisional Rest Station, and thence to Casualty Clearing Station here; about a thirty-kilometre drive. This is a special hospital for gas cases, staffed by specialists: awfully good sorts. Mine punched a great hole in my right ear as a means of introducing himself, took a sample of blood, tested the blood-pressure in my right arm with a sort of inflatable elastic stocking, clapped a dollop of castor oil into me, and departed. Very up-to-date and cheery.

So here I am. If it wasn't necessary to breathe, I'd be all right. I have found the only position in which it is possible at all: like this:-

So they have propped me up with bed-rests and things, and there I sit all day and night, and cough like a sick monkey and pant like a Douglas two-stroke engine, 100 revs to the minute. A grotesque state for a man made in God's image, isn't it?

Capt. Ramsay told me that 'emotionalism', as he tactfully called it, was an invariable symptom of this particular gas (which it appears is DICHLORETHYLARSINE – well, I couldn't stand against that, could I!), so I needn't reproach myself for my recent breakdowns.

Now I've told you the absolute worst of the picture, so don't go imagining horrors. The pain in my lungs will pass away in a day or two, and I shall probably be back with the battalion inside ten days. (I shall not wear a wound-stripe for this.) Meantime I'm drinking tubsfull of lime-juice (that's all I can billet in the 'present disturbed state of the interior'), and though I can't talk which is perhaps a good thing nor breathe (which'll teach me to appreciate it when I can) for the present, there's not the slightest scrap of a reason for you to worry about anything. I'm expecting to be convalescent before you get this.

This is a big marquee-hospital about fifteen kilometres from Calais, within a stone's throw of the place where I got a job for a bit after the Ypres fight last year. All sunny and peaceful. No chance of a 'blighty,' of course; it's the specialist gas-hospital for the whole B.E.F. and the ultimate destination for gas-cases. Nothing beyond it. Rotten luck.

The pains I had after falling into the beck were gas pains, not rheumatics as I thought. The whole forest was rotten with gas.

Later. Orders just arrived for me to be 'evacuated lying to base.' Capt. Ramsay says I shan't be fit to return to duty for at least a month or six weeks. They must really be thinking I'm an interesting case!

Watten, 28 May 1918
No fixed date for our evacuation yet, but as it's six days since they had one it can't be long. Meanwhile I'm much better, and am allowed to smoke to-day, even encouraged and presented with free Stramonium cigarettes. [. . .] They taste like dead cods' heads. However, they do ease the breathing a lot.

Capt. Ramsay told me this morning he had orders that all patients not likely to be fit for seven days were to be sent down the line; so that looks like anticipating a rush. But the point is:- if they're clearing out the C.C.S.' s, they may be clearing out the Base Hospital as well, and then . . . well, then the next step would be arriving one fine night at Charing Cross or Victoria station; who knows? It's the slenderest Chinaman's chance, but as things are at the moment it's just within the bare bounds of the possible.

The following particulars are from my official tally, so you'll see there's no reason to worry.

Name, Age, Unit, etc.	. . . (duly filled in) . . . ..
Diagnosis:	Gassed (shell): Dichlorethylarsine
Conjunctivitis:	Slight
Laryngitis:	Slight
Cyanosis:	Nil
Dyspnoea:	On slight exertion
Blood Pressure:	120 : 50
Temperature:	103
Blood:	All counts within normal limits
Religion:	C. of E. (I don't know why gas should have any effect on this)

Temperature chart has a rather curious appearance. On the 25th it was 103 (a.m.) and 101.4 (p.m.); on the 26th, 98.8 and 103.2; and to-day 97.6 both morning and evening. Pulse last night was 88, this morning 45. Not very consistent, what?

No more news. I suppose you'll have heard from the W.O. by this. Hope you're not worrying too much.

No.5 British Red Cross Hospital, Wimereux, Boulogne-sur-Mer, 29 May 1918
A day's march nearer . . . ! (I daren't say it, for fear the gods hear me.)

Yesterday Ramsay took a polygraph tracing of my heart. It's such a fascinating toy that at the risk of boring you I'm going to describe it. Imagine a machine like a tiny nickel phonograph, without a horn but carrying a bar attached to it like the outrigger of a canoe. From this bar go two rubber leads; one ends in a black rubber stethoscope–cup, the other in a thing resembling a wrist-watch with straps and dial. At the junction of each lead with the outrigger-bar there is adjusted a thin trembling sliver of steel, projecting back over the phonograph. Instead of a record, a roll of paper is inserted into the machine, exactly like a tape-machine in a club.[2]

The wrist-watch is fastened on my right wrist, the stethoscope is placed against my neck, and the phonograph wound up, started, and placed on the bedside table. One of the steel tremblers (which is inked, and pressed on the moving strip of paper) vibrates in accordance with the (arterial) pulse in my wrist; the other reproduces that in my neck, which comes from a vein. When the machine is shut off and the tape gathered up and examined, it shows three wavy lines: one made automatically by clock-work, called the time-register, showing an indentation every fifth of a second, the second reproducing the action of the auricles (as taken from the neck-pulse), and the bottom line tracing the action of the ventricles (from the wrist). So it presents a picture of the separate workings of the upper and lower parts of the heart, as well as their synchronisation with each other (by comparing them with the time-line at the top). I have a few inches of the tape, which I will show you some time.

At 2.30 the ambulance came for me, and I was rolled in a blanket, dumped on a stretcher, and driven off to ST. OMER, about 8 kilometres, in company with the rest of the evacuation. Here the patients from half-a-dozen neighbouring C.C.S.'s were also brought, to be picked up by the hospital train when it came through.

Like most big French railway-stations, there is a large stone *salle* which you enter direct from the square outside. On the floor of this they laid us all down. There are two entrances, one at each side of the *salle*, and the procedure reminded me of a game of dominoes. A stretcher would be brought in 'L' [left] and laid carefully down. Immediately another would appear 'R' [right], and be placed at the first one's feet. So they went on, matching body for body, till there were 350 of us neatly laid out in rows on the stone floor. The place had glass windows and a glass roof, and the sun poured down upon us, and if all the rest wanted a drink as badly as I did – and I expect they did – I'm sorry for them. There was one solitary poster on the wall, in the middle of a vast expanse of brown plaster, at which we all gazed dumbly. *'Ah! Quand supprimera-t-on l'alcool?'*[3] it demanded passionately, of what was probably the most unresponsive audience ever gathered together.

At last the train came in, and the dominoes started to unpack. They melted away from each side of me, and at last my turn came and I was hoisted into the air, out on to the platform, and into a hospital coach.

I've told you about hospital trains before, so we'll skip on until I arrived at this place. I'm afraid I made rather a sensational entry.

You see, there was a lot of delay about unloading the train, and when I did get into an ambulance at last it was vilely driven and horribly bumpy and went to two wrong hospitals on the way. So when I was finally dumped down in the entrance-hall here among doctors and sisters and things, I was coughing and choking rather badly, and it must have been fairly obvious what my diagnosis was, even if it hadn't been written on my tally and pinned to the blanket for anyone to see.

However, in spite of this a dear old bean had to bend over me and say winningly, 'And what is the matter with *you*? Is it gas?' Well, I wasn't feeling awfully cheery just then, and besides, that particular question had begun to irritate me. Everyone asked it, from the Field Ambulance downwards. So I opened my eyes and looked up at him. 'No, no, no,' I gasped weakly, 'I'm a midwifery case' – and collapsed. Tableau; though I couldn't see.

Later. M.O. just arrived. And he tells me he is going

TO SEND ME
OVERSEAS
TO
BLIGHTY
IN A DAY
OR
2
!!!

Wimereux, 30 May 1918

This is one of the privately endowed hospitals, lent and run by Lady Hadfield.[4] It is really an annexe or overflow of No. 14 General Hospital, which is just up the road. Probably it was a hotel before the war; looks like it, anyway.

I am in a room with three others, on the third floor. Reading from left to right, they would be described by Dr. Watson as 'No. 1. The Adventure of the Boy with the Blue Spectacles.' 'No. 2 The Adventure of the Major Who Limped.' 'No.3. The Adventure of the Synovitic Queenslander.' 'No. 4. The Adventure of the Gassed Gravelpusher (me).' The Boy with the Blue Spectacles and the Major Who Limps are already convalescents and out all day, so I don't see much of them. The Synovitic Queenslander arrived the same day as I did and has a knee which he contracted ragging up the line. He goes for little hobbles in the afternoon for an hour or two, and returns to bed. Lastly there is me, who may not even go for little hobbles, and so am left alone through the afternoon with a commanding view of the third-floor windows of the house opposite and the trolleys of passing tramcars.

On the window-sill of the house opposite (which is some sort of A.S.C. Headquarters) there is a fine cageful of singing canaries. I see them put out first thing, in the morning, by a brown-haired girl in WAAC uniform. She is assisted by a young corporal of the A.S.C. Thenceforward throughout the day I see the two heads bent over the table in the window. Occasionally they take a stand-easy and come to the window together to survey the street below. In the evening they lift in the canaries; she takes one end of the cage and he takes the other.

On the floor below them there is a little iron balcony projecting from the window, which I can just see if I sit up in bed. Now and again an elderly and pompous-looking A.S.C. colonel comes out and takes a breather on it. He lights a cigarette and stands Napoleonically with his arms folded, allowing the passing girls to look up from the street below and admire him. He is, I suppose, the boss of the couple on the floor above, and hasn't an idea what a good time they are having.

All this doesn't interest you a bit, does it? – but I'm only scribbling to pass the time, and there's nothing else to write about. I'm going to England as soon as ever I'm fit to travel (or at least as soon as the M.O. says so; I'm quite fit now), and until then I'm naturally not much interested in anything else.

Wimereux, 1 June 1918
Nothing whatever to write about; days very hot and long and uninteresting; temperature constant at 96.4 (queer it should keep so low) and pulse at 40; and still not even allowed to sit up in bed. Only four hours from London, and yet kept here day after day – wouldn't that make you wild?

The Major Who Limps has gone away this morning, and I am to be moved into his bed to-night, where I can see out into the street below all day; so that'll be something.

We're so close to London here that we can get to-day's papers to-day, and letters only take a single night to get across. After being separated by a six-day post, it makes you feel absolutely next door.

Boche was over last night, and the night before, but confined his activities to Boulogne and didn't touch us.

I wish you could write, but it wouldn't be any use; I shall be away from here before you get this – at least I hope so. I wrote to the regiment yesterday and asked them to forward any letters that might be waiting for me, but I don't even suppose I'll get those.

12 Ward, Ruskin Park 4th London General Hospital, Denmark Hill,
London, S.E., [No date]
A 'blighty one' at last! — and back in London in summertime; fancy.
Some people have all the luck, don't they?

I had a very comfortable journey, though tedious. Left Wimereux in
an ambulance at 9.45 yesterday morning, and was embarked at Boulogne
by 10.30. There we lay in our cots till 4 in the afternoon, when we sailed.
Arrived Dover 6.30, and was transferred into a hospital train, where we
lay for another three-and-a-half hours, finally pulling out at about 10 at
night. We went round by Sidcup and Gravesend, and reached Charing
Cross at 1.30 a.m. Unloading took an hour, and it was 2.30 before my
ambulance drove out of the station, and nearly 3.30 before I arrived here.

I think you know this house, Ruskin Park; so there's no need to describe
it. I sent a note round to Edie[5] this morning, but of course I haven't seen
her yet.

Preliminary investigation by the M.O. this morning at 10. There's
nothing wrong that time won't correct, but at present of course I'm bed-
ridden.

I don't know what the W.O. said when they first notified you. My tally
is marked 'Gassed – severe,' but if they told you that, don't pay any attention. There is no choice between the official descriptions 'Slight,' 'Severe'
and 'Dangerous;' and I was in rather a bad way just at first, so they probably didn't care to mark it 'Slight;' but of course that's all cleared up long
since now, and there's nothing 'severe' on earth wrong with me.

I'll tell you more when I get settled down. I've only been in the place
nine hours so far.

Ruskin Park, 5 June 1918
Twenty four hours in London have done me more good already than all
the gas-hospitals and special treatments in France. Just to lie here and
see the sunshine on the trees and hear the birds and know that London
is all round me – it's everything.

Edie and Myah[6] came to see me yesterday afternoon (as soon as ever
they knew I was here, bless them), and brought some exquisite flowers.
Edie said she was writing to you, so you'll have the assurance of an
independent witness that there's nothing to worry about. Short, sharp,
and soon over, that's my experience. Now I'm well on the road to convalescence, and feeling an awful fraud.

This is the M.O.'s entry on my case-sheet to-day, after he had
examined me:-

Diagnosis: Gassed –France –23/5/18 and subsequently.

History: Conjunctivitis, laryngitis, dyspnoea, and occasional rhonching.

Present condition: Pains in chest (right), shortness of breath on exertion; heart and chest, nil.

The 'shortness of breath on exertion' is the only complication that's delaying things now; and there we'll just have to wait till the heart pulls itself together again. But as I'm in bed all day, it's having every chance.

Just one story of some of our gallant allies[7] which may amuse you. As you know, they came in for one of Fritz's smacks up north about a month ago, and in accordance with their best traditions at once beat it smartly to the rear. So we sent a cyclist brigade at full speed to stop the rot. These rode up to a rendezvous behind the lines, dismounted, parked their cycles, and went forward on foot (pushing their way through the stream of west-bound fugitives), and were presently engaged with the advancing Hun. Meanwhile our brave allies, in their headlong westward course, came upon the rows of parked bicycles waiting by the roadside. With grateful cries of 'Caramba! What forethought! What considerateness! How excel-lent is the British staff-work!' they leapt upon the cycles and continued their flight for Calais, home, and beauty.

A scandalous story. Don't repeat it.

A yarn that has an instructive moral for the opponents of reprisals is the following, which I can vouch for.

At a certain town in France there is a Chinese Labour Company, whose compound adjoins a Prisoners-of-War Camp where about sixty Huns were interned. One night, less than a month ago, the nocturnal Gotha, while dropping its usual quota of bombs, happened to score a direct hit on the Labour Company's compound and knocked out seventeen Chinks. The remainder endured with Stoic fortitude, and said nothing to anybody. However, the next night they arose and girded up their loins, patiently hacked through the wire fence, and proceeded deliberately and with great thoroughness to cut the throat of every single Hun prisoner. This done, they returned in the same impassive silence to their own quar-ters and went back to bed — still without saying a word to anyone.

It is borne in upon me that there are things to be learnt from the Celestial mind.

Of course there was a frightful scandal, and several Chinks were shot, and the rest deported. Still, the good work was done.

Ruskin Park, 5 June 1918

[. . .] I've had shoals of letters since appearing in the 'Roll of Honour'(!), and am busy answering them. Otherwise there's no news; I'm just steadily convalescing.

[. . .] *Later.* M.O. just been round, and I'm to have a Medical Board to-morrow, which will recommend me for a Convalescent Home.

Ruskin Park, 9 June 1918

[. . .] I'm allowed up and around the ward in my dressing-gown now. I don't want anything better than just to lie in a long chair on the verandah with a pipe and watch the clear green spaces in the evening sky for an hour or two at sunset. Everything is absolutely hushed and still; the leaves on the trees don't even rustle, and there isn't a bird singing anywhere; just peace, perfect peace and a summer's evening – in England. And to know that I can sit there for exactly as long as I choose, without having to get up and do something or go somewhere, is more than half the joy. They let you do just exactly what you like here the whole day long: get up when you want, have a bath at any hour of the day, go back to bed or not as you please – nobody bothers you from morning to night. It's Nirvana: the perfect bliss of simply being let alone. Most of the day I do nothing but sit and watch the grass grow.

When I leave here I am to go to a Convalescent Home for three weeks or a month, and then have three weeks' leave. They let you choose your own Convalescent Home; I suppose Harrogate is about the nearest to you, unless there's one at Saltburn – is there, do you know? Or I might go to Windermere; I believe there's one there.

One of the patients in this ward had an amputation yesterday. It occurred to me for the first time to wonder, as I sat and watched the sunset, what they do with amputated arms and legs and things after the operation. Are they given to the cat, or what? I wondered for an hour, but came to no conclusion.

Mrs Mitchison's Hospital, 29 June 1918

This is an idyllic month, and my spirits are increasing in inverse proportion to my bank balance. Enid[8] and I spent an extremely jolly afternoon on the river yesterday, and returned to town for dinner. We went to a pothouse near Piccadilly Circus where I am on fairly good terms with the management, and managed to secure a mixed grill without coupons or cards of any sort, whereat I displayed pardonable pride and Enid was duly impressed. We garnished it with lobster salad and Pêche Melbas and coffee, and after a cigarette or two I motioned languidly to the waiter for the bill, put my hand in my pocket – and found I hadn't a bean! Absolutely Tableau; and 'Query: What should A do?' This, too, after creating a helluvan impression over my supper achievement.

I preserved a nonchalant sang-froid [. . .] and looked about me. Not a soul I knew; nothing but the wild, free notes of the stockbroker surprised while drinking soup, or the chorus-girl calling to her mate. How true it is, as Shakespeare or somebody has remarked, that it is just when everything in the garden looks lovely that Fate is waiting round the corner with the stuffed eel-skin.

However, I sent my card to the manager, and having familiarised myself with him in my ill-spent youth all was well. I borrowed a fiver off him and departed; not the stately exit I should have liked, but one rather recalling a scrambled egg slipping off a bit of toast.

Moral: make to yourselves friends of the mammon of unrighteousness, in the shape of restaurateurs, when possible.

This afternoon, being Sunday, I took my new gloves and a cane and went poodle-faking.[9] It was blazing hot, and I sat for an hour in a strange drawing-room balancing a minute tea-cup on my knee and breathing heavily, or else conversing with a strangled smile to perfect strangers. One of them was Lady North, and she discovered I had been at the House with her son Dudley, and opened out at once; and for the life of me I couldn't remember a single incident in Dudley's University career that wasn't highly discreditable, because he was as complete a young tough as ever I remember. Eventually I emerged, with a strong conviction that I wasn't intended for Mayfair success. Altogether a clammy afternoon.

2, Chatsworth Road, West Norwood,[10] 18 July 1918
Just returned from Medical Board; given leave till August 8th, and then Active Service again, beginning by rejoining the 5th Battalion at Glencorse, Edinburgh.

[. . .] Had 'bad' (?) luck with my Board. Struck the only 'unamenable' member of it, was the only one of our contingent of five to be passed fit for service. However, it's 'all in the seven,' as they say.

Chapter 17

'A roaring, surging wave of sound':
Portsmouth and Peace, August 1918
to December 1985

While Staniforth had been recovering from the effects of gas, the 2nd Leinsters had continued to rotate between camp and the front near Hazebrouck before moving to Ypres in late June. There, in September, they would take part in the operation which became known as the Battle of Ypres 1918. On 28 September, the 2/Leinsters marched to their assembly point near Hooge 'pipers playing and flag flying'.[1]

When the attack began, the 29th Division plus the 9th Division and the Belgian 8th drove all before them, advancing behind a creeping barrage, despite heavy rain making the ground difficult. The battalion then also took part in the Battle of Courtrai, specifically at Ledeghem on 14 October, and saw their last action at Staceghem six days later. They suffered heavily after joining the 29th Division on 23 April, with 175 fatalities between then and the end of the war.

However, Staniforth saw no further action after he had recovered from the effects of gas. When certified fit for service, he was posted to the 5th (Extra Reserve) Battalion of the Leinsters at Glencorse in Scotland. The telegram he sent to the War Office explains succinctly what happened:

PROCEEDED GLENCORSE TODAY JOIN 5ᵀᴴ LEINSTERS AFTER SICK LEAVE UNDER INSTRUCTIONS 3ᴿᴰ LONDON GENL HOSPITAL DATED 18/7/1918. LEINSTERS UNKNOWN THERE. AM INFORMED THEY ARE DISBANDED. PLEASE WIRE INSTRUCTIONS.[2]

It soon transpired that the 5/Leinsters had been merged with the 3rd (Reserve) Battalion, who were in Portsmouth as part of the garrison there. His next letters home explained in more detail how he came to join them, and how his time in Portsmouth would change his life for ever when he met Ruby Di

Stephens, known to her family as 'Biddie', but whom Staniforth would later call Dinah.

The Royal British Hotel, Princes Street, Edinburgh, 9 August 1918
[. . .] As I telegraphed you, I found no trace of the Leinsters at Glencorse; apparently they had been amalgamated some weeks ago with another battalion (I suspect the 3rd at Portsmouth); anyway, they had left those parts, and no one knew or cared anything about them. So I returned here, wired to the War Office for instructions, booked a room for the night, and settled down to await orders. Meanwhile this is a jolly place, and I propose to take myself to see 'The Private Secretary'[3] to-night, and don't care how long the W.O. is in replying – if I can recapture my valise.

The Royal British Hotel, Edinburgh, 10 August 1918
[. . .] This has been a day not without its tense moments. This morning I realised that the financial situation, unless heavily reinforced, makes it impossible to quit this hostelry with honour; wherefore my anguished telegram to you. (I needn't say that bitter experience has taught all Banks to look with disfavour on one of Mr Cox's cheques[4] when presented by a total stranger.) All day I waited in my spacious apartment for a reply from you. At 5 p.m. it came: a lengthy and expensive wire about mail-carts and. things, but containing no hint of £.s.d. I took it to the G.P.O. and enquired, but they assured me it had at no time contained money.

Pride – and other circumstances into which we need not enter – forbade me to wire again. You will next picture your only son racking his brains for the names of any friends or acquaintances in this unspeakable town. Presently I recalled the existence of a near and dear relative who conceals his identity under a quaintly-arranged trio of gilded spheres.[5] To him accordingly I betook myself, unashamed before a Saturday-evening-crowded street. My signet-ring, four pennyweights at six shillings per dwt., my cigarette case, badly crabbed by the crest on it (I wish people wouldn't put identification-marks on gifts of jewellery; it's cost me a lot of good money in my time), say five shillings at most; and my wrist-watch, retail price £3, wholesale perhaps thirty shillings, pledge-value about ten; the three together ought to tot up to forty shillings, which was good enough. So I demanded £2, and the goods passed into my uncle's safe-keeping. I emerged with a brace of Bradburys,[6] returned to the hotel, and found your money-order for £3! So I went straight back to the Mount of Piety. The pawnbroker appeared mildly surprised to see me. (It was perhaps ten minutes since my last visit.) I gravely produced the pledge-ticket and laid down £2.0.10 on the counter and asked for my valuables. He produced them with a slightly stupefied air, and as I departed I saw him conferring anxiously with his assistant. I think he would have liked to place me under mental observation for a while.

Then I went to the station, extracted a warrant from the R.T.O. on the strength of my W.O. telegram, rescued my valise from the Lost Props (I'd spent most of the morning exchanging telegrams with the Glencorse station-master about it), booked a berth in the sleeper, returned and dined, and now I'm waiting for train-time.

I'm sorry I couldn't come back to Hinderwell and see you, but there wouldn't have been any use in it after receiving explicit instructions from the War Office, would there? I'll write again from Portsmouth, if I do find the regiment there and don't have to turn round and go off to Inverness or Sligo or somewhere.

Fort Nelson, Fareham, Hampshire, 23 August 1918
This is only a change of quarters, as you surmised. There is a ridge of hills behind the low ground on which Portsmouth is built, crowned with a number of forts which command the harbour and dockyard. They are garrisoned by detachments from the troops in the town, periodically relieved.

This particular fort, of which I am in command, is used also as a Garrison School for young officers. Batches of about thirty arrive out here, spend three weeks receiving instruction, and are replaced by another class. The primary duty of the Commandant is to act as schoolmaster to these budding Von Moltkes,[7] and organize tactical schemes and field exercises among the surrounding hills for them to break their young brains upon, and between-whiles to fill them up with lectures and book-larnin'. Apart from that I have about sixty troops to look after (mostly men sent out from the battalion in Portsmouth for misdemeanours of one sort or another).

It's a jolly place to be in, and much healthier than Pompey,[8] which lies down at our feet among the marshes. Of course the fort is too big for us (it is built to accommodate about a thousand men, and we're only a skeleton garrison), and half the casemates, keeps, caponiers and galleries are simply locked up and left unused, while it takes us all our time to keep the remaining half in decent order. But at least one has a job to do, which isn't the case in Portsmouth, and is left to do it in one's own way. For which much thanks.

Whitehead was down here the other day, on his way back to the Battalion in France. He tells me they're still in practically the same place: just one divisional front to the left of where I left them, which brings them just about opposite Merris. A quiet time since I left; they did one raid at Vieux Berquin some time ago, that's all. He's still adjutant, and was only at Brigade for a fortnight during the staff captain's absence on leave. He says leave is only being granted now every seven months, not every three as formerly. Rather a jag.

During the course of the next month, Staniforth made the acquaintance of the Stephens family in Southsea, and was invited for weekends at their holiday cottage in the Isle of Wight.

Fort Nelson, 23 August 1918
The influenza[9] here is fearful. The weekly death-rate in the town has gone up from its normal 60 or 70 to between 400 and 500 for the last three weeks now. Consequently it's out of bounds for all troops not actually stationed inside the town; so we're isolated in our little fort out here, with no prospect of release until the epidemic has run its course. Cheery prospect. [. . .]

Fort Nelson, 25 October 1918
You've always given me your love all my life; I want lots more love and congratulations now. Can you guess why? I'm sure you can. The dearest and sweetest girl – no, I won't say in the world; in *my* world – has promised to marry me (in about ten years' time, I suppose!).

You'll say this is a sudden way of breaking the news to you. You see, I had to be quite sure, first of myself and then of Biddie, before I could tell you.

I think I mentioned her to you before, when I first met the Stephens family; though I didn't think at the time how things would turn out. I wish you knew her and could judge for yourselves; as you don't, I can only tell you of her as a very loving, sweet-souled, gentle girl – exactly what you would wish your own daughter to be. She's only a child yet – she'll be twenty next February – though a very sweet one, and with a child's pure and loving heart, and twenty thousand times too dear for me.

I couldn't see her father (Paymaster-Captain Stephens, C.B., R.N., stationed at Southampton; I've only met him once), but I've told her mother frankly that I've no money and no prospects, and in spite of that she has consented to trust me with Biddie, though of course there's no prospect of marriage for ages to come.

We've often talked of it, haven't we; I suppose I knew all the time it was bound to come some day; and now it's happened at last for better or worse. [. . .] You're very lucky to have a daughter like her; sweet, shy, trustful, and affectionate. I'm longing for the day when you'll see her; I shall be awfully proud.

During the day she's working in the tracing-office at the Dockyard here.

P.S. Aren't you relieved that after all I don't propose to bring a musical-comedy actress[10] into the family?

[. . .]

News of peace at 11am on 11 November 1918 took time to spread and for soldiers at the front, the fighting continued until the very last minute. The 2/Leinsters, though not losing men in doing so, continued to march forwards to the last. Because one condition of the armistice was that the line reached at 11am on 11 November would be the front line, 88 Brigade tried to secure as much ground as possible. The 2/Leinsters' war diary noted that 'By a dashing exploit' the brigade commander 'with a few cavalrymen' crossed the river Dendre at Lessines, adding, 'Our troops were everywhere received with the greatest enthusiasm.[11]' Staniforth explained in a letter to his parents how he celebrated the news.

Fort Nelson, 12 November 1918[12]
[. . .] I had been spending the week-end at Portland Terrace, and had an appointment for an interview with the G.O.C. at Portsmouth Headquarters at 11 o'clock on Monday morning. With no other thought but that, I left the house at about half-past ten. There was no news then; not a whisper of it in the streets. Then I thought I heard a man say to a passer-by, 'Well, they've done it at last.' Fifty yards further on there were two or three more who'd heard. Then it flew from lip to lip; in five minutes the whole street knew it; a man was already fixing a Union Jack on the top of a house; a motor-cyclist went past with a flag on his handle-bars. And then the newsboys flooded the streets with an 'Extra Special Peace Edition.' Knots of people closed round them at once; I pushed into one of the groups, threw the boy a shilling, snatched a paper and tore it open at the 'Stop Press' column. There it was, in the blurred grey type peculiar to late stop-press insertions:- 'The Mayor of Portsmouth

has been officially informed by the Admiralty that an armistice with Germany was signed at 4.45 this morning. Hostilities will cease at 11 a.m. to-day. The Mayor asks all citizens to assemble at the Town Hall at noon.'

I looked at my watch and found I had just five minutes to spare. Fortunately the Post Office is quite close to the Garrison Headquarters, so I slipped inside and telegraphed to you. Then I went into the telephone cabinet and rang up the Dockyard, told Biddie (but she knew already; trust the Navy to be first on the spot in Portsmouth!), and arranged to pick her up at 12 o'clock, and also telephoned Fort Nelson and spread the glad tidings there. After that I had to go and see the General.

He kept me waiting about the office, fuming with impatience, for twenty minutes, while outside I could hear the gathering crowds in the street and see the bunting beginning to break from the houses. At last I was admitted; five minutes question and answer, and I was out in the street again. By the greatest piece of luck in the world a disengaged taxi was cruising past, the driver more interested in the sights around him than in possible fares. I boarded him, and we headed full speed for the Dockyard gates.

Now, the Dockyard *is* Portsmouth, of course. Ninety per cent of the families in the town have a brother or a son or a daughter – or the whole lot – employed there. So it was a big and ever-growing crowd that swayed and pushed and shouted round the closed gates when we got there, all wanting to carry off their particular man or woman and rejoice together. Very slowly my taxi-man worked his way through the press till we were right up to the gates, and then he switched off his engine and we sat down to wait. 'As soon as we pick up our passenger,' I told him, 'get out of this one-time and drive like hell to the Town Hall.' Then I got out and sat on the bonnet of the cab, where I could get a good view and also stave off people who wanted to collar the taxi for themselves.

Slowly the minutes dragged on. At about five to twelve the noise began to swell steadily. First one ship's siren, then two, then six, then a score joined in. The locomotives in the Harbour Station took it up, and all the little picket-boats and small fry chimed in with their whistles. It was a roaring, surging wave of sound that grew and grew, until right on the crest of it the great Gates opened and the flood of workers poured out, hundreds of figures all running and tumbling and discharging themselves into the big pool of humanity outside. Among the first fifty I spotted Biddie, running and breathless in the stream. She saw me at once, and made a bee-line for the taxi and flung herself panting and laughing and sobbing into my arms. In a minute I had her in the cab, the door slammed, the wheels began to revolve, and we drew slowly away from the crowd.

Then I think we were rather incoherent for a moment or two . . .

We reached the Town Hall square in four or five minutes (it's only a short drive), but the taxi was stopped at the approaches to the square and we had to get out and go on foot.

Imagine Sheffield's Fitzalan Square jammed and stuffed with people till you wouldn't think there was room for another human being, and more hundreds hurrying and pouring every second from the side-streets.

We hung on tightly to each other and made a small flying wedge, and in due time got a fairly good position where we could at least see, if not hear, what was going on on the steps of the Town Hall itself. Here we established ourselves on the kerb, and like Moses 'surveyed the landscape o'er.'

And it was worth surveying. Every man, woman and child in that vast concourse had a small Union Jack, and they all waved them wildly and incessantly. From side to side the square was alive with a tossing sea of flags that rippled and swayed and shook wherever the eye turned. Hemming it in on three sides were walls of tall houses, each blanketed with banners, and a cluster of heads at every window. The lamp posts, telegraph poles, and electric light standards rose here and there like strange fruit-trees, loaded with their burdens of hardy climbers. The sun glinted on the bayonets of the guards of honour (naval and military) that lined the Town Hall steps, and the steps themselves were submerged in tiers of fortunate spectators who had secured their places an hour or more before.

The ceremony was brief and soon over. First the Mayor appeared and spoke a few words; then Admiral Sir Stanley Colville, K.C.B. (commander of the port); and finally Major-General Sir Douglas Smith (G.O.C. Portsmouth Garrison, whom I'd been interviewing half-an-hour previously). Cheers for the King, the Allies; the Navy and the Army were called for, and various anthems sung, and then the crowd began to break up slowly and went off to parade the streets in groups and detachments.

When it was at last possible to navigate, Biddie and I made a move to Portland Terrace. It wasn't until we turned into the quieter streets towards the end of our journey, away from the noise and emotions of the crowd, that we woke up to the fact that we were walking along with our arms round each other like a pair of small children.

Later that evening we went to dinner at the Queen's Hotel, and had a rotten menu and a bottle of indifferent champagne. But most of the time we preferred to sit quietly at home and do our own thanksgiving in our own way – and not least for that we were together on that day. Yet I wished you could have been there too. Then indeed it would have been a Day.

I'm too tired to write any more. Goodnight, and a world of love from both of us.

Though engaged, Staniforth and Biddie, or 'Dinah' as he came to call her, did not marry until 1922. Before this, he had to complete his studies and find employment, having been formally discharged from the army on 29 March 1919. He arrived back in Oxford in late April 1919, and in a letter to his parents dated 28 April he described his efforts to recover his possessions, which had been left there throughout the war.

[. . .] They've given me rooms back in Meadow Buildings again, where I was when I first came in 1912. Not so bad, considering I had to be jammed in somewhere at the last moment. On Saturday I got my belongings back. The College had put them in store after Christmas 1914, so a few things are gone, but not many really. It could have been much worse, if the blood-curdling tales of my scout are true. He says the first contingent who were billeted here, in autumn 1914, were Territorials (officers).

They made the most frightful havoc of the undergraduates' rooms; looted clocks and books and valuables, drank every drop of wine that was left, broke furniture, ruined sheets and tablecloths, and smashed glass and china past all counting. Then the authorities moved all undergraduates' possessions into the bedrooms, locked the doors on them, and made the Terriers sleep in the depleted sitting-rooms. Within ten days the carpenter had been called to repair more than *thirty* burst locks and smashed-in doors! They had simply battered in the bedroom doors and looted again. However, very fortunately my things were in my rooms in Tom Quad, which at that time happened to be reserved for staff officers, and they seem to have been a comparatively honest crew. A few of my choicest books were too much of a temptation, and I missed three small Greuze[13] engravings, but otherwise my chief casualties seem to be among the glass, china and cutlery departments, as is only to be expected.

There was, however, one Gladstone bag, containing half-a-dozen football and hockey shirts and a dozen pairs of football stockings (Charterhouse colours and others), and some assorted caps, flannel shorts, scarves, vests and drawers. My dears, the moths had got into it,

and browsed undisturbed for nearly five years! You can't imagine the
result. Everything is absolutely ruined, of course; all eaten to lacy shreds
and tatters. Luckily it was only old sports gear.

[. . .] Traditions are all gone by the board, naturally. I suppose they'll
come back in time. But it's rather distressing to see people smoking all
over Tom Quad, and having Oxford ladies to lunch in their rooms, and
treating third and fourth year men with a cheerful equality, and there are
wonderful visiting-cards printed in attractive Old English black-letter
nailed up over gentlemen's doors. This is snobbery, of course. They're
only small things, I know; but in Oxford, and in this college, they're a bit
painful.

*Staniforth did not remain at Christ Church for long. The University of
Oxford's War Decree (7) stated that any University member who, after his
matriculation, was absent on military service for three terms or more could
supplicate (apply) for a Bachelor of Arts, provided that he could prove that
he was, or would have been, qualified for admission to the examination in any
Final Honour School. Staniforth had already achieved a Second in Classical
Moderations in 1913 and so he was eligible for finals in Classics. Those suppli-
cated for degrees also had to pay a fee of £4 to the University Chest and the
student register records that Staniforth's fee was paid on 19 June 1919, the
date on which his BA was conferred upon him.*[14]

*Following graduation, Staniforth found work with a coal-shipping firm in
South Wales. He married Dinah on 1 July 1922,*[15] *and they lived in Cardiff.
In order to demonstrate the quality of their coal, his employers trained him as
an engine driver, and he put his skills to use during the General Strike of 1926.
In an interview for* Hampshire, The County Magazine, *published in 1983,
Staniforth recalled:*

On several occasions I drove the Fishguard Express from Neath, where
it changed crews after the journey from Paddington, to Fishguard. I
had to collect my locomotive from the sheds which were on a little spur
line running along the backs of the railwaymen's cottages. They were,
of course, all on strike and one borrowed his son's catapult and waited
for us in his garden. He wasn't a very good marksman at first, but he
was getting better every day and before the strike was over my firemen
and I had to lie on the floor of the cab to avoid his missiles![16]

*After the General Strike, Staniforth settled in Argentina. Having visited the
country to sell coal, he had liked it, and found work with the Entre Rios railway*

(rising to the role of assistant traffic manager) before he lost his job during the global depression of 1931. Just before Christmas that year he joined the International Broadcasting Company (IBC), Leonard Plugge's commercial rival to the BBC, broadcasting from Fécamp in Upper Normandy, mostly introducing dance music records. His formal job title was 'announcer', but when the BBC later commemorated fifty years of popular music broadcasting, Staniforth was dubbed the first 'Disc Jockey'.

After a year with the IBC, the Staniforths returned to England so that their daughter, Rosamund, who had been born in Argentina, could be educated there. He continued to work in the IBC's London office and then moved to publishing. During that time he came to the view that his calling in life was as a priest in the Church of England and he enrolled at Chichester Theological College, being ordained in 1937. After two curacies, at Graffham, a West Sussex village, and Bognor Regis, he held a living at Flimwell on the Kent/Sussex border, during which time his home was destroyed by a doodlebug (in 1944), and the family had to live with parishioners. Later, he was chaplain to two girls' schools in Sussex before moving to Sixpenny Handley in Dorset in the mid-1950s. There, he was Vicar and Rural Dean of Blandford until retirement, when he and Dinah moved to Boldre in the New Forest in 1963, into a property which abutted the home of their daughter and her husband.

Staniforth's retirement saw him continuing to conduct church services. Dinah died in 1970, three weeks before he had been due to serve as Chaplain and Lecturer in Classics on a Swan Hellenic cruise of the eastern Mediterranean. He decided to go and his daughter accompanied him. On his return, he moved in with his sister Maisie for two years before accepting an offer to live in a parish almshouse close to his home. He lived there for the remainder of his life, helping the parish in various ways and translating for Penguin Classics the works of Marcus Aurelius and the early Christian writings of the Apostolic Fathers.[17] He was 92 when he died on Boxing Day 1985.

Further reading

Good starting points for Ireland during the Great War are:

Dungan, Myles, *Irish Voices from the Great War* (Dublin, 1995).

Dungan, Myles, *They Shall Grow Not Old: Irish Soldiers and the Great War* (Dublin, 1997).

Gregory, Adrian and Pašeta, Senia (eds), *Ireland and the Great War: 'A War to Unite Us All'?* (Manchester, 2002).

Horne, John, ed., *Our War: Ireland and the Great War* (Dublin, 2008).

Jeffery, Keith, *Ireland and the Great War* (Cambridge, 2000).

Johnstone, Tom, *Orange, Green and Khaki: The Story of the Irish Regiments in the Great War, 1914–18* (Dublin, 1992).

Terence Denman has written extensively on the 16th (Irish) Division:

'The 10th (Irish) Division 1914–15: A Study in Military and Political Interaction', *Irish Sword* 17, 66 (1987), pp. 16–25.

'An Irish Battalion at War: From the Letters of Captain J. H. M. Staniforth, 7th Leinsters 1914–18', *Irish Sword*, 17 (1989), pp. 165–217.

'The Catholic Irish Soldier in the First World War: the "Racial Environment"', *Irish Historical Studies*, XXVII, 27. (1991), pp. 352–65.

Ireland's Unknown Soldiers: The 16th (Irish) Division in the Great War (Dublin, 1992).

A Lonely Grave: The Life and Death of William Redmond (Blackrock, Co. Dublin, 1995).

'The 16th (Irish) Division on 21 March 1918: Fight or Flight?' *Irish Sword*, 69 (1999), pp. 273–87.

Other useful studies of specific units/battles/issues affecting Irish units on the Western Front are:

6th Connaught Rangers Research Project, *The 6th Connaught Rangers: Belfast Nationalists and the Great War* (Belfast, 2008, 2nd edition 2011).

Bowman, Timothy, *Irish Regiments in the Great War: Discipline and Morale* (Manchester, 2003).

Burke, Tom, *The 16th (Irish) and 36th (Ulster) Divisions at the Battle of Wijtschate – Messines Ridge, 7 June 1917* (Dublin, 2007).

Grayson, Richard S., *Belfast Boys: How Unionists and Nationalists Fought and Died Together in the First World War* (London, 2009).

Orr, Philip, *The Road to the Somme: Men of the Ulster Division Tell their Story* (Belfast, 1987).

Documents at The National Archives, Kew, are increasingly available to download online. Others are available for consultation by anybody with a reader's ticket (see the Kew website for details on which personal documents should be shown to obtain one of these). The main items relevant to this study are:

WO 158/416	16th Division, Narrative of Operations 7th to 9th June 1917
WO 339/15145	Capt. J.H.M. Staniforth
WO 339/23115	Lieut J.H.M. Staniforth
WO 95/1955 & 1956	16th Division General Staff War Diary
WO 95/1969	47th Brigade HQ War Diary
WO 95/1969	6th Connaught Rangers War Diary
WO 95/1970	7th Leinsters War Diary
WO 95/2308	2nd Leinsters War Diary

Appendix

Archives at the Imperial War Museum used for this book were as follows:

IWM Documents J.H.M. Staniforth, 67/41/1-3

IWM Documents J.F. Blake O'Sullivan, 77/167/1

IWM Documents W.A. Lyon, 80/25/1

Acknowledgements

I would like to thank Mrs Rosamund Du Cane, Max Staniforth's daughter, for allowing me to edit her father's letters, and for making me so welcome at her home. Her enthusiastic collaboration with the project from first to last has been invaluable and it has been a pleasure both meeting her and working with her.

I am very grateful to Terry Denman for his advice on a number of points regarding this project. All writers on the 16th (Irish) Division owe him a debt of gratitude for opening up the field with his work. His article on Staniforth was a valuable alert to the existence of letters which were not in Staniforth's typescript.

Thanks are due to Judith Curthoys, the Archivist at Christ Church, for providing information on Staniforth's degree, and to Jeremy Hargreaves, who kindly explained some Christ Church terminology.

At the Imperial War Museum, Elizabeth Bowers, Madeleine James and Anthony Richards have been very helpful throughout. I am especially grateful to Madeleine for arranging for photographs to be taken of various items held in the IWM's collection. I would particularly like to thank Amanda Mason for her helpful comments on a draft of this volume. Rod Suddaby provided useful information at a seminar on Staniforth held at the IWM in November 2011. Thanks are also due to Emily Fuggle for organising that seminar. The Reverend Clive Hughes, formerly of the IWM, collected the letters from Max Staniforth in 1981 and I am grateful to him for the time he took to discuss his recollections with me over the phone. I am also grateful to Barbara Levy, the IWM's literary agent, for arranging the contract with Pen & Sword, where thanks are also due to Rupert Harding for his guidance.

I continue to be grateful to Seán O'Hare, Harry Donaghy and all others involved in the 6th Connaught Rangers Research Project, for their inspirational enthusiasm for the memory of the 16th (Irish) Division. Thanks are due to Julian Putkowski for sharing with me his 2005 paper which, in the context of a wider discussion of the Second Battle of Ypres, addressed the phenomenon of Germans allegedly being found wearing British uniforms.

Permission to quote from the Staniforth letters and to reproduce images of them is provided by Mrs Rosamund Du Cane. The Imperial War Museum has provided permission to reproduce photographs from its collections. The 1982-3 pictures of Staniforth in his study are from *Hampshire, The County Magazine* and are reproduced by kind permission of Jon Benson of the Mark Allen Group.

Finally, I would like to thank my wife and son, Lucy and Edward, for tolerating the mental absences which such a project involves, and my Mum, Jannat, for supporting us all.

Notes

Editor's Introduction

1. Staniforth was known in his family as 'Max', from his middle name, Maxwell. His father's diary, held by his daughter, was begun in 1902 and refers to Staniforth as 'Max' from that point. However, he signed all his letters to his parents during the war 'John' and was called that by other officers. Not until March 1920 did Staniforth sign himself 'Max' in letters to his parents.

2. The most positive response recited the current economic situation as a factor. A letter dated 1 October 1985 said, 'I am afraid only a limited number of people are buying books like this at the moment.' Ironically, this was from Leo Cooper, whose imprint Pen and Sword agreed, a quarter of a century later, to publish the book.

3. The National Archives, Kew [TNA]: WO 339/15145, File on Capt J.H.M. Staniforth.

4. On this subject, see Thomas Hennessey, *Dividing Ireland: World War I and Partition* (London, 1998), pp. 80-124.

5. Richard S. Grayson, *Belfast Boys: How Unionists and Nationalists Fought and Died Together in the First World War* (London, 2009), p. 17

6. *Irish News*, 12 February 1915, p. 4.

7. The letters have the Imperial War Museum reference 67/41/1-3 and were deposited with the museum in March 1981 by Staniforth himself. In addition to those described for the May 1917 to March 1918 gap, there are also four from April, two from May and one from September 1918. One other letter is filed with that dated 8 September 1917 but its date is unclear.

8. See p.19.

9. A number of the author's editorial comments from his typescript are included in the notes (clearly labelled as being the author's).

Author's Foreword

1. Staniforth added: 'William Hamilton Maxwell (1792-1850), of the Maxwells of Nithsdale; author of *Wild Sports of the West, Stories of Waterloo, A History of the Rebellion of 1798*, and a variety of novels on sporting and military subjects. His *Life of Wellington*, on whose staff he had served in the Peninsular campaign and at Waterloo, has been many times re-issued, and has few equals as a biography of a soldier by a soldier.'

237

2. Maisie's real name was Mary, but she was always known within the family by her nickname. She was born on 27 May 1902.
3. Hilda Maureen was born on 7 October 1908.
4. 1889-1944; writer, barrister and five-times a Liberal parliamentary candidate.
5. 1889-1959; socialist theorist, historian and writer, and Chichele Professor of Social and Political Theory at Oxford, 1944-57.
6. 1882-1964; geneticist and winner of the Darwin Medal in 1952; a member of the Communist Party of Great Britain the 1940s, he served in the Black Watch in WWI.
7. 1890-1971; humorous writer and activist for law reform; Independent MP for Oxford University 1935-50; served in Royal Navy in WWI and WWII.
8. 1893-1964; publisher and author, editor of the Conservative *English Review* 1931-36, and a prominent supporter of Franco.
9. 1892-1969; served in WWI with Oxfordshire and Buckinghamshire Light Infantry; Cabinet Secretary 1938-46; Permanent Secretary to the Treasury and Head of the Home Civil Service 1946-56.
10. 1892-1974; Conservative MP 1935-55, junior minister 19036-45 and 1951-55.
11. 'The House' is an informal name for Christ Church used by its undergraduates and postgraduates, though nowadays less commonly than in Staniforth's time. It derives from the Latin for Christ Church, 'Ædes Christi' in which 'Ædes' means 'House'. I am grateful to Jeremy Hargreaves for explaining to me some intricacies of this and other Christ Church terminology.

Chapter 1
1. Timothy Bowman, *Carson's Army: The Ulster Volunteer Force, 1910-22* (Manchester, 2007).
2. 1858-1923; Member of Parliament 1900-23; Prime Minister 1922-23.
3. Formally, the alliance between the Conservative Party and the Liberal Unionist Party which existed from the late 1880s until the outbreak of WWI.
4. *Belfast Evening Telegraph*, 17 January 1913, p. 6.
5. 1854-1935; Member of Parliament, 1892-1921, then as Baron Carson a Judge 1921-29.
6. 1775-1847; leading campaigner for Catholic Emancipation in the early nineteenth century; Member of Parliament 1828-30, 1832-36 and 1837-41.
7. 1856-1918; Member of Parliament 1881-1918; Leader of Irish Parliamentary Party 1900-1918.
8. *Hansard*, HC Deb 3 August 1914, vol. 65 col. 1829.
9. *Irish News*, 16 September 1914 p. 5.
10. *Irish News*, 21 September 1914 p. 5.

11. 1867-1945; academic and founder of the Gaelic League and the Irish Volunteers, imprisoned after Easter Rising, Member of Parliament 1918-22 (but did not take seat due to Sinn Féin policy of abstention and instead sat in Dáil Éireann until 1927, for a time as Minister of Education); Northern Ireland Parliament 1921-25 (also abstained).

12. University College Dublin, Eoin MacNeill Papers, LA1/P/2; *Belfast Evening Telegraph*, 25 September 1914 p. 6. See also reservations expressed by Redmond supporters: National Library of Ireland, Moore Ms 10,561(8): Moore to Devlin, 28 September 1914.

13. Charles Hannon, 'The Irish Volunteers and the Concepts of Military Service and Defence 1913–24' (University College Dublin, unpublished PhD thesis, 1989), p. 105.

14. Terence Denman, *Ireland's Unknown Soldiers: The 16th (Irish) Division in the Great War* (Dublin, 1992), p. 38.

15. Dr J. Staniforth's diary, in possession of Mrs. R. Du Cane.

16. Lieutenant Colonel J.S.M. Lenox-Conyngham.

17. Staniforth is referring to the conflict between 'Redmondites' who supported recruitment to the British Army and more radical nationalists who supported Sinn Féin and opposed the British war effort.

18. 'Shebeen' was originally used for a bar selling illegal home-produced alcohol, but had by this time entered usage as a general term for a bar, sometimes one in which music was performed.

19. The Battle of Mons, 23 to 24 August 1914.

20. Both in Co. Cork.

21. 'All in the seven' meant 'to be expected', drawing on the notion that normal army service was seven years, although in 1914 volunteers signed up for three years, or, if the war lasted longer, its duration.

22. A town in Co. Cork which gave its name to a march popular with Irish regiments.

23. Go to the toilet.

24. Pipeclay was used to make belts white.

25. Dwight Lyman Moody and David Sankey were late nineteenth century evangelical preachers and singers who also published hymns.

26. Cloths placed over the tops of chair backs or arms to protect them from dirt.

27. The Irish Volunteers landed 3,000 rifles at Howth, Co. Dublin, on 26 July 1914, bought from Germany, with ammunition. Some of these weapons were later used during the Easter Rising.

28. Laxative.

29. Night clothes.

30. On leave.

31. Lieutenant T. Hughes.

32. Brigadier General P.J. Miles.

33. Lieutenant General Sir Lawrence Parsons, commander of the 16th Division.

34. Six years at this time.
35. A personal sewing kit.

Chapter 2

1. Timothy Bowman, *Irish Regiments in the Great War: Discipline and Morale* (Manchester, 2003), pp. 83–85.
2. Honour Moderations, exams taken at Oxford prior to final examinations, the precise timing varying from subject to subject.
3. Subaltern: a general term for commissioned officers below the rank of captain, effectively 2nd lieutenant and lieutenant.
4. Originally a naval term for midshipmen but used in the army for junior officers, especially when in training.
5. Sections of trenches built at angles to prevent an enemy capturing part of a trench and then firing along the full length of it.
6. Supporting walls along the length of trenches.
7. The side of the trench facing the enemy, usually lined with sandbags.
8. Colonel A.H. Wood.
9. 2nd Lieutenant J. Johnstone.
10. A leading brand of Irish whiskey.
11. The early stages of the effects of withdrawal from alcohol.
12. Probably a reference to the Mexican Revolution which began in 1910.
13. Dismissed from the army.
14. Within two miles of Fermoy.
15. Staniforth meant 'pickets', a type of guard.
16. In a few letters, Staniforth used the battalion war diary format of writing place names in capital letters.
17. Colonel A.H. Wood.
18. Captain W.E. Phillips.
19. Thomas 'Tom' Kettle (1880–1916), an Irish nationalist MP 1906–1910 and a member of the Irish Volunteers. Killed at Ginchy on 9 September 1916 as a Lieutenant with the 9th Royal Dublin Fusiliers. After the Easter Rising, Kettle famously commented, 'These men will go down in history as heroes and martyrs; and I will go down – if I go down at all – as a bloody British officer.' See J.B. Lyons, *The Enigma of Tom Kettle: Irish Patriot, Essayist, Poet, British Soldier, 1880–1916* (Dublin, 1983), p. 293.
20. Stephen Gwynn, rather than 'Gwynne', (1864–1950), Irish nationalist MP 1906–18. He trained in the cadet corps of the Leinsters and served as an officer with the 6/Connaughts.
21. William Redmond (1861–1917), the younger brother of John Redmond, Irish nationalist MP from 1883 to 1917. He was killed at Messines on 7 June 1917 while a Major in the 6/Royal Irish Regiment. Aged 56, he had had to obtain special permission to be at the front with his battalion. See Terence Denman,

A Lonely Grave: The Life and Death of William Redmond (Blackrock, Co. Dublin, 1995).

22. In theory, soldiers were issued with discs by the War Office but they often became lost and many soldiers acquired others privately. See David O'Mara's article on the Western Front Association website at: www.westernfrontasso-ciation.com/great-war-on-land/73-weapons-equipment-uniforms.html [accessed 29th July 2011].
23. Possibly Lieutenant H.K. Purcell but more likely Lieutenant N.N. Purcell, as Staniforth refers to Noel Purcell later.
24. Captain W.E. Phillips.
25. 2nd Lieutenant L.J.M. Studholme.
26. Christ Church, see above p. 238 n. 11.
27. 2nd Lieutenant H.F. Wilmot.
28. Lieutenant C.T. Denroche.
29. A signalling system utilising reflection of the sun.
30. Parsons.

Chapter 3
1. Bowman, *Irish Regiments*, pp. 79-80.
2. The pen-name of Francis Sylvester Mahony (1804-1866) who wrote the poem 'The Bells of Shandon'.
3. Lieutenant Colonel G.A.M. Buckley.
4. The Battle of Neuve Chapelle, 10 to 13 March 1915.
5. A House at Charterhouse.
6. *The Boy's Friend* was a popular story paper of the early twentieth century. It included information on issues relating to camping and survival.
7. Strictly, 'to juke' is to deceive, but in this context, it also involves ducking down.
8. This line was added by Staniforth in the original.
9. Staniforth was formally promoted to Lieutenant on 24 May.
10. A junior officer.
11. Presumably Finn.
12. Literally, 'the whole shop', simply meaning 'everything'.
13. Staniforth brought his bull terrier back to Fermoy from his leave.
14. Lord Wimborne, Lord Lieutenant (the monarch's representative) of Ireland, 1915-18.
15. The photograph has not been located by the editor or Staniforth's daughter.
16. Christ Church.
17. Presumably an Irish society at Oxford.

Chapter 4
1. See, for example, *Irish News*, 27 October 1916, p. 6 & 17 December 1915, p. 3.

2. In ancient Rome, deities (guardian and domestic respectively). Staniforth is perhaps referring to whatever soldiers took with them as symbols of their faith or as good luck charms.
3. Hundredweight: 112 pounds.
4. A play on a quotation from Jonathan Swift's *Gulliver's Travels*, 'whoever could make two ears of corn, or two blades of grass, to grow upon a spot of ground, where only one grew before, would deserve better of mankind, and do more essential service to his country, than the whole race of politicians put together.' See Jonathan Swift, *Gulliver's Travels: A Voyage to Lilliput and Brobdingnag*, (London: 1726, 1863 edition), p. 161.
5. The information was not in fact deleted. Staniforth wrote the original letter in this letter to make the point that such information would be deleted if he included it.
6. Now Dún Laoghaire.
7. Now Port Laoise.
8. The first two sentences of this paragraph are very badly damaged in the original, but that might have happened between Staniforth's transcription and the letters going to the IWM, so the words are from the typescript.
9. One of the Charterhouse cricket teams.
10. Probably 'Deo gratia', or 'Thank God' in Latin.
11. A musical term to indicate repetition from the beginning.
12. There had been problems filling 49 Brigade, partly because some of its members had volunteered to transfer to the 10th Division so that they could go overseas sooner. In November 1915 it was decided that 49 Brigade would remain in England after 47 and 48 had left for France, so that it had more time to recruit. They joined the 16th Division in late February 1916. See, Denman, *Ireland's Unknown*, pp. 55 & 61-2.
13. Major General W.B. Hickie.
14. The detachable front of a gun–carriage, which could be used as a small cart.
15. Kipling's poem 'Boots' was about the movement of an infantry column.

Chapter 5
1. References to the precise location and movements of the battalion are taken from TNA, WO 95/1970: 7/Leinsters War Diary.
2. Staniforth enclosed a menu card.
3. Lady of the house.
4. Pavement.
5. A German military aeroplane used for reconnaissance.
6. The first day of the Battle of Loos and accompanying diversionary attacks at various points on the British part of the front.
7. The towers were part of a pithead in the Loos area and became known as 'Tower Bridge'. By mentioning Sherlock Holmes, Staniforth was hinting

that his parents could use this information to form a general idea of his where-abouts.

8. A reference to his fellow officer, Billy Cullen, who was known to Staniforth's parents.
9. A German lancer regiment.
10. This crucifixion story spread widely in the trenches in 1915, but no conclusive evidence of it was ever provided. See Heather Jones, *Violence against Prisoners of War: Britain, France and Germany, 1914-1920* (Cambridge, 2011), p. 79. Staniforth's own words bear a close resemblance to those used in what may be the original source of the story, Ian Hay, *The First Hundred Thousand*, (London, 1915), p. 180. This said, 'But the grim realities of war are coming home to us. Outside this farm stands a tall tree. Not many months ago a party of Uhlans arrived here, bringing with them a wounded British prisoner. They crucified him to that self-same tree, and stood round him till he died. He was a long time dying. Some of us had not heard of Uhlans before. These have now noted the name, for future reference – and action.' The similarity is so close that Staniforth must have read this account at some point. The material was originally published in articles in *Blackwood's Magazine*, and then later in 1915 in a book. Of course, it would also have been reviewed so there are many ways in which Staniforth could have encountered the material before he included it in his letter in slightly amended form.
11. The villages Staniforth used as pseudonyms were in the Whitby area.
12. Lieutenant General Sir Henry Rawlinson, commander of IV Corps.
13. A British weekly tabloid which included the popular 'Old Bill' cartoons depicting an elderly British Tommy.
14. A regular census of who was available for active service.
15. After Mr Wong, a character in W. Carlton Dawe's *Kakemonos: Tales of the Far East* (1897).
16. A Bordeaux wine.
17. Without dissent.
18. The French hero of a series of humorous short stories by Arthur Conan Doyle, set during the Napoleonic wars.
19. Excuse me, sir. The soldiers . . . .
20. Yes, madame, the soldiers . . . ? Continue, madame.
21. They always pee on the wheat.
22. Really? That's bad, that. But perhaps the Captain can settle everything.
23. Ah, well, then. Thank you, sir . . . thank you, sir . . . sorry, sir.
24. Staniforth had written 'IX' after the date, presumably to indicate his location.
25. A term from *The Jungle Book* for a deserted settlement.
26. Shells used to light up an area battlefield at night, often to detect enemy raids.
27. Probably at Houchin.
28. Staniforth added in an editorial note to his typescript: 'The German heavy

shells exploded in a cloud of black smoke, causing the Army to nickname them after this Negro boxing champion.' This was a reference to John Arthur 'Jack' Johnson (1878-1946), the first African-American world heavyweight boxing champion.

29. Staniforth added: '"Coal-boxes" was another name for the German high-explosive shells.'
30. Staniforth added: 'The Staniforths' middle-aged cook.'
31. A medicine used to combat colds and fevers.
32. 47th (2nd London) Division.
33. Used in the same way as rubber/plastic bullets to control riots.
34. Cigarettes.

Chapter 6

1. *Irish News*, 23 March 1916, p. 5 & 1 April 1916, p. 4.
2. 'Flame thrower', first used by the Germans in October 1914, and more widely from the middle of 1915.
3. Presumably a supplier of medical equipment, possibly Burroughs Wellcome & Co., known to be a supplier to the British Army.
4. Private 1519 J. Comiskey, killed on 17 February 1916.
5. Identity not known.
6. A former pupil of Robinites House at Charterhouse, Staniforth's own House there.
7. Possibly a reference to the early stages of the Battle of Verdun, which began the previous month.
8. Perhaps referring to the role of the 1st Canadian Division at Festubert in May 1915, which was the previous major battle involving the Canadians.
9. Plays on 'chique' and 'bizarre'.
10. Brigadier General G. Pereira.

Chapter 7

1. Imperial War Museum, IWM Documents J.F. Blake O'Sullivan, 77/167/1: 'At Rest in Philosophe'.
2. See above, p. 240 n.20.
3. Julian Putkowski has said, writing of the Second Battle of Ypres, that 'The appearance of the Germans dressed in British uniforms features sporadically in a number of war diaries accounts and soldiers' letters. They tend to infer that the cross-dressers may have been either macabre apparitions or a subterfuge by the enemy, intended to sow confusion.' He advances an 'alte-native hypothesis' which is that confusion might play a role in identifying people in British uniforms as Germans. These are wide-ranging and include, for example, in the case of Scottish regiments, ignorance of the Gaelic tongue. Meanwhile, soldiers who had escaped from German lines having been in hiding might be believed to be Germans trying to advance using the

cover of a British uniform. These arguments were set out in a paper, 'Toxic Shock: The British Army's reaction to German discharges of poison gas during the Second Battle of Ypres', presented at the *Innocence Slaughtered* 2005 Conference at the 'In Flanders Fields' Museum, Ieper.

4. Staniforth is using 'chatty' in the traditional sense of talkative, although it is interesting to note that the word was also used to describe lice infestation, and the author might have been conscious of some irony in its use here, precisely because after such a time he might well have been infested with lice.

5. Slang for anti-aircraft fire.

6. Likely to have been chlorine gas.

7. The German attack and British counter-attack was in the Hulluch sector, which included trenches at Philosophe in which the 16th Division had recently been.

8. Michael Foy & Brian Barton, *The Easter Rising* (Stroud, 1999), p. 325.

9. French 'pour prendre congé': leave-taking.

10. 'B' Type London buses were used as auxiliary motor transport behind the front line. An example is housed at the Imperial War Museum, London.

11. Carbon-copy paper.

12. It is not clear precisely what this piece of equipment was. However, the shape and purpose suggests that it might be some kind of speaker, and more correctly described as a 'broadcaster' than as a 'recorder'. Having a 'recorder' of such information seems unlikely given the available technology.

13. This letter was just one line.

Chapter 8

1. TNA, WO 95/1969: 6/Connaughts War Diary

2. TNA, WO 95/1969.

3. There does not appear to have been a Captain Lynch in the Leinsters (the 7th or other battalion) in 1916 so this person was in all likelihood temporarily attached from another regiment.

4. *Belfast Evening Telegraph*, 14 October 1916 p. 3.

5. This letter is only in the typescript.

6. Or O'Donnell Abu, a traditional Irish march.

7. For context, see Jones, *Violence against Prisoners of War*.

8. There are sixty-four days between 27 May and 31 July, so Staniforth meant fifty-one.

9. A reference from Tennyson's 'The Charge of the Light Brigade'.

Chapter 9

1. www.nhs.uk/conditions/Scabies/Pages/Introduction.aspx [accessed 28 July 2011].

2. TNA, WO 339/15145.

3. A play on 'Ich Dien'.

4. TNA, WO 339/15145; www.1914-1918.net/hospitals.htm [accessed 28 July 2011].
5. This letter, although not the enclosure, is only in the typescript.
6. It seems that P.O.W. and R.C. were inserted by Staniforth to make humorous references to captures of members of the battalion by the enemy so that they were now Prisoners of War, and to the battalion's religious character, Roman Catholic.
7. Staniforth noted on the original: 'P.U.O. ('Pyrexia; Unknown Origin,' or vulgarly translated, trench-fever) and N.Y.D. ('Not Yet Diagnosed') constituted 50% of the total cases in any Field Ambulance or C.C.S.'
8. A reference to Cullen now being based in Rhyl.
9. Staniforth noted on the original: 'Gold Flake and Woodbine cigarettes.'
10. May there be no evil omen.

Chapter 10
1. Staniforth's service record (TNA, WO 339/15145: Staniforth, Capt J.H.M.) does not quite match with his next letter. His individual record shows him being at base at Étaples from 4 to 7 September. However, such records were often compiled well after the events they document, and at a distance, and are well known to contain inaccuracies about precise dates. His own letter to his parents dated 12 September suggests that he was back with his battalion by 3 September after a brief time at Étaples, in time to take part in the attack on Guillemont. There is of course, always the possibility that the individual record is accurate and that he did not rejoin his battalion until 8 September and did not want to admit to not having been at Guillemont. However, even if he did not arrive back until 8 September, he was with his unit in time for the attack on Ginchy the next day. There was no shame in having been at Ginchy but not Guillemont, and Staniforth was not a man to talk up his war record in his letters. In the editor's judgement it seems exceptionally unlikely that Staniforth's letter about Guillemont is not accurate. The inaccuracy of precise dates in service records is seen later where it is suggested that Staniforth rejoined the 7/Leinsters after sick leave on 29 June. In fact, a detailed letter about his journey back shows that it was 26 June. See letter of 30 June 1917.
2. IWM Documents W.A. Lyon, 80/25/1: Memoirs, p. 63.
3. IWM Documents J.F. Blake O'Sullivan, 77/1617/1: letter to his mother 10 to 13 September 1916.
4. *London Gazette*, 26 October 1916.
5. Denman, *Ireland's Unknown*, p. 82; Richard Doherty & David Truesdale, *Irish Winners of the Victoria Cross* (Dublin, 2000), p. 122.
6. TNA, WO 95/1970.
7. IWM Documents W.A. Lyon, 80/25/1: Memoirs, p. 64.

8. Sir Philip Gibbs (1877-1962), a notable war correspondent who wrote for *The Daily Telegraph* and *Daily Chronicle*.
9. William Beach Thomas (1868-1957), war correspondent for *The Daily Mail*.
10. This figure was reached using *Soldiers Died in the Great War* and *Officers Died in the Great War* (originally published as a listing in 1921 by His Majesty's Stationery Office, now available as a CD-Rom from the Naval and Military Press). It includes all twelve infantry battalions in the division, plus the division's engineers, but information on specific RAMC and RFA units is rarely present.

Chapter 11
1. TNA, WO 339/23115: Staniforth, Lieut J.H.M.
2. A former pupil of Charterhouse School.
3. Up the Kaiser.

Chapter 12
1. TNA, WO 95/1970.
2. Staniforth was concerned that after his return from sick leave, he might be sent to a battalion other than his old one, possibly even in another regiment.
3. A Biblical reference, to Isaiah, 52:7 'How beautiful on the mountains are the feet of those who bring good news, who proclaim peace, who bring good tidings . . . '
4. Or Tilques, but in fact the battalion went to Tatinghem, close by.
5. Tanks were first used in the later stages of the Battle of the Somme, and again at Arras and Messines in April and June 1917. At Passchendaele they quickly bogged down in the thick mud and their future value was doubted by many until their successful deployment at Cambrai in November 1917.
6. The maximum speed is generally cited as being much lower than this, around four mph.
7. Ready to go.
8. A nautical term used to indicate something unnecessary.
9. Drawing on the Bradshaw compiled railway timetables, the term was also used to indicate a complete and authoritative reference source.
10. *Battle Lines, The Journal of the Somme Association*, 17 (2000), p. 10.
11. *Battle Lines*, 4 (1991), pp. 30-31.
12. *Battle Lines*, 17 (2000), pp. 9-11.
13. XIX Corps.
14. Tinned turnip and carrot stew, which often made up part of soldiers' rations at the front.
15. Shirkers.
16. As Staniforth seems to have been close to Eringhem, this is probably either Merckeghem or Millam.
17. TNA, WO 95/1969.

Chapter 13

1. Tom Johnstone, *Orange, Green and Khaki: The Story of the Irish Regiments in the Great War, 1914–18* (Dublin, 1992), p. 303.
2. TNA, WO 95/1970.
3. A type of overcoat favoured by officers. It was three-quarter length, wool and double-breasted.
4. Metal cages used to strengthen sections of trenches.
5. Notes accompanying transported goods.
6. A type of high riding-boot.
7. Shells from field howitzers.
8. This letter has three further pages but they are so badly damaged as to be illegible.

Chapter 14

1. After the loss of Calais to France in 1558, Queen Mary I was so distraught that she said it, and the name of her husband, would be found on her heart when she died.
2. Capt. E.L.L. Acton and probably Major J.D. Mather.
3. A 1917 Hodder & Stoughton publication by Michael MacDonagh, with a foreword by John Redmond.
4. There is some doubt over which battalion some men killed at that time, and listed as '7th Leinsters', were actually serving with.
5. This letter is only in the typescript.
6. A member of the Royal Engineers' specialist Railway Operating Division.
7. French infantryman.
8. 'The coal burns much better like this; is has more heat, you see, does it not?'
9. A mildly risqué Parisian magazine.

Chapter 15

1. Roughly, 'Get in the carriage. Get in the carriage everyone. The train leaves soon. Quickly, quickly. In the carriage . . . quick, quick.'
2. 'Poor Bloody Leinsters', a play on 'Poor Bloody Infantry'.
3. Leinster Regiment.
4. Brigadier-General Bernard Freyberg, who had been awarded the Victoria Cross for actions on the Somme in November 1916 while a Lieutenant-Colonel, later a Lieutenant-General during the Second World War and in 1946-52, Governor-General of New Zealand.
5. The full name of the Leinsters was the Prince of Wales's Leinster Regiment (Royal Canadians) due to one of its predecessors regiments being Canadian and so it used the Canadian maple leaves as part of its regalia.
6. Meaning the average British soldier, 'Tommy Atkins'.

7. The raid was 'minus the trenches' because by this stage of the war, as the allies pushed the Germans back, fighting was now more often over open ground which had not previously been fought over.
8. 2nd Lieutenant C.A.N. Holden.
9. One of five children of Mr and Mrs Bruce. Mr Bruce was the manager of Grinkle Ironstone Mine of which Dr Staniforth was the doctor. It has not been possible to establish precisely what happened to Clayton Bruce, though he had clearly received a 'Blighty' wound so that he was, as Staniforth said, 'out of it', meaning that he was home wounded, possibly permanently.
10. Probably, 2nd Lieutenant S. O'C. Mallins.
11. 2nd Lieutenant A. Chapman.
12. This letter is only in the typescript.
13. Slang for one pound.
14. Especially too.
15. Of course, we will never see them again.
16. Death on the battlefield.
17. An incorrect form of j'ai pensé, 'I think'.
18. Very bad character. Very little intelligence.
19. 9 years old. Excellent little boy. Not an absence for the entire year.
20. Paul loves Melanie.
21. Paul is a fool.
22. The original is barely visible, so this is taken from the typescript.
23. A German 5.9 shell.
24. Charles Blondin (1824–1897), the French tightrope walker.
25. Literally 'The Day' in German, and used to indicate a momentous event. The battalion war diary notes that a German attack was expected between 25 and 28 May. TNA, WO 95/2308: 2/Leinsters War Diary.

Chapter 16
1. A type of herbal cigarette.
2. A ticker-machine which would have brought news and information such as prices of stocks and shares.
3. 'Ah! When will we do away with alcohol?', a poster produced by 'L'union des Françaises contre l'alcool', a French campaign against alcohol.
4. Née Frances Belt Wickersham (1862–1949), the American wife of Sir Robert Hadfield, who ran Hadfields, one of the major British arms manufacturers, and donated £100,000 towards war hospitals run by his wife.
5. Staniforth's Aunt Edith.
6. Another aunt, Myah was sister to Edith and Staniforth's father.
7. Possibly a reference to Portuguese soldiers.
8. Staniforth's later note described Enid as 'An actress who was a temporary acquaintance at that time.'

9. A slightly derogatory term meant to imply that an officer was being more attentive to women than was considered polite.
10. The home of Staniforth's Aunt Edith and her husband, Frank Newell.

Chapter 17
1. TNA, WO 95/2308.
2. TNA, WO 339/15145.
3. An 1883 play by Sir Charles Hawtrey.
4. See letter of 6 December 1914 for an explanation of Cox and Co., p. 21.
5. Staniforth had gone to a pawnbroker and is referring to the sign of the trade.
6. Two pounds.
7. Helmuth von Moltke (1848-1916), Chief of the German General Staff, 1906-14.
8. A colloquial term for Portsmouth.
9. The Spanish flu which hit many parts of Europe as the war drew to a close.
10. See reference to 'Enid', above p. 220.
11. TNA, WO 95/2308.
12. This letter is only in the typescript.
13. Jean-Baptiste Greuze (1725-1805), a French painter.
14. Information provided to author by Judith Curthoys (Archivist, Christ Church) in emails of 20 & 27 September 2011.
15. Information on Staniforth's later life is largely drawn from family material provided by his daughter, including her publication, Rosamund Du Cane, *Sicklemiths & Spear Carriers: Being an account of the Staniforths of Hackenthorpe with notes on other Staniforth and allied families* (Newbury, 2002), in addition to the *Hampshire* article cited in the next reference.
16. Michael Kennet, 'Pop radio's first disc jockey is alive and well in Hampshire', *Hampshire, The County Magazine*, 23, 4 (February 1983), pp. 28-29 & 32.
17. Marcus Aurelius, *Meditations: Translated with an introduction by Maxwell Staniforth* (Harmondsworth, 1964); Maxwell Staniforth, *Early Christian writings: The Apostolic Fathers* (Harmondsworth, 1968).

Index